The idea of the city
in nineteenth-century Britain

Birth of Modern Britain series

General editors:

A. E. Dyson
Senior Lecturer in English Literature,
University of East Anglia

and

R. T. Shannon
Reader in English History,
University of East Anglia

The idea of the city in nineteenth-century Britain

Edited by

B. I. Coleman

Department of History,
University of Exeter

Routledge & Kegan Paul

London and Boston

301.36
C 69 i

First published in 1973 MN
by Routledge & Kegan Paul Ltd
Broadway House, 68–74 Carter Lane,
London EC4V 5EL and
9 Park Street,
Boston, Mass. 02108, U.S.A.

Printed in Great Britain by
Unwin Brothers Limited, The Gresham Press,
Old Woking, Surrey, England.
A member of the Staples Printing Group

ISBN 0 7100 7591 X (c)
ISBN 0 7100 7592 8 (p)

Library of Congress Catalog Card No. 73-77561

To my parents

General editors' preface

The series is concerned to make the central issues and topics of the recent past 'live', in both senses of that word. We hope to appeal to students of history and of literature equally, since each has much to offer, and learn from, the other. The volume editors are encouraged to select documents from the widest range of sources, and to convey the 'feel' of particular controversies when passion ran high. One problem for the modern student is hindsight: often, we fall back on over-simplified visions of history—Whig or Marxist, progressive or conservative—because we fail to imagine events as they were. We hope here to re-create situations through the passions and commitments of participants and contemporary commentators, before the outcome was known. In this way, students are encouraged to avoid both oversimplified judgments and that dull sense that whatever happened was inevitable which can so devitalize our understanding of any period's history, or its art.

We believe that this treatment of the recent past, bringing out the sense of immediacy and conflict, is also the soundest basis for understanding the modern world. Increasingly, we realize that continuity is more striking than discontinuity: nothing could be more naive than a claim for 'modernity' which assumes that the past is 'irrelevant' or dead. It was during the age of Arnold and Gladstone, Disraeli and Tennyson, Darwin and Chamberlain that our most distinctive modern problems defined themselves—the growth of great cities and technology; the battle between individualism and collectivism; the coming of democracy, with all its implications for education, class, vocation and the ordinary expectations of living; the revolutions in travel and communication; the shifting relationships between individuals and the state. Many of the major ideas that shape our world were also born: and in the ferment of day-to-day crises and perplexities, prophetic and widely ranging hopes and fears, we see the birth of modern Britain, the emergence of our world of today. Volume editors have been encouraged in their selection of material from contemporary

sources to illuminate that density and complexity of things which
is the essence of 'reality'.

Of all the phenomena of change confronting the Victorians,
none had a more immediate impact, or was more concrete and
oppressive, than the growth of great cities. At first bewildered by the
onset of mass urbanization and suburbanization, the Victorians were
increasingly oppressed by the sheer immensity of the unprecedented
social problems. The image which filled their minds was predominantly that of a hungry sea, remorselessly eroding and flooding,
beyond all power of human control. The challenges raised by the
conurbations of modern Britain ranged from matters such as
sewerage, education and public transport to a sense of the city as
a portent of cultural doom. Original fears that great shifts of the
population would change the rural nature of most human living
gave place to fears that man himself would be dehumanized and
reshaped. Both the utopias and nightmares surrounding twentieth-
century industry and technology have their origins in the writings
to concern us here.

Contents

Preface and acknowledgments

The subject of this book is the argument, or series of arguments, in nineteenth-century Britain about cities—their growth and their nature, their causes and their consequences, and their relationship with human nature and with the rest of society. During the century of the 'urban transformation' these questions were current in certain intellectual circles and the discussion was sometimes impassioned and particularly revealing about the participants. The question overlapped with other subjects of controversy and interacted with them, so that some of the comments collected here were contributions to other controversies about, for example, religion, poverty and the industrial system. The argument about cities did, however, have an existence and a continuity of its own, with some distinctive preoccupations, and it is curious that despite Asa Briggs's brief treatment in *Victorian Cities* a decade ago it has attracted relatively little attention in its own right. The growing interest in the history of urbanization justifies a further look at the intellectual and controversial response to the growth of the cities.

Several points should be made clear. First, 'city' (of which the English legal definition has always been unhelpful) is used here to mean, as it often did in contemporary parlance, much what the mid-century census reports designated 'large towns and populous districts'. Though the general process of urbanization provided the setting for the argument about cities, it was generally accepted that there was a fundamental difference (which the term 'city' underlines) between the great towns and the more numerous, smaller and often older ones which figured little in the controversies about cities except when (as with Oxford in mid-century) some pointed contrast with the cities was being made.

Secondly, attitudes to particular cities are considered here only as they contributed to the debate about 'the city' in general or about certain types of city. The exception is London which, as the exemplar and archetype of the great city, could hardly, then or now, be excluded from the consideration of cities in general. Thirdly, no attempt has been made to represent the actual experience of the cities by ordinary people. The subject is the intellectual reflection and controversy within the higher culture, among literary and professional men, politicians and polemicists. It is thus social history only to the extent that the history of ideas is social history.

The introduction to the selections is necessarily too brief to exhaust a subject that is not easily exhausted anyway, and it provides little more than a framework of periodization and a few lines of analysis. The selections themselves merely skim the surface of the contemporary debate, though taking, I hope, some of the cream. They have been made lengthy rather than snippetty, for the most part, in order to show something of the context and development of arguments instead of just isolated ideas and comments. Other items might well have been included, and the bibliography provides some guidance for those who wish to read more extensively for themselves.

The book was conceived at a formal dinner some time ago when Dr R. T. Shannon, in an effort (as I then thought) to keep up his spirits and the conversation, invited his neighbour to write it. Since then he has often been helpful, as has Mr A. E. Dyson. No other individual bears much responsibility for what follows, but I am indebted to my former colleagues, the Master and fellows of Trinity Hall, Cambridge, where I began work on the book, and to my special-subject pupils in the History department of the University of Exeter whose interest and enthusiasm helped to sustain my own.

I am grateful to the following for permission to reproduce extracts from copyright material: The Estate of H. G. Wells for *The Sleeper Awakes* and for *Anticipations*; The Estate of C. F. G. Masterman and Methuen & Co. for *The Condition of England* by C. F. G. Masterman; Faber and Faber Ltd and the M.I.T. Press for *Garden Cities of To-morrow* by Ebenezer Howard; Allen & Unwin for *The Evolution of Modern Capitalism* by J. A. Hobson; Macmillan, London and Basingstoke, for the paper by Patrick Geddes in *Sociological Papers* by F. Galton and others; and Nelson for *Poverty* by B. Seebohm Rowntree.

All possible care has been taken to trace the ownership of copyright in *The Heart of the Empire* and to make acknowledgment for the use of extracts from it.

B. I. Coleman

Introduction

During the nineteenth century Britain experienced what has been called 'the urban transformation'; it changed from an overwhelmingly rural society to a predominantly urban one. Though even in 1800 Britain (excluding Ireland) had been more urbanized than any other nation, and though the extent of urbanization was to vary regionally, the transformation was remarkable, unprecedented anywhere in its scale and duration. It could not have been reasonably anticipated in 1800, and a century later men were still struggling to grasp the nature of the change and its implications.

The urban population increased both absolutely and in relation to the rural one. The population of urban districts with over 5,000 inhabitants increased from 2·3 millions in 1801 to 19·7 millions in 1891.[1] By 1901 some twenty-five million people, 77 per cent of the population, lived in urban districts. In the century before 1901 the numbers living in cities of at least 50,000 inhabitants, had grown from 1·46 millions to 15·1 millions. By one estimate 21·3 per cent of Englishmen had lived in towns of 20,000 or more inhabitants in 1801, but the figure had reached 61·7 per cent by 1891.

Though small towns remained numerous, the most dramatic feature of urbanization was the increase in both number and size of the large towns and cities. In 1801, the year of the first official census, London had been the only city with over 100,000 inhabitants, and only five others had exceeded half that figure; by 1901 there were thirty cities above 100,000 and nineteen others over 50,000. Some of them had long been considerable towns, but others had been created or had risen to importance only during the nineteenth century. The large town of 1900 was several times more populous than its equivalent of 1800, and most cities had spread considerably in area. The term 'the city', which once had commonly denoted London alone, had almost become a synonym for urban society generally. The 1901 census report observed that in general 'the more populous the urban district, the higher is the rate of growth', and some foresaw a society composed of cities of metropolitan scale.

London remained easily the largest city throughout, with over one-tenth of the English population. In 1801 Liverpool with 82,000 inhabitants was the nearest rival to London's 1·1 million; by 1901 greater London contained 6·6 million people to greater Birmingham's 890,000. London was always a special case both in size and in character and it dominated discussion at the start and at the end of the century, though in between attention shifted to the fast-growing industrial cities of the provinces whose special character coloured the controversy about cities for several decades.

The major factor in shifting the demographic balance was migration from the countryside and the smaller towns to the cities. The latter had little natural increment through an excess of births over deaths, and without immigration they would hardly have grown. At least half the inhabitants of nearly every large town in mid-century had been born outside its boundaries. The rural population, which until then had been increasing, though more slowly than the urban population, began to decline after mid-century, and many rural areas experienced substantial depopulation in the century's closing decades.

The process of urbanization and the rise of the cities constituted a profound social transformation of which the early stages had occasioned controversy well before Victoria's accession. Though attitudes were always diverse, the whole argument was affected by several changes of mood. Attitudes to the cities were influenced by the current state of the 'condition of England' question, and so successive phases of pessimism and optimism matched the familiar periodization of nineteenth-century history—a mid-century 'age of equipoise' sandwiched by more troubled periods.

It is sometimes argued that British culture had, and perhaps still has, an anti-urban bias, but contemporary opinion was far from uniformly hostile to the urban transformation. The city always had admirers even if the critics sometimes had the majority. For most of the century the liberal side of politics tended to defend the large towns where it believed its own strength to lie, and the literary depiction of the cities was not always unappreciative. Though there were critics aplenty, some of the fiercest wished to improve the cities rather than to reject them entirely.

Scotland at least was not instinctively hostile. On the whole, Scottish intellectual society came to terms with the cities more easily than its English counterpart, for reasons which probably included the disasters suffered by Highland society, the location of the leading universities in major cities, the harshness of the climate and terrain, and the lower prestige of the landed aristocracy than in England. Their relatively easy acceptance of urban and commercial life assisted the major contribution of Scots, especially economists, to the ideology of British liberalism in the early nineteenth century.

The representative character of the selections printed here is problematical. The public controversy which they illustrate was for the most part conducted by educated and prominent figures from politics, literature and the professions. Only rarely could they claim to speak for significant sections of society. The literary figures were especially idiosyncratic, though even Cobbett, for all the mud on his boots, was perhaps striving to give a shape to dimly-conceived grievances of the countryside rather than stating a commonly-accepted analysis of its problems.

To take one illustration, Arcadianism was a familiar device for denigration of the cities, yet rural life was, and had always been, far from idyllic for many people. There were rural discontents as well as urban ones, and one factor in the drift citywards was probably the migrants' recognition of those advantages of city life which Howard labelled 'the urban magnet', though sometimes rural discouragements may have been a more potent influence than city allurements. Either way the comments collected here on this theme and many others should be treated as reactions to social developments rather than as manifestations of social realities as most people experienced them.

We can do little more than guess at what ordinary people of town and country thought of the cities and their phenomenal growth. The educated and the articulate who publicized and recorded their attitudes to the cities were sometimes influential but they were in a very limited sense representative figures. What the selections and this introduction can do is indicate the nature of their concern, the gist of their argument and the changes in their mood and their interests.

The early nineteenth century

Before 1800 the argument had been less about cities than about London. A certain suspicion inevitably attached to the capital as the one great city in a predominantly agrarian society. As the centre of government and parliament, of court and fashion, of

finance and commerce, it had its admirers, but stern moralists
tended to blame it for the ills they detected in society at large
as well as for its own shortcomings. The critics identified London
in particular and cities in general with political and moral corruption,
cupidity and ambition, luxurious excess, sexual exploitation and
irreligion. Worst of all was London's influence on rural society.
The interests of the countryside were paramount, and its disruption
by city men, manners or money provoked condemnation of the
city and sometimes inspired, by reaction, an Arcadian idealization
of the countryside past or present. Despite London's position as
the centre of intellectual life and artistic patronage, an antithesis
between country good and city evil was already something of a
literary convention.

Tensions between city and countryside were not unique to
England, but here the social and economic influence of London,
the greatest city of its time, encountered a rural society long-
settled, prestigious and with determined and articulate defenders.
The sense of conflict and incompatibility increased early in the
nineteenth century as a phase of social disturbance in the countryside, intensified by the economic effects of prolonged war, coincided
with the rapid growth of London and other large towns.
Meanwhile Paris's role in the French Revolution, following
London's Gordon Riots of 1780, had underlined the danger of the
mob and the problem of political control in cities. After 1815 the
post-war depression in agriculture and the recurrent commercial
crises, which sparked off disorders and agitations in many towns,
encouraged both jeremiads of rural decay and anticipations of
urban insurrection, while the increase of pauperism and the extent
of religious indifference among the poor helped to make the cities
a cause of serious concern.

The two decades after 1815 saw a development and extension of
the argument about cities. With the unprecedented increase in the
number and size of the industrial and commercial cities in northern
England and the Midlands, London was first rivalled and then
replaced as the main preoccupation. The provincial cities, some
of a size only London had attained before, suggested that cities,
far from being as ephemeral as biblical and ancient history had
seemed to indicate, were become a permanent and increasingly
important feature of society. The industrial city also seemed
significantly different from London. It was less conspicuously a
centre of moral and political corruption, it was productive, and

it was not obviously parasitical upon the countryside, while it did not arouse provincial distrust as the capital did. Whether or not the new cities were dangerous developments, they made novel demands on powers of analysis and comprehension. Already a new spirit of social enquiry had established the official census of population, which produced statistical illustration of urban growth, and developed the study of 'political economy'; now the burgeoning of the cities, the proliferation of their problems and a curiosity about the new industrialism encouraged the statistical and impressionistic investigation of urban society.

London had always been seen as a city of social extremes, but now attention was directed to the bottom of society and critics became more alarmed by urban poverty than by 'excess', especially when pauperism strained the poor-relief system and destitution created suffering intolerable to humanitarian conscience. The trade cycle, by creating intense and widespread destitution, advertised the problems of the industrial towns dramatically. The city began to seem a complex of social problems involving the lower classes primarily and including class conflict, vice and crime, irreligion, disease and high mortality, as well as political disorder. Some problems needed urgent and positive action, and from the 1820s measures of social control and amelioration, some of them involving municipal or central government, were being advocated and sometimes implemented. The 'condition of England' controversy of the century's second quarter involved the country-side as well as the large towns, but at least the cities now attracted attention for their own sake. The question of the cities had gained autonomy of agrarian preoccupations.

Its ideological content increased, partly through the impact of the doctrines of Ricardo and his fellow economists. 'Political economy' and its commitment to competitive individualism helped to give the cities confident and capable defenders, though the strong hostile reaction to its teaching increased the polarization of the controversy. The new economic doctrines became identified with the defence of the industrial towns, and the whole argument became entangled with questions of capitalist industrialism, competition and the factory system. The main case for the city became the assertion of the values of economic competition and social individualism, while opponents attacked such theories and practices as mere palliatives of the city's evils, if not the cause of them. Attitudes to the cities and to political economy did not always correspond, but the intrusion of economic theory linked the debate about cities with questions of economic organization, government action and parliamentary politics. Indeed around 1830, with the development of a political divide between reformers and conservatives, there emerged fairly distinctive Whig and Tory attitudes to the cities. Macaulay's disagreement with Southey anticipated features of the Reform Bill debates and of later controversies over the Corn Laws and factory legislation, though some of the Tory arguments were echoed by various radicals and socialists.

By the 1830s the main lines of argument were clear. In the cities the critics saw tendencies towards anarchy, the denial of social responsibility by the wealthy, and the breakdown of community as it had traditionally been understood. Economic competition seemed to be causing or intensifying mass destitution, popular unrest and class conflict as well as leaving the poor in a deplorable religious and moral condition, and the economists' defence of the working of market forces appeared, when stripped of its pretensions, to be mere mammon-worship. For a check upon economic individualism the critics looked sometimes to legislative interference or, more often, to an ideal of social duty and cohesion, a system of social control, which some located in the hierarchic paternalism which they believed to exist in rural society or to have existed in historic times. Pastoralism and mediaevalism were strong among the city's detractors.

The city's advocates stressed the importance to national wealth and strength of urban industry and commerce and their provision of livelihood for a population grown too large for the land to sustain. They pointed not to destitution and the breakdown of social cohesion but to the prosperity and comfort enjoyed by sizeable classes and to the multifarious social institutions of large towns. Economic freedom was only one aspect of the personal independence enjoyed in the cities which nurtured political and intellectual liberty too and claimed to represent intelligence and invention against the stupidity and obscurantism of rural life. Destitution and squalor, far from being inherent features of the cities, would be remedied in time by the economic growth which the Corn Laws were condemned for impeding, though even in the meantime any comparisons with rural society were seen as redounding to the city's advantage.

The argument easily became one between quality and quantity.

The case for the city's commercial civilization lay mainly in material achievement and aggregation; the critics rejected such criteria as pernicious or irrelevant and stressed less tangible matters of social relationships and psychological conditions. Sometimes the idea of progress was at issue. The city's admirers were usually confident of the inevitable advance of civilization; some of their opponents were convinced of social decay and thought major changes necessary to halt the downward slide. They were not always clear, however, whether the cities should and would disappear when social regeneration came. The city's critics indeed divided into those who saw the countryside or various types of model communities as alternatives to the cities and those who sought the amelioration of the existing cities.

Some old preoccupations survived alongside the new ones in the century's second quarter. Economic depression and political agitation, especially Chartism, sustained fears of political violence, though the danger now seemed to be self-conscious political disaffection rather than the brutal irrationality of the mob. City irreligion and immorality attracted increasing attention, though now the Church of England was mounting an effort to convert the city masses to Anglican observance and moral respectability. More novel in its impact was the growing problem of public health, now dramatized by cholera outbreaks and by the new system of registration of births and deaths which showed the highest mortality concentrated in the cities. The 1840s, which saw the rise of the public health movement, provided the climax to the phase of alarm and controversy, but the decade also saw continuing progress in tackling some of the city's problems. The provision of schools, churches and professional police forces and the start of sanitary improvement scarcely amounted to a transformation of urban society, but at least they helped to suggest that the cities could be controlled and improved.

The mid-Victorian period

The century's third quarter corresponded roughly to a period of relative optimism and confidence. Increased prosperity and stability after decades of economic depressions brought an easing of political conflict and social tension. The cities came to appear in a happier light. Their admirers had always insisted that trade expansion would solve most of their problems, and in these buoyant years when free trade and Britain's commercial supremacy went virtually unchallenged the city of industry and commerce seemed less like a volcano and more like a cornucopia.

As the initial shock of rapid urbanization passed, the 'large towns and populous districts' became accepted as one side of the national coin, meriting consideration, even respect, comparable to that accorded to rural society. The acceptance of the cities was unenthusiastic in some cases, but the worst prophecies of earlier years had proved unfounded and the remaining problems seemed less urgent and less threatening. The bitterness and the polarization of the argument became less. Despite the agricultural community's resentment of Corn-Law repeal in 1846, the sense of political confrontation and economic competition between urban and rural interests soon lessened. The countryside had little grievance against the cities as agricultural prosperity returned and the railways linked agricultural producers and city markets. The 1847 Ten Hours Act ended the passionate argument about the factory system and freed the industrial city of some of its guilt-by-association, while the 1848 Public Health Act provided reassurance that sanitary problems would be tackled in districts of high mortality. The public-health reformers, environmentalists in their approach to social problems, argued that improved sewerage, drainage and water-supply would promote the material and moral well-being as well as the physical health of the urban poor, and, despite the piecemeal character of sanitary improvement, its promise of urban amelioration helped to generate optimism and anticipation transcending the immediate achievements.

The new mood was encouraged and symbolized by the railways, for which the 1840s were a decade of dramatic development. They not only encouraged the expectation of social benefits through technological development and business enterprise, but also by extending and strengthening the transport and communications networks centred on the cities showed the inevitability of a continuing concentration of population and economic activity. The recognition of the city's inevitability did not in itself stifle criticism—arguably the city's amendment became even more necessary if there was no alternative to its further growth—but the emotional impetus necessary for reform was lost as the intensity of the early-Victorian preoccupation with social problems declined. The betterment of the condition of the urban poor was left largely to religious institutions, to private philanthropy, to the self-help of individuals and to the working of economic forces in whose beneficence there was general confidence. There was to be little or no outside interference with the economic and social processes which were shaping the cities. Even sanitary reform, which required the action of municipal government, left business enterprise substantially unregulated, imposed no alien ideal or authority upon urban society and did not call into question the totality of city civilization. The cities were to be left to work out their own salvation.

Criticism of the cities lost much of its edge. Arcadian romanticism retreated, and the countryside no longer seemed to provide a model of social organization; nature itself, however much the citizen suffered from the deprivation of its benefits, offered no alternative way of life to the cities. Ideals of rural paternalism and hierarchy became less appealing, and the individual independence which the cities were held to foster became accepted as a positive virtue. The cities were now being measured against their own standards and aspirations, and the assumption that their best hope lay in reproducing the norms of rural society became less common. Comparisons with the countryside rarely suggested that rural society as a whole found the cities wanting. Even romantic mediaevalism gained an urban dimension as the Gothic revival, tiring of ruined abbeys, discovered the mediaeval city and Ruskin urged architects and artists to transform its modern counterpart by the light of Gothic principles.

The self-assurance of the city's spokesmen grew through the mid-Victorian years. No longer reliant on cosmopolitan Whiggery to make their case, urban radicals like Bright and Cowen took the lead in what Arnold called 'glorifying the great towns', and civic pride found warrant in the visible achievements of the industrial cities and in their place in the vanguard of advancing political liberalism. The high-point of confidence and assertion came in the 1870s when Chamberlain's civic gospel celebrated the city as a *polis*, a self-conscious community with a will and a capacity of its own. Under his leadership urban radicalism even aspired to remodel rural society in its own image.

The other side of the political spectrum was less articulate. The Tories spent the years after 1846 absorbing the lessons of free trade and political economy, and electoral expediency came to dictate some accommodation with the interests of the large towns. Many Conservatives, especially those zealous for the Church of England, continued to distrust the cities, but their leaders, aware of the potentialities of 'villa Toryism', tried to give the party an image more congenial to the urban electorate. Views overtly hostile to the cities and what they represented became muted.

The counter to the cities' eulogizers came largely from those literary and artistic figures who now saw the city not as the centre of cultural achievement but as the expression of materialism, acquisitiveness and ethical corruption. The prominence of social questions around 1840 gave literature an inexhaustible supply of material and an absorbing interest in the cities, and a spate of 'social-problem novels' provided vehicles for humanitarian sympathy with human suffering and debasement and for the social environmentalism encouraged by the public health movement. In the third quarter of the century Dickens, Ruskin and Arnold, sceptical of the social values of political economy, sustained both the humanitarian conscience and the aesthetic and intellectual aspiration which adjudged the cities physically repulsive and culturally barren. In their contempt for what the city represented there survived something of the 'condition of England' concern of earlier years, but it was not always clear what transformation of society the critics wanted or by what means. Most critics could see no alternative form of social organization to the cities their preaching did so little to reform.

The late-Victorian and Edwardian periods

By the 1880s the mid-Victorian optimism had evaporated. With the largest cities growing especially fast, the problems, instead of disappearing, seemed to become greater and more intractable. Since mid-century the rural population had been decreasing and the balance between town and country populations shifting rapidly. The question of the cities loomed larger for the prospect (confirmed by the contemporary experience of other advanced societies, notably America) of a society predominantly urbanized. With urbanization apparently accelerating and irreversible, few warmed to the idea of a population compressed into cities no longer supported by a flourishing and stable rural society.

Whether or not these years experienced a 'great depression', much of the old confidence in economic expansion disappeared. The 1880s saw the prominence of the questions of 'the unemployed' and the slums, and, as electoral reform gave the city population more political weight, the increase of unrest and agitation revived fears for society's stability. By now the argument that sustained economic growth would remedy the city's acknowledged ills had worn thin; the long period of stability and expansion since the 1840s had not eliminated destitution, squalor, disease and discontent. Sanitary reform too, despite considerable progress, had not produced spectacular improvements in health and mortality, let alone the promised material and moral elevation of the masses. Instead the limitations and difficulties of environmental improvement had become clear, and the advances of social conscience and investigation were defining problems of housing provision, income levels and nutritional standards which lay beyond the public health movement and even questioned the sufficiency of self-help, philanthropy and business enterprise. The temptation was to despair of the cities, even to look to alternative forms of social organization.

London became the main preoccupation again. It had gained little credit even in the mid-Victorian period when civic optimism had been derived mainly from experience or contemplation of the provincial cities. The city of finance and high society, London provided the most glaring contrasts of wealth and poverty, splendour and squalor, especially in the great contrast between the West End and the East End. By the 1880s the condition of its slums was being dramatically publicized and its employment problems were contributing to the spread of socialist ideas and political militancy. Though the metropolis remained in many ways unique, the rapid growth of the largest cities suggested that London was the shape of cities to come and that its conditions and problems, if not yet typical, were anyway archetypal. With the large city a nationwide, even international, phenomenon, London began to seem just 'the city' writ larger than the rest. The individuality and diversity of cities seemed less evident, and phrases like 'the abyss', 'the ghetto' and 'the vortex' had currency as synonyms for cities in general.

The change of mood reflected particularly the evolution of the political left as the old Whig/Liberal arguments were undermined. Just when electoral reforms dictated a political concern for the urban masses, it became clear that the confidence in economic growth had been exaggerated. Its benefits seemed to have been too narrowly concentrated, and support grew for the view that the condition of the 'submerged tenth' invalidated some of the verities of economic individualism. A generation of 'advanced Liberal' intellectuals became disenchanted with the social consequences of industrialization and urbanization, all the more so as the cities weakened as bastions of Liberal causes with the Tories gaining electoral ground and various kinds of socialism taking root.

A socialist critique of the cities was elaborated too, not wholly distinct from the Liberal one but tending to question the free enterprise system as a whole and not just some of its social effects. The modern city appeared as the creation of business capitalism and the embodiment of its values and tendencies, and the revolutionary element in socialism anticipated a rising of the city populace to overthrow the system of exploitation. Most socialists, however, some of them informed by the London County Council's experiences, advocated various collectivist controls, enterprises and services to modify existing society.

The city's unfavourable image was attributable to more than the extent of destitution and squalor. Its sheer size seemed to dwarf the individual, destroying his sense of community and leaving him insignificant before the forces of technology, capital and government. If socialists feared the tyranny of capital, liberal individualists, fearful perhaps of democracy, sometimes saw a different tyranny latent in the passions of the crowd. A prevailing sense of the city's 'artificiality' was matched by the difficulty of comprehending its nature, of conceiving that anything like intelligence had created and was controlling it. An apocalyptic note crept into the discussion and the suspicion revived that cities were somehow doomed. The alternative seemed to be a national slide into physical degeneracy as the cities exhausted the countryside's resources of men, vitality and health.

The depopulation of the countryside and the pessimism about the cities combined to produce a perceptible nostalgia for rural life. A back-to-the-land impulse, of which radical demands for the creation of a new peasantry were symptomatic, took a variety of forms. There was the added poignancy that an essential Englishness seemed to be in process of being lost through the decline of the countryside and the triumph of the city, international as a phenomenon and cosmopolitan in character.

The gloom was not unrelieved, even outside the revolutionary left which hoped for the city to cure its own disease. The conservative side of politics, though alarmed by socialism, was disturbed less by the cities than some Liberals and socialists were. The Conservative party, strong in the suburban constituencies, was absorbing the leaders of commerce and industry who had always provided apologists for the cities. Conservatism moved towards the *laissez-faire* stance from which the Liberals were uncertainly retreating, and it was a renegade Liberal, Charles Booth, who was provoked by the city's bad press to defend its economic organization. Other social investigators, less enamoured of the cities, questioned society's faith in economic individualism and looked to collectivist action to tackle the ghetto. Some of this thinking influenced the Liberal government's legislation after 1906. Not for the first time the cities were forcing-houses for theories and practices of government.

Science and technology provided another source of hope by offering means of environmental transformation well beyond the old concepts of sanitary reform. The disparity between existing conditions and what was technically feasible, though sometimes depressing, also promoted speculation about the creation or evolution of cities fundamentally different from the existing ones. Society's technical inventiveness and economic vitality, in which confidence was reviving by the Edwardian period, seemed capable of remodelling the cities, notably through the decentralization of the overcrowded city population by new transport and communications systems.

The vision of urban man's industrial and technological capacities being harnessed for the general welfare was only one element in the returning optimism before 1914. 'Civics' and other forms of social investigation were beginning to direct society's creative energies towards the city's transformation. The idea of 'town planning' was gaining acceptance, and the 1909 Housing and Town Planning Act gave an earnest of government's intention to deal with the slums. The possibilities of suburbanizing much of the city population and reducing residential density were becoming clearer. As for the urban poor, Liberal governments had provided various social services designed to benefit the poor directly, and a different prospect was opening up from the steady worsening of the social and physical condition of the city's labour force which some had once anticipated. It was beginning to seem that the cities could once again be reconciled with aspirations to social progress.

Politics and government

Some preoccupations persisted throughout the successive changes
of mood and interest. One perennial was political worry, sometimes about the social stability of cities themselves, at other
times about their influence on national politics. Though mob
violence was a traditional hazard of cities, by 1800 a deeper fear
of the city's insurrectionary potential was developing. The decades
of unrest and agitation after 1815 confirmed the 'volcano' image
of the cities and manufacturing districts, and political prudence
helped to motivate the investigation of urban society and the
search for means of controlling its troublesome manifestations.
Although the century's second quarter developed agencies for
controlling and moralizing the urban poor, the fear of disorder
eased only with the more settled economic conditions in mid-
century. Political unease revived in the 1880s when the virtual
democratization of the representative system coincided with an
extension of trade unionism and an increase of militant socialism,
and once again it stimulated the investigation and reform of the
cities. By 1914, however, the mass electorate had proved itself
more conservative than some had expected, and with the new Labour
party, strong in the cities and backed by most trade unions,
accepting electoral alliance with the Liberals the political forces
of the cities seemed to have been incorporated into the parliamentary
system.

At first the organized and articulate radicalism of more respectable
sections of urban society had also posed problems for government
and for the landed classes. Struggles over parliamentary reform,
the church establishment and the Corn Laws took on at times
something of the character of conflict between the respective
leaders of urban and rural society. The sense of conflict weakened
after the 1840s, only to revive temporarily in the eighties, but
the landed classes and the Church of England suffered a steady
erosion of their political and social influence through the progress
of urbanization. Though the radicalism of the cities never dominated
the political system, it contributed to the ideology and the
parliamentary dominance of the mid-Victorian Liberal party, and
governments came to recognize and cultivate the economic and
social interests of the cities. Later in the century the suburban vote
and business interests moved more to the Tory side, and the cities
seemed to be posing a new political problem—the polarization of

interests and attitudes between capital and labour and the great
gulf between wealth and poverty.

Although the cities were identified with the doctrines of
laissez-faire economics in the early Victorian period, the very
growth of the cities and of capitalist industrialism dictated
extensions of government's role in society. By 1830 the nature
and degree of legislative and administrative intervention were
subjects of controversy, and in time both local and central
authorities enjoyed an accretion of powers with respect to various
aspects of the cities. The spokesmen of the cities did little to
assist this process. They tended to distrust central government
and to lack a positive philosophy of municipal government,
emphasizing instead the 'local self-government' of their communities
and the defence of individual liberties. Toryism too, after
dallying with notions of activist government, did little to provide
a programme or policy for the cities, and its own attitudes to
legislative interference became increasingly defensive. Only
public health reform generated much enthusiasm and impetus until
the 1870s when Chamberlain symbolized a growing faith in the
ability of the cities to transform themselves. The exaltation of
municipal government was naturally the first response to the
recognition of the cities' need for more active and creative
government; it was more compatible with civic pride and the sense
of civic autonomy than 'centralization' would have been. The
creation of the London County Council in 1888 provided a much
vaster challenge to civic government and furthered the idea of
'municipal socialism', but the financial and political limitations
of local government and the recognition that some problems
of the cities required action outside municipal boundaries suggested
the need for a more active and extensive involvement of central
government and for the development of national policies. The
social legislation of the Edwardian period, though still piecemeal
in character, marked a significant extension of central government's
responsibilities in society, though the question whether such
collectivist measures were or needed to be compatible with
economic individualism remained controversial.

The poverty question

From the 1820s the question of mass poverty was integral to the
argument about the cities. Poverty itself was not necessarily seen

as a problem, but the cities dramatized and publicized destitution by concentrating and localizing it, by putting it beyond the reach of traditional paternalism, and by associating it with political disaffection, class conflict, irreligion and public health problems. In particular the industrial towns' vulnerability to the trade cycle produced widespread 'distress' of a kind hard to ignore, and the 'social problem novels' of mid-century depicted the plight of the urban poor as a humanitarian problem. The advocates of the city and of *laissez-faire* economics argued that, given trade expansion, self-help and business enterprise would remedy the worst poverty; the critics of the cities sometimes suspected that the economic forces which were swelling the towns were actually creating intolerable poverty and squalor, but their motley panaceas, ranging from paternalism to legislative interference, were mostly impractical or politically unacceptable. The environmentalism of the public health movement alone won much support, perhaps because it promised the social elevation of the poor without direct interference with the economic process, but it stressed government's duty to suppress nuisances rather than to make positive social provision. The condition of the urban poor attracted less attention during the mid-Victorian phase of economic optimism, but in the 1880s the revelation of the gulf between the rising standards of society at large and the condition of the slum population shattered much of the complacency. The provision of working-class housing, for example, had lagged behind the population increase of the larger cities and now the extent of 'overcrowding' cast doubt on the efficacy of supply-and-demand economics in social matters. The controversy aroused by the condition of the slums and the more systematic analysis of urban poverty helped to make a case for direct action by government upon the income levels, housing provision and welfare of certain social groups. The social legislation of Liberal governments before 1914 made steps in those directions, though some saw the reduction of city-centre congestion as the prerequisite for raising the condition of the slum-dwellers. By then the poverty question had done much to qualify the faith in economic individualism as the regulator of the life of cities and as the social ideal towards which city experience pointed.

The religious question

Religious concerns were another constant feature. Religion was not easily separated from political considerations at first, for one of its recognized functions was to keep society harmonious and easily governable, and the disorders of the early nineteenth century suggested that religious influences and agencies, especially those of the Church Establishment, needed to be strengthened in the large towns. Prudence apart, most influential people were Christians of a sort and expected Britain to be a Christian nation, so that the spectacle of religious indifference, immorality and vice concentrated in the cities was often a prick to conscience. The concern at 'religious destitution' embraced the provincial cities as well as London, long notorious for impiety, and it focused on the poorer classes amongst whom religion seemed least satisfactory.

As the establishment, the Church of England had most to lose from the growth of irreligion or of hostile faiths and recognized a duty towards the cities which its parochial system already attempted to serve. After 1815 the Church was anxious to remedy its own weaknesses in the large towns and to be their healer and stabilizer, but parliamentary support for its efforts was limited by nonconformist hostility and other political pressures. The Church was closely identified with political conservatism, its strength lay in rural society, and its spokesmen tended to distrust the cities on many counts. Despite the churches and schools it built, the parishes it sub-divided, and the novel evangelistic methods it used, the Church never brought the masses to worship in numbers sufficient to remedy its own sense of inadequacy in the cities. Despite its comparative success in prosperous residential districts, by 1900 it felt that its influence at all levels of urban society was weakening and the cities remained more than ever a problem and a puzzle to zealous Anglicans.

Protestant dissent not only lacked Anglicanism's spurs of political expediency and social duty but was also less alarmed by the cities. Nonconformity was strong in the large towns, it valued them as bastions of political and religious liberty against Anglican Toryism, and in general it shared the Liberal optimism about their future. It had reservations, however, about the moral and spiritual condition of the city poor, especially after the disturbing evidence of the 1851 official census of religious worship. Despite their efforts in urban evangelism, the nonconformist denominations themselves were suffering a decline of membership, vitality and confidence by the end of the century, and their disillusionment contributed to the more critical tone of Liberal opinion towards the cities.

By then the distrust of the cities as man's work, not God's, was no longer the prerogative of the pious Anglicans who had long seen religious associations and influences in the countryside but had believed the city less conducive to spiritual faith and experience. There had always been uncertainty whether these deficiencies were inherent or remediable, though it was widely agreed that Christianity was especially necessary in the city to guard against its peculiar difficulties and temptations, but by 1900 the noticeable decline of religious commitment and vitality was posing even more strongly the question whether the life of cities was not essentially materialistic and, in its effects, secularizing. Such suspicions increased the unease about the cities at the century's turn and encouraged regret at the passing of the old rural order. That ethical advance seemed to accompany spiritual decline only compounded the puzzle for some Christians.

Countryside and city

Much of the argument about cities was always in terms of an antithesis between city and countryside, a 'dual image' which varied in its nature and intensity. A society with the village, the estate and the country town its normative communities was seeing itself transformed into a nation dominated by large towns and the balance of its population transferred from countryside to city. At the century's beginning the city was the cuckoo in the nest of rural society, and even when the urban transformation was nearing completion the sense of a rural order recently lost, indeed still decaying, remained strong. Comparisons between city and countryside were inevitable and constant, often excluding any consideration of the smaller towns.

At first most commentators on the cities had identified with the countryside where they originated or resided, whose way of life they took for granted, and to whose ruling classes they belonged or deferred. By mid-century most writers of note acknowledged the city as significant in its own right and had the experience and confidence to write about it from the inside. The countryside had become less immediate and its interests less important. When pastoral nostalgia coloured the discussion of cities later on, it was for an idea of the countryside as much as for its actuality.

In the first half of the century the argument about city and countryside had been, in part, about political authority. The landowners who ruled rural society also bore the responsibilities of national government, and their associations with the universities and the professions helped their prestige in intellectual circles. Tory critics of the cities saw the aristocracy as the embodiment of social duty, order and continuity and used the ideal of landlord paternalism as a stick with which to beat the leaders of urban society; conversely the city's admirers detected aristocratic reaction in the criticism of the cities and the praise of rural society, and they warned that the corollary of aristocratic paternalism was subordination and deference. One difficulty was that the 'local self-government' and social individualism for which the cities stood seemed to provide no acceptable alternative to the landed classes in national government; the democratization of the representative system, which the growth of the cities helped to promote, was accepted only slowly and painfully. The wider acceptance of liberal and individualistic values in the mid-Victorian period meant that the countryside as a social system became less attractive, though the countryside as nature still figured prominently in discussion of the cities. At the end of the century the wistfulness occasioned by the problems of rapid urbanization and the decay of rural society was for man's experience of nature, for the scale and intimacy of rural communities, and for traditional skills and values, rather than for hierarchy and squirearchy. Even the cities' critics saw a simple return to the rural society of the past as neither feasible nor desirable.

After the transformation

There are echoes of nineteenth-century arguments in modern controversies about, for example, urban decay and renewal, pollution, conservation and crime, but the basic situation has changed. Britain is no longer an agrarian society in process of urbanization and industrialization, with all its difficulty and excitement, but a largely urbanized nation which has grown accustomed to its condition and the problems of regulating itself. Cities no longer alarm us by their number, their size and their divergence from an older ideal of social organization, nor do they excite and elate us

by their novelty and by the economic energies and social freedoms
which they once represented.

If the controversies of even the Edwardian era now seem redundant,
it is partly because the structure and character of cities have
changed. The 'loosening of the city texture' which some foresaw
has occurred. The residential suburbs have grown vastly, a
development which, with the slower rate of population growth and
of migration from the countryside, has facilitated the easing of
city overcrowding and the redevelopment of slum areas. The
creation of the welfare state and the wider distribution of the
growing material benefits of the industrial economy have relieved
most of the poverty, disease, squalor and human debasement which
depressed observers of the slums only decades ago. The cities still
have social problems, but we no longer feel helpless before them.
Government is now much stronger, its sensitivity to social questions
is greater, and the need for its action to regulate social and
economic life is widely accepted. The business enterprises concentrated in the cities have become subject to public controls and
influences so that the controversy over economic individualism
has waned. On the other hand the social freedoms of which the
city once boasted have become commonplace. In other respects too
the cities no longer promise or threaten so much. The fear of
democracy has passed, and the political energies of the cities have
been safely institutionalized for the most part. The decline of
Christian commitment has left the cities less conspicuous for their
religious deficiencies, and changes in personal morality have
lessened another source of concern. The unease that remains about
society's values is scarcely focused on the cities as such.

We have indeed lost much of our consciousness of 'the city'—
perhaps inevitably so when there is no longer a distinctively
different (and in some ways rival) social order alongside the cities
and when the spreading suburbs are scarcely identifiable as city
at all. London and the provincial cities are not ready-made scape-
goats for society's problems as they were during the urban transformation. Equally they scarcely hold out the prospect of a
society radically different from what we know already. Even
by 1914 the sense of any alternative to the piecemeal improvement
of existing society was disappearing, and since then the decline
of utopianism has confirmed our commitment to social pragmatism.
The cities, in Britain at least, no longer inspire extremes of
optimism or pessimism, of praise or of criticism. In that sense we

seem to have reached almost an end of ideology, and the ideas, attitudes and responses which the nineteenth-century cities produced among the people who experienced and observed them seem as multifarious and as diverse, as curious and as distant, as those cities themselves.

Note

1 There are difficulties in defining and calculating the 'urban' population: here the urban sanitary districts created by the Public Health Acts are the criterion. Some of the figures (all referring only to England and Wales) are from A. F. Weber, *The Growth of Cities in the Ninteenth Century* (New York, 1899).

One   To the 1820s: The proliferation of the wens

The development of attitudes between Cowper's *The Task* (1) in the 1780s and the writings of the 1820s was considerable. For Cowper, London was the only contemporary English city of much significance. He admired its cultural achievement and pre-eminence, but feared the influence of its modes and morals on rural society, especially on the landowning classes, and condemned its moral corruptions. The city was identified with 'excess' rather than with destitution as it became later. Rural life was the social norm and the foundation of the nation's well-being, and the countryside stood for moral virtue against the unnatural evil of the city. Cities, despite some attractions, seemed to Cowper to be inconsistent with the divine plan as well as with the basic needs of human nature. Wordsworth, a poet of a different generation and background, shared many of these attitudes, though *The Prelude* (2) showed how far the troubled decade of the 1790s had heightened fears of popular disorder in the cities. His sense of London's potential for anarchy was one component of his exploration of the psychology of city life; another was the 'lonely-amidst-the-crowd' theme of human alienation and the breakdown of natural social relationships which was to become one of the staples of the argument about the cities. Wordsworth's retreat from his earlier radicalism to conservatism was matched by his reaction from the 'chaos' of London to the spiritual experiences of nature and the idealization of peasant virtue.

The pseudonymous *Letters from England* (3) by another erstwhile radical, Southey, showed the new industrial towns beginning to alter the terms of debate. An alarmist about the danger of popular insurrection, Southey criticized the physical circumstances and capitalist organization of large-scale industrialism as well as the lack of social discipline in the fast-growing industrial communities. From now on the cities' critics were to focus much more on the condition of the lower classes, though a preoccupation with London as the centre of government still coloured the article by the

Monthly Magazine's editor, Richard Phillips, in 1811 (4). The influence of the new 'science of political economy' showed perhaps in his effort to analyse the causes and constituents of London's growth and in his impatience with the untidy and wasteful sprawl of metropolitan development, but he saw London's expansion as primarily a consequence of its functions as the capital city and he held the view, already becoming archaic, that its decline and fall, the experience of all 'overgrown' cities of the past, were inevitable.

A different historical sense informed Southey's *Quarterly* article of 1820 (5) advocating church extension in the large towns. His admiration for features of pre-Reformation England, especially the sufficiency of its ecclesiastical system, exemplified a new mediaevalistic enthusiasm, encouraged perhaps by Scott's novels, among some of the cities' critics. The growing interest in religious institutions reflected the hope that religion would help to soothe and stabilize a turbulent society as well as the unease of the Church of England at its own failure to adapt to the growth of the cities and at the strength of Dissent there. For all his romanticization of aspects of the past, Southey, unlike most earlier writers, was concerned with practical problems of the cities, particularly the condition and behaviour of the poor, and was seeking practical remedies. So was the Glasgow minister Chalmers in writing one of the earliest major works of urban sociology (6). He too saw the industrial and commercial cities as a peculiar problem and looked to the ecclesiastical establishment to provide much of the solution. An exponent of 'political economy', Chalmers saw the religious and moral deficiencies of the city populace as the result of institutional inadequacies rather than of an inherent inferiority to the rural population, though he admired the parochial system of the countryside and wanted its operation to be reproduced in the cities. His 'moral regimen' of new parishes, schools, domestic visitation and 'Malthusian philanthropy' left little scope for government interference, unlike the schemes of Southey, an opponent of *laissez-faire* theories.

Another Scot, the landowner Sinclair (8), summarized criticisms of the cities, particularly on the score of their unhealthiness, but declined to join the chorus of condemnation himself. He saw urban industry and commerce as providing essential employment for an increasing population and, arguing the benefits to rural society of urban growth, he gave a qualified blessing to the town-wards drift of the population.

A very different agriculturist, Cobbett (7), sought to articulate the grievances of rural society during the post-war agricultural depression. He blamed the politicians and financiers of 'the great wen' for the dislocation caused by successive inflation and deflation and saw taxation of the land to pay interest on the national debt as the worst example of the exploitation of the countryside by city interests as well as one cause of London's continuing growth. The growth of large towns seemed to be inconsistent with the interests of rural society. The working of the land was man's natural activity and the city was a perversion of natural energies, a cancer on the body of agrarian society draining it of people, produce, wealth and vitality. Initially hostile to the factory 'slavery' of the industrial towns and to their competition with rural domestic industry, he later conceded some merit to industrious and productive towns like Sheffield which were sympathetic to his cause of parliamentary reform. By then it was becoming obvious that the 'wens' were not going to disperse by a natural process as Cobbett had once hoped.

1   God made the country, 1785

Extracts from William Cowper, *The Task* (1785), books i, iii and iv.

William Cowper (1731–1800), the poet, came from the landed and professional classes, but he lived and wrote largely outside London literary society. Living at Olney, Buckinghamshire, he came under the influence of the Evangelical movement. In *The Task* he acknowledged London's cultural pre-eminence but condemned its moral corruption and, above all, its influence on rural society.

> But though true worth and virtue, in the mild
> And genial soil of cultivated life
> Thrive most, and may perhaps thrive only there,
> Yet not in cities oft,—in proud and gay
> And gain-devoted cities; thither flow

As to a common and most noisome sewer,
The dregs and faeculence of every land.
In cities foul example on most minds
Begets its likeness. Rank abundance breeds
In gross and pamper'd cities sloth and lust,
And wantonness and gluttonous excess.
In cities, vice is hidden with most ease,
Or seen with least reproach; and virtue taught
By frequent lapse, can hope no triumph there
Beyond the achievement of successful flight.
I do confess them nurseries of the arts,
In which they flourish most; where in the beams
of warm encouragement, and in the eye
Of public note they reach their perfect size.
Such London is, by taste and wealth proclaim'd
The fairest capital of all the world,
By riot and incontinence the worst.
. . . Where has commerce such a mart,
So rich, so throng'd, so drain'd, and so supplied
As London, opulent, enlarged, and still
Increasing London? Babylon of old
Not more the glory of the earth, than she
A more accomplish'd world's chief glory now.
    She has her praise. Now mark a spot or two
That so much beauty would do well to purge;
And show this Queen of Cities, that so fair
May yet be foul, so witty, yet not wise.
It is not seemly, nor of good report
That she is slack in discipline,—more prompt
To avenge than to prevent the breach of law.
That she is rigid in denouncing death
On petty robbers, and indulges life
And liberty, and oft-times honour too
To peculators of the public gold.
. . . nor can it come to good.
That through profane and infidel contempt
Of holy writ, she has presumed to annul
And abrogate, as roundly as she may,
The total ordonance and will of God;
Advancing fashion to the post of truth,
And centering all authority in modes

And customs of her own, till sabbath rites
Have dwindled into unrespected forms,
And knees and hassocks are well-nigh divorced.
   God made the country, and man made the town.
What wonder then, that health and virtue, . . .
. . . should most abound
And least be threatened in the fields and groves?
Possess ye therefore, ye who borne about
In chariots and sedans, know no fatigue
But that of idleness, and taste no scenes
But such as art contrives,—possess ye still
Your element; there only ye can shine,
There only minds like yours can do no harm.
   . . .
   There is a public mischief in your mirth,
It plagues your country. Folly such as yours
Graced with a sword, and worthier of a fan,
Has made, which enemies could ne'er have done,
Our arch of empire, steadfast but for you,
A mutilated structure, soon to fall.

. . . Cities then
Attract us, and neglected Nature pines
Abandon'd, as unworthy of our love.
But are not wholesome airs, . . .
. . . yet secure
From clamour, and whose very silence charms,
To be preferr'd to smoke, to the eclipse
That metropolitan volcanoes make,
Whose Stygian throats breathe darkness all day long,
And to the stir of commerce, driving slow,
And thundering loud, with his ten thousand wheels?
They would be, were not madness in the head
And folly in the heart; were England now
What England was, plain, hospitable, kind,
And undebauch'd. But we have bid farewell
To all the virtues of those better days,
And to all their honest pleasures. Mansions once
Knew their own masters, and laborious hinds
That had survived the father, served the son.
Now the legitimate and rightful Lord

Is but a transient guest, newly arrived
And soon to be supplanted. He that saw
His patrimonial timber cast its leaf,
Sells the last scantling, and transfers the price
To some shrewd sharper, ere it buds again.
Estates are landscapes, gazed upon awhile,
Then advertised, and auctioneer'd away.
The country starves, and they that feed the o'ercharged
And surfeited lewd town with her fair dues,
By a just judgement strip and starve themselves.

    Ambition, avarice, penury incurr'd
By endless riot, vanity, the lust
Of pleasure and variety, dispatch,
As duly as the swallows disappear,
The world of wandering knights and 'squires to town.
London ingulfs them all. The shark is there
And the shark's prey; the spendthrift and the leech
That sucks him: there the sycophant and he
That with bare-headed and obsequious bows
Begs a warm office . . . .
These are the charms that sully and eclipse
The charms of nature. 'Tis the cruel gripe
That lean hard-handed poverty inflicts,
The hope of better things, the chance to win,
The wish to shine, the thirst to be amused,
That at the sound of Winter's hoary wing,
Unpeople all our counties, of such herds
Of fluttering, loitering, cringing, begging, loose
And wanton vagrants, as make London, vast
And boundless as it is, a crowded coop.
    Oh thou resort and mart of all the earth,
Checquer'd with all complexions of mankind,
And spotted with all crimes; in whom I see
Much that I love, and more that I admire,
And all that I abhor; thou freckled fair
That pleases and yet shocks me, I can laugh
And I can weep, can hope, and can despond,
Feel wrath and pity, when I think on thee!
Ten righteous would have saved a city once,
And thou hast many righteous.—Well for thee,—

That salt preserves thee; more corrupted else,
And therefore more obnoxious at this hour,
Than Sodom in her day had power to be,
For whom God heard his Abraham plead in vain.

   The town has tinged the country. And the stain
Appears a spot upon a vestal's robe,
The worse for what it soils. The fashion runs
Down into scenes still rural, but alas!
Scenes rarely graced with rural manners now.
Time was when in the pastoral retreat
The unguarded door was safe. Men did not watch
To invade another's right, or guard their own.
Then sleep was undisturb'd by fear . . . .
Increase of power begets increase of wealth,
Wealth luxury, and luxury excess;
Excess, the scrofulous and itchy plague
That seizes first the opulent, descends
To the next rank contagious, and in time
Taints downward all the graduated scale
Of order, from the chariot to the plough.
The rich, and they that have an arm to check
The licence of the lowest in degree,
Desert their office; and themselves intent
On pleasure, haunt the capital, and thus
To all the violence of lawless hands
Resign the scenes their presence might protect.

'Tis born with all. The love of Nature's works
Is an ingredient in the compound, man,
Infused at the creation of the kind.

. . .

It is a flame that dies not even there
Where nothing feeds it. Neither business, crowds,
Nor habits of luxurious city life,
Whatever else they smother of true worth
In human bosoms, quench it or abate.
The villas with which London stands begirt
Like a swarth Indian with his belt of beads,
Prove it. A breath of unadulterate air,
The glimpse of a green pasture, how they cheer

The citizen, and brace his languid frame!
Even in the stifling bosom of the town,
A garden in which nothing thrives, has charms
That soothe the rich possessor . . . .
What are the casements lined with creeping herbs,
. . . are they not all proofs
That man, immured in cities, still retains
His inborn, inextinguishable thirst
Of rural scenes, compensating his loss
By supplemental shifts, the best he may?
The most unfurnished with the means of life,
And they that never pass their brick-wall bounds
To range the fields and treat their lungs with air,
Yet feel the burning instinct; over head
Suspend their crazy boxes planted thick
And water'd duly. There the pitcher stands
A fragment, and the spoutless tea-pot there;
Sad witnesses how close-pent man regrets
The country, with what ardour he contrives
A peep at nature, when he can no more.

2   The strife of singularity, 1805

Extracts from William Wordsworth, *The Prelude, or, Growth of a Poet's Mind* (1805 version), books vii and viii.

William Wordsworth (1770–1850), the poet, was the son of a Cumberland attorney and agent. After Cambridge he saw London and Paris during the turbulent years of the French Revolution which he welcomed at first. Later, disillusioned with radical politics, he became increasingly conservative and retreated to the Lake District where he lived for the rest of his life. His verse autobiography *The Prelude*, first published in a revised version in 1805, described the poet's response to 'the deformities of crowded life' in London. Though intellectually and emotionally excited by the metropolis, he feared the atomization of society and the latent force and passion of the crowd.

> I glance but at a few conspicuous marks,
> Leaving ten thousand others, that do each,
> In Hall or Court, Conventicle, or Shop,
> In public Room or private, Park or Street,
> With fondness rear'd on his own Pedestal,
> Look out for admiration. Folly, vice,
> Extravagance in gesture, mien, and dress,
> And all the strife of singularity,
> Lies to the ear, and lies to every sense,
> Of these, and of the living shapes they wear,
> There is no end. . . .
>
>   But foolishness, and madness in parade,
> Though most at home in this their dear domain,
> Are scatter'd everywhere, no rarities,
> . . . one feeling was there which belong'd
> To this great City, by exclusive right;
> How often in the overflowing Streets,
> Have I gone forward with the Crowd, and said

Unto myself, the face of every one
That passes by me is a mystery.
Thus have I look'd, nor ceas'd to look, oppress'd
By thoughts of what, and whither, when and how,
Until the shapes before my eyes became
A second-sight procession, such as glides
Over still mountains, or appears in dreams;
And all the ballast of familiar life,
The present, and the past; hope, fear; all stays,
All laws of acting, thinking, speaking man
Went from me, neither knowing me, nor known.
And once, far-travell'd in such mood, beyond
The reach of common indications, lost
Amid the moving pageant, 'twas my chance
Abruptly to be smitten with the view
Of a blind Beggar, who, with upright face,
Stood propp'd against a Wall, upon his Chest
Wearing a written paper, to explain
The story of the Man, and who he was.
My mind did at this spectacle turn round
As with the might of waters, and it seem'd
To me that in this Label was a type,
Or emblem, of the utmost that we know,
Both of ourselves and of the universe;
. . .
. . . What say you then,
To times, when half the City shall break out
Full of one passion, vengeance, rage, or fear,
To executions, to a Street on fire,
Mobs, riots, or rejoicings? From these sights
Take one, an annual Festival, the Fair
Holden when Martyrs suffer'd in past time,
And named of Saint Bartholomew; there see
A work that's finish'd to our hands, that lays,
If any spectacle on earth can do,
The whole creative powers of man asleep!
. . . what a hell
For eyes and ears! what anarchy and din
Barbarian and infernal! 'tis a dream,
Monstrous in colour, motion, shape, sight, sound.
. . .

Oh, blank confusion! and a type not false
To what the mighty City is itself
To all except a Straggler here and there,
To the whole Swarm of its inhabitants;
An indistinguishable world to men,
The slaves unrespited of low pursuits,
Living amid the same perpetual flow
Of trivial objects, melted and reduced
To one identity, by differences
That have no law, no meaning, and no end;
Oppression under which even highest minds
Must labour, whence the strongest are not free;
But though the picture weary out the eye,
By nature an unmanageable sight,
It is not wholly so to him who looks
In steadiness, who hath among least things
An under-sense of greatest; sees the parts
As parts, but with a feeling of the whole.
. . . Attention comes,
And comprehensiveness and memory,
From early converse with the works of God
Among all regions; chiefly where appear
Most obviously simplicity and power.
. . .
This did I feel in that vast receptacle.
The Spirit of Nature was upon me here;
The Soul of Beauty and enduring life
Was present as a habit, and diffused,
Through meagre lines and colours, and the press
Of self-destroying, transitory things
Composure and ennobling Harmony.

With deep devotion, Nature, did I feel
In that great City what I owed to thee,
High thoughts of God and Man, and love of Man,
Triumphant over all those loathsome sights
Of wretchedness and vice; a watchful eye,
Which with the outside of our human life
Not satisfied, must read the inner mind;
For I already had been taught to love
My Fellow-beings, to such habits train'd

Among the woods and mountains, where I found
In thee a gracious Guide. . . .

3 Sleeping upon gunpowder, 1807

Extracts from (Robert Southey), *Letters from England* (1807), letters
36 and 61.

Robert Southey (1774–1843), writer and controversialist, was the
son of a Bristol linen-draper. Educated at Westminster School
and Oxford, he was an extreme radical in the 1790s and became
closely acquainted with Coleridge and Wordsworth. By 1807 he
was moving towards Toryism in reaction against the French
Revolution's consequences on the continent and against economic
and social developments within English society. His *Letters from
England*, written and published as letters from a fictitious Spanish
gentleman touring England, showed Southey's distaste for the
manufacturing cities and his fear of popular insurrection.

BIRMINGHAM

You will perhaps look with some eagerness for information concerning
this famous city, which Burke . . . calls the grand toy-shop of Europe.
. . . I am still giddy, dizzied with the hammering of presses, the clatter
of engines, and the whirling of wheels; my head aches with the
multiplicity of infernal noises, and my eyes with the light of infernal
fires,—I may add, my heart also, at the sight of so many human beings
employed in infernal occupations, and looking as if they were never
destined for anything better. Our earth was designed to be a seminary
for young angels, but the devil has certainly fixed upon this spot for
his own nursery-garden and hot-house.

When we look at gold, we do not think of the poor slaves who
dug it from the caverns of the earth; but I shall never think of the
wealth of England, without remembering that I have been in the
mines. Not that the labourers repine at their lot; . . . incredible as it
may seem, a trifling addition to their weekly pay makes these short-
sighted wretches contend for work, which they certainly know will

in a very few years produce disease and death, or cripple them for the remainder of their existence.

I cannot pretend to say, what is the consumption here of the two-legged beasts of labour; commerce sends in no returns of its killed and wounded. Neither can I say that the people look sickly, having seen no other complexion in the place than what is composed of oil and dust smoke-dried. Every man whom I meet stinks of train-oil and emery. . . .

The noise of Birmingham is beyond description; the hammers seem never to be at rest. The filth is sickening: filthy as some of our old towns may be, their dirt is inoffensive; . . . But here it is active and moving, a living principle of mischief, which fills the whole atmosphere and penetrates everywhere, spotting and staining everything, and getting into the pores and nostrils. I feel as if my throat wanted sweeping like an English chimney. Think not, however, that I am insensible to the wonders of the place:—in no other age or country was there ever so astonishing a display of human ingenuity: but watch-chains, necklaces, and bracelets, buttons, buckles, and snuff-boxes, are dearly purchased at the expense of health and morality: and if it be considered how large a proportion of that ingenuity is employed in making what is hurtful as well as what is useless, it must be confessed that human reason has more cause at present for humiliation than for triumph at Birmingham.

You may well imagine what such people as these would be in times of popular commotion. It was exemplified in 1791. Their fury by good luck was in favour of the government; they set fire to the houses of all the more opulent dissenters whom they suspected of disaffection, and searched everywhere for the heresiarch Priestley, carrying a spit on which they intended to roast him alive. . . .

. . . there is more excuse to be made for dishonesty in Birmingham, than could be pleaded anywhere else. In no other place are there so many ingenious mechanics, in no other place is trade so precarious. War ruins half the manufacturers of Birmingham by shutting half their markets. . . . Even in time of peace the change of fashion throws hundreds out of employ. Want comes upon them suddenly; they cannot dig; and though they might not be ashamed to beg, begging would avail nothing where there are already so many mendicants. It is not to be expected that they will patiently be starved, if by any ingenuity of their own they can save themselves from starving. . . .

Two causes, and only two, will rouse a peasantry to rebellion; intolerable oppression, or religious zeal . . . no other motive is powerful enough. A manufacturing poor is more easily instigated to revolt. They have no local attachments; the persons to whom they look up for support they regard more with envy than respect, as men who grow rich by their labour; they know enough of what is passing in the political world to think themselves politicians; they feel the whole burthen of taxation, which is not the case with the peasant, because he raises a great part of his own food; they are aware of their own numbers, and the moral feelings which in the peasant are only blunted, are in these men debauched. A manufacturing populace is always ripe for rioting,—the direction which this fury may take is accidental; in 1780 it was against the Catholics, in 1790 against the Dissenters. Governments who found their prosperity upon manufacturers sleep upon gunpowder.

Do I then think that England is in danger of revolution? If the manufacturing system continues to be extended, increasing as it necessarily does the number, the misery, and the depravity of the poor, I believe that revolution inevitably must come, and in its most fearful shape. But there are causes which delay the evil, and some which may by an easy possibility avert it, if government should aid them.

That [manufacturing[system certainly threatens the internal tranquillity and undermines the strength of the country. It communicates just knowledge enough to the populace to make them dangerous, and it poisons their morals. The temper of what is called the mob, that is, of this class of people, has been manifested at the death of Despard,[1] and there is no reason to suppose that it is not the same in all other great towns as in London. It will be well for England when her cities shall decrease, and her villages multiply and grow; when there shall be fewer streets and more cottages. The tendency of the present system is to convert the peasantry into poor; her policy should be to reverse this, and to convert the poor into peasantry, to increase and to enlighten them; for their numbers are the strength, and their knowledge is the security of states.

Note

1 Colonel Despard, an aggrieved officer who had plotted to overthrow and murder the government, was executed in 1803.

4   The rise and fall of imperial London, 1811

Extracts from an article by 'Common Sense' (Sir Richard Phillips)
in the *Monthly Magazine*, February 1811, pp. 1 ff.

Richard Phillips (1767–1840, knighted 1808) was a radical politician
and publisher in Leicester and later in London. He was one of the
earliest purveyors of cheap literature for popular instruction, much
of it republican in tone. His article in the *Monthly Magazine*, which
he founded and edited, sought to explain the contemporary growth
of London in terms of the new 'science of political economy'.

No question is so common as, *whence come the inhabitants of all the
new houses built in the suburbs of London?*

Nothing can be more rational than such an enquiry; at least one
thousand houses per annum having been finished in the suburbs of
London during the last forty years—yet every new house is taken
and occupied before it is finished, or its walls dry! This rate of increase
being ten times greater than it was between the death of Elizabeth
and the accession of the Hanoverian family, the causes may be deserving
of investigation, not only as a matter of curiosity, but with reference
to their connection with the science of political economy.

As the new houses are generally of respectable size, and may be
taken at the full number of eight souls to a house, the population of
the metropolis is ascertained ... to have increased in the present age
upwards of three hundred thousand souls. So rapid an increase of
inhabitants is not therefore to be accounted for on ordinary principles;
and it obviously involves a variety of considerations.

... I refer to seven causes chiefly. ...

1 London is not only the ancient metropolis of England and Wales,
but it is now the new metropolis of the added kingdoms of Scotland
and Ireland; and moreover, of our increased colonies in all parts of
the world. In the reign of Elizabeth, it was the metropolis of about
seven millions of people, but it is now the metropolis of an aggregation
of *twenty* millions. It is not therefore to be wondered, without referring

to other causes, that London has increased to treble its size since that time, and that the population ... should be four times greater. All the colonists consider London as their home; it is the focus of their correspondence and interests; their fortunes are remitted to it; and here they find pleasanter means of spending them than among their native wilds, whether in Scotland, Ireland, Yorkshire, or other districts. . . .

2 The increase of our government establishments, the treasury, the customs, the excise, army, navy, and tax-offices; and of our great trading companies, the Bank, the India-house, and others of bill-brokers, bankers, and private establishments, furnishes at least three thousand competent occupiers of the new houses. . . .

3 Persons who live upon annuities derived from the increased public funds, and from the numerous stock companies created in the metropolis within the last twenty or thirty years, are a large class of new metropolitan housekeepers. . . .

4 The general increase of the metropolis, by adding to the mass of luxury, has increased the number of artizans, and persons employed on objects of luxury, such as painters, engravers, jewellers, embroiderers. . . .

5 Another distinct large class of residents, in the immediate environs of London, are French, Dutch, Spanish, German, Italian, and other emigrants who, during the late wars and revolutions, have fled to England, as a place of security. . . .

6 The sixth class of independent residents in the suburbs, are an increased number of persons who have made fortunes of various amounts in trade. . . .

7 The enormous increase of the army and navy, and the consequent increase of officers living on half-pay, and on pensions, leads to the occupation of at least two thousand houses ... not only for the advantages of society, but for the convenience of receiving their annuities, and improving their interests with administration.

Having thus accounted for the augmented population of twenty thousand houses, it is easy to conceive that as many more are greedily taken by tradesmen and others, who purpose to obtain a living out of those by trade and labour of various kinds. There will be bakers, butchers, fruiterers, grocers, public-houses ... all the varieties which compose the industrious and enterprising part of a community, supporting themselves out of the wants of the twenty thousand independent families. . . .

To what extent this increase can be advantageously carried, it is impossible to anticipate. . . . I suspect there never existed so large and populous a city as London, or as London will be, within seven years, when the new streets and squares are erected which have lately been planned on every side of the town. . . . If we retain our foreign colonies, and the continent of Europe continues to be disturbed by revolutions and military conquest, . . . I have no doubt but in another twenty or thirty years, the fields and roads between London and the above-mentioned villages, will be filled by houses, and the population increased from three quarters of a million to a million and a half. This is the necessary consequence of increased empire, of insular security, of civil and religious liberty, and of public confidence.

It is idle to talk of limiting the extent or size of the town by law, unless you could prevent colonists, aliens, and annuitants, from coming to dwell among us. Whether the increased population should be provided for by improvements in the internal parts of the town, or whether by indefinite enlargement, is however a question worthy of consideration. Already the town is found to be of inconvenient size for social and trading purposes . . . There has long ceased to be any common interest between the remote parts of so immense a city: the inhabitant of Mary-le-bone is a foreigner in Wapping; and so is the inhabitant of Spital Fields in Westminster. There are thousands who have arrived at old age in one half of London, who never visited the other half; and other thousands who never saw a ship, though London is the first port in the world. Of course, these are beings of very different habits and characters; and they possess even a varied pronunciation and peculiar idioms. For convenience of trade and association, it would be desirable that the town should be more compact; but it is desirable in regard to health, that it should spread itself to the neighbouring villages. It is however worthy of consideration, whether the interior of the town does not draw more attention, and there can be no doubt but good streets near the centre of business would be preferred . . . to similar streets in remote parts of the town. . . . most of the old streets in the centre of the town, are as worthy of building-speculation as scites in the suburbs. Cross streets are every where wanted; and half a dozen squares northward of the city, would answer as well as Finsbury Square: . . . It is impolitic and senseless to carry the town to Highgate, Hampstead, and Clapham, when so bad a use is made of its internal parts; where whole districts consist almost of waste ground, or are occupied by beggary and wretchedness.

I have often marvelled at the want of concert and general plan with which the extensive suburbs are raised. . . We see street on street rising every where, without any general design; every under-taker building after his own fancy, and to suit the patch of ground of which he is the master. Perhaps it is now too late for parliament to prescribe the plan of future erections; or rather, in this free country magnificence must yield to convenience, and a fancied public good, to private interest.

In conclusion . . . great cities contain in their very greatness, the seeds of premature and rapid decay. London will increase, as long as certain causes operate which she cannot control, and after those cease to operate for a season, her population will require to be renewed by new supplies of wealth; these failing, the houses will become too numerous for the inhabitants, and certain districts will be occupied by beggary and vice, or become depopulated. This disease will spread like an atrophy in the human body, and ruin will follow ruin, till the entire city is disgusting to the remnant of the inhabitants; they flee one after another to a more thriving spot; and at length the whole becomes a heap of ruins! Such have been the causes of the decay of all overgrown cities. Ninevah, Babylon, Antioch, and Thebes are become heaps of ruins, tolerable only to reptiles and wild beasts. Rome, Delhi, and Alexandria, are partaking the same inevitable fate; and London must some time, from similar causes, succumb under the destiny of every thing human.

5   Every parish a little commonwealth, 1820

Extracts from the unsigned article 'New Churches', by Robert
Southey, in *Quarterly Review*, **23**, 1820, pp. 553–4, 557 and 564.

See document 3. By 1820 Southey, now Poet Laureate and a
regular contributor to the Tory *Quarterly Review*, was turning to the
religion and organization of the Church of England as a means of
social control and influence. His article reviewed, among others,
two influential pamphlets by Rev. Richard Yates which had called
for church extension in the cities and helped to bring about the
government's 'Million Act' of 1818 to promote church-building
and the subdivision of populous parishes.

We have . . . adverted to the service which the monastic orders
formerly rendered in aid of the church in this country. While they
existed the church had in itself a principle of growth which kept pace
with the growth of cities, the general increase of population, and the
necessities of society. . . .

From the time of the abolishment of the Regulars the ill consequence
of having diminished the number of religious instructors has been felt.
It was more glaringly manifest in the capital. . . . If even then there
were parishes which . . . 'were grown madly disproportionate,' what
should be said in these days when those parishes have increased twenty
fold! when it appears that, in the metropolis, there are seven parishes
containing each from twenty to thirty thousand inhabitants more than
their respective places of worship can contain,—six wherein the
excess amounts to from thirty to forty thousand; two in which it is
from forty to fifty thousand, and one parish, that of Mary-le-bone,
which has not room in its church and chapels for nine thousand out of a
population of seventy-five!—Nor is this deficiency confined to the
metropolis. In Liverpool, out of 94,000 inhabitants only 21,000 can be
accommodated in the churches; in Manchester, only 11,000 out of
seventy-nine. . . . The deficiency is greatest in growing towns and
cities, the very places where religious instruction is more peculiarly

required: it is an evil which has arisen with the commercial prosperity of the country and keeps pace with it. Our forefathers built convents and cathedrals,—the edifices which we have erected are manufactories and prisons, the former producing tenants for the latter.

Looking back . . . upon England, as it was before the Reformation, we find that the population did not, in all probability, reach to a fourth part of its present amount; that the number of religious instructors was at least twofold of what it is now . . . and that the religion of the country, by means of its forms and ceremonies, was interwoven with the whole business of life. The habits of the people were not migratory at that time. A peasant, perhaps, scarcely ever went thirty miles from the place where he was born, unless he were called away upon military service. There were then no overgrown cities, and the few manufactures which existed were carried on upon a small scale, and in a manner which was neither incompatible with private comfort, nor with public peace and safety.

The diseased growth of parishes frustrated the political as well as the religious purposes of our old parochial system, if we may be permitted to consider apart things which are, strictly speaking, inseparable. Every parish being in itself a little commonwealth, it is easy to conceive, that before manufactures were introduced, or where they do not exist, a parish, where the minister and parochial officers did their duty with activity and zeal, might be almost as well ordered as a private family. Indeed there cannot be a more practicable or a more efficient means of reform than this system of our ancestors would afford, if it were brought fairly into use. Mr. Yates has well pointed out the essential and important benefit of that sort of preventive policy which the parish minister and parish officers were designed to exercise, but which cannot possibly be exercised in our huge city or manufacturing parishes, because 'it is necessarily dependant upon, and derived from a personal knowledge and inspection of all the poor and labouring classes.'

6   The principle of locality, 1821

Extracts from Thomas Chalmers, *The Christian and Civic Economy of Large Towns* (Glasgow, 1821–6, 3 vols), i, pp. 24–9, 95–9, 126–7 and 342–3.

Thomas Chalmers (1780–1847), later Professor of Divinity at Edinburgh University and a leading figure in the Scottish kirk, was minister of a Glasgow parish in 1821. His *Christian and Civic Economy* was intended to reconcile the established churches and the doctrines of political economy and to suggest methods of tackling the poorer classes of the industrial and commercial cities. His insistence that the parochial system of the countryside could and should be reproduced in the large towns encouraged the church extension movements in both Scotland and England. For Chalmers the parochial organization was to be the basis not only of religious and moral influence but also of a 'Malthusian philanthropy' which, with the abolition of statutory poor relief, would encourage self-reliance among the poor.

. . . we believe the difference, in point of moral and religious habit, between a town and country population, to be more due to the difference, in point of adequacy, between the established provision of instruction, for the one and the other, than to any other cause . . . The doctrine of a celestial influence . . . calls for a terrestial mechanism, to guide and extend the distribution of it; and it is under the want of the latter, that a mass of heathenism has deepened, and accumulated, and attained to such a magnitude and density in our large towns. . . . Nor do we think it more rational to look for the rise of Christianity in Pagan lands, without . . . missionary labour, than to look for its revival among the enormous, and now unpervaded departments of the city multitude, without such a locomotive influence, as shall bring the Word of God into material contact with its still, and sluggish, and stationary families.

We hold the possibility, and we cannot doubt the advantage of assimilating a town to a country parish. We think that the same moral regimen, which, under the parochial and ecclesiastical system of Scotland, has been set up, and with so much effect, in her country parishes, may, by a few simple and attainable processes, be introduced into the most crowded of her cities, and with as signal and con-spicuous an effect on the whole habit and character of their population ... in a word, that there is no such dissimilarity between town and country, as to prevent the great national superiority of Scotland, in respect of her well-principled and well-educated people, being just as observable in Glasgow or Edinburgh, for example, as it is in the most retired of her districts ... So that, while the profligacy which obtains in every crowded and concentrated mass of human beings, is looked upon by many a philanthropist as one of those helpless and irreclaimable distempers of the body politic, for which there is no remedy—do we maintain, that there are certain practicable arrange-ments which ... will stay this growing calamity, and would, by the perseverance of a few years, land us in a purer and better generation.

One most essential step towards so desirable an assimilation in a large city parish, is a numerous and well-appointed agency. . . . in a small country parish, the minister alone, or with a very few coad-jutors of a small session, may bring the personal influence of his kind and Christian attentions to bear upon all the families. Among the ten thousand of a city parish, this is impossible; and, therefore, what he cannot do but partially and superficially in his own person, must, if done substantially, be done in the person of others. And he, by divid-ing his parish into small manageable districts—and assigning one or more of his friends, in some capacity or other, to each of them—and vesting them with a right either of superintendence or of enquiry, as will always be found to be gratefully met by the population—and so, raising ... a steady intermedium of communication between himself and the inhabitants of his parish, may at length attain an assimilation in point of result to a country parish, though not in the means by which he arrived at it. . . . In this way, an influence, long unfelt in towns, may be speedily restored to them . . . .

. . . There is no large city which would not soon experience the benefit of such an arrangement. But when that city is purely com-mercial, it is just the arrangement which, of all others, is most fitted to repair a peculiar disadvantage under which it labours. In a provincial capital, the great mass of the population are retained in kindly and immediate dependence on the wealthy residenters of the place. It is the resort of annuitants, and landed proprietors, and members of the law, and other learned professions, who give impulse to a great amount of domestic industry, by their expenditure; and, on inquiring into the sources of maintenance and employment for the labouring classes there, it will be found that they are chiefly engaged in the immediate service of ministering to the wants and luxuries of the higher classes in the city. This brings the two extreme orders of society into that sort of relationship, which is highly favourable to the general blandness and tranquillity of the whole population. In a manufacturing town, on the other hand, the poor and the wealthy stand more disjoined from each other. . . . they meet more on an arena of contest, than on a field where the patronage and custom of the one party are met by the gratitude and good will of the other. When a rich customer calls a workman into his presence, for the purpose of giving him some employment . . . the feeling of the latter must be altogether different from what it would be, were he called into the presence of a trading capitalist, for the purpose of cheapening his work, and being dismissed for another, should there not be an agreement in their terms. We do not aim at the most distant reflection against the manufacturers of our land; but . . . their intercourse with the labouring classes is greatly more an intercourse of collision, and greatly less an intercourse of kindliness, than is that of the higher orders in such towns as Bath, or Oxford, or Edinburgh. In this way, there is a mighty unfilled space interposed between the high and the low of every large manufacturing city, in consequence of which, they are mutually blind to the real cordialities and attractions which belong to each of them; and a resentful feeling is apt to be fostered, either of disdain or defiance, which it will require all the expedients of an enlightened charity effectually to do away. Nor can we guess at a likelier, or a more immediate arrangement for this purpose, than to multiply the agents of Christianity amongst us, whose delight it may be to go forth among the people, on no other errand than that of pure good-will, and with no other ministrations than those of respect and tenderness.

So much for the question of a religious establishment over a country at large. But . . . it has a special advantage in towns, which has been, in a great measure, overlooked, or, at least, been wofully defeated in the practical management of towns.

In our last chapter, we made a comparison between local and general Sabbath schools. Now, a church is, or easily might be, in effect, a local Sabbath school. Its district is, or ought to be, the parish with which it stands nominally associated, and its sitters ought to be the inhabitants of that parish. The established ministers of a large town, should be enabled each to concentrate the full influence of his character and office, on his own distinct and separate portion of the whole territory. . . .

The influence of locality may be resolved into two influences . . . The first is, that by which the minister obtains a more intense feeling of his relationship to his people. The second is, that by which the people obtain a more intense feeling of their relationship to their minister. It is incalculable how much this last is promoted, by the mere juxta-position of the people to one another . . . in a number of contiguous families, all related by one tie to the same place of worship, and the same minister. It would go to revive a feeling, which is now nearly obliterated in towns, whereby the house which a man occupies, should be connected, in his mind, with the parish in which it is situated, and an ecclesiastical relationship be recognized with the clergyman of the parish. In these circumstances . . . attendance upon the parish church, would at length pass into one of the habitual and established proprieties of every little vicinage. Old families would keep it up, and new families would fall into it; and the demand for seats . . . would become more intense every year, so as to form a distinct call for more churches, whenever they were called for by the exigencies of a growing population.

There is nothing in the mere circumstance of being born in a town, or of being imported into it from the country, which can at all reverse any of the laws of our sentient nature. . . . In towns, everything has been done to impede the reiteration of the same attentions upon the same families. The relationship between ministers and their parishes has, to every moral, and to every civilising purpose, been nearly as good as broken up. Every thing has been permitted to run at random; and, as a fruit of the utter disregard of the principle of locality, have the city clergyman and his people almost lost sight of each other. . . . it were giving way to a mystic imagination altogether, did we not believe that the treatment of human nature, which leads to a particular result in the country, would, if transplanted into towns, lead to the same result on their crowded families. We have no right to allege a peculiar aptitude to moral worthlessness, in the latter situation, when we find that every moral influence, which bears upon the former, has, in fact, been withdrawn from our cities. The moral regimen of the one, is diametrically the reverse of what it is in the other; and, not till they are brought under the operation of the same causes, can we estimate aright the question, whether the town or the country is most unfavourable to human virtue.

. . . for many years previous to the extension of this [Sunday school] system, a woful degeneracy was going on in the religious habit and character of our country . . . the religious spirit, once so characteristic of our nation, has long been rapidly subsiding—that, more particularly in our great towns, the population have so outgrown the old ecclesiastical system, as to have accumulated there into so many masses of practical heathenism:—and now the state of the alternative is not, whether the rising generation shall be trained to Christianity in schools, or trained to it under the roof of their fathers; but whether they shall be trained to it in schools, or not trained to it at all. It is whether a process of deterioration, which originated more than half a century ago, and has been rapid and resistless in its various tendencies ever since—whether it shall be suffered to carry our people still more downward in the scale of moral blindness and depravity; or whether the only remaining expedient for arresting it shall be put into operation. . . . as the matter stands, in many a city and in many a parish, the Christian philanthropist is shut up to an effort upon the young, as his last chance for the moral regeneration of our country. In despair . . . of operating, with extensive effect, on the confirmed habit and obstinacy of manhood, he arrests the human plant, at an earlier and more susceptible stage, and . . . showers upon their heads and hearts the only Christian influence they ever are exposed to. He is . . . rearing many young, who, but for him, would have been the still more corrupt descendants of a corrupt parentage, to be the religious guides and examples of a future generation.

7   All-devouring wens, 1821–30

Extracts from William Cobbett, *Rural Rides* (1853 edn), sections for 1821–30.

William Cobbett (1762–1835), the radical journalist and politician, was the son of a Farnham labourer. After 1815 he became a leading agitator for reform of parliament and government. Concerned for the interests of rural society, which was then suffering from the post-war agricultural depression, Cobbett detested a financial and economic system which seemed to favour the towns, London above all, at the expense of the countryside. He also hated the new textile towns for damaging domestic industry in the countryside, though Sheffield's metal industries, complementary rather than inimical to rural production, won his respect. The *Rural Rides*, accounts of horseback tours of England, were first published in collected form in 1830.

[4 December 1821]   This Chatham has had some monstrous wens stuck on to it by the lavish expenditure of the war. These will moulder away. . . . [I learned] of the house-distress in that enormous wen [Portsea], which, during the war, was stuck on to Portsmouth. Not less than fifty thousand people had been drawn together there! These are now dispersing. The coagulated blood is diluting and flowing back through the veins. Whole streets are deserted . . . Is this the 'prosperity of the war?' Have I not, for twenty long years, been regretting the existence of these unnatural embossments; these white swellings, these odious wens, produced by *corruption* and engendering crime and misery and slavery? We shall see the whole of these wens abandoned by the inhabitants, and, at last, the cannons on the fortifications may be of some use in battering down the buildings.—But what is to be the fate of the great wen of all? The monster, called, by the silly coxcombs of the press, 'the metropolis of the empire?' What is to become of that multitude of towns that has been stuck up around it? The village of Kingston was smothered in the town of Portsea;

and why? Because taxes, drained from other parts of the kingdom, were brought thither.

The dispersion of the wen is the only real difficulty that I see in settling the affairs of the nation and restoring it to a happy state. But dispersed it *must* be; and if there be half a million, or more, of people to suffer, the consolation is, that the suffering will de divided into half a million parts. As if the swelling out of London, naturally produced by the funding system, were not sufficient . . . our pretty gentlemen must resort to positive institutions to augment the population of the Wen. They found that the increase of the Wen produced an increase of thieves and prostitutes, an increase of all sorts of diseases, an increase of miseries of all sorts; . . . they must have a *'penitentiary,'* . . . to check the evil, and that they must needs have in the Wen! So that here were a million of pounds, drawn up in taxes, employed not only to keep the thieves and prostitutes still in the *Wen*, but to bring up to the Wen workmen to build the penitentiary, who and whose families, amounting perhaps to thousands, make an addition to the cause of that crime and misery, to check which is the object of the penitentiary! People would follow, they must follow, the million of money. However, this is a piece with all the rest of their goings on. They and their predecessors, ministers and *House*, have been collecting together all the materials for a dreadful explosion; and if the explosion be not dreadful, other heads must point out the means of prevention.

[8 January 1822] In quitting the great Wen we go through Surrey . . . From *St. George's Fields*, which now are covered with houses, we go, towards Croydon, between rows of houses, nearly half the way, and the whole way is nine miles. There are, erected within these four years, two entire miles of stock-jobbers' houses on this one road, and the work goes on with accelerated force! To be sure; for the taxes being, in fact, tripled by Peel's Bill[1], the fundlords increase in riches; and their accommodations increase of course. What an at once horrible and ridiculous thing this country would become, if this thing could go on only for a few years! And these rows of new houses, added to the Wen, are proofs of growing prosperity, are they? These make part of the increased capital of the country, do they? But how is this Wen to be dispersed? I know not whether it be to be done by knife or by caustic; but dispersed it must be! And this is the only difficulty, which I do not see the *easy* means of getting over.

[5 May 1823] More and more new houses are building as you

leave the Wen to come on this road. *Whence come* the means of building these new houses and keeping the inhabitants? Do they come out
of *trade* and *commerce*? Oh, no! they come from *the land* . . . .

[1 August 1823]   As to linen, no farmer's family thinks of buying
linen. The lords of the loom have taken from the land, in England, this
part of its due; and hence one cause of the poverty, misery, and
pauperism that are becoming so frightful throughout the country. A
national debt, and all the taxation and gambling belonging to it, have
a natural tendency to draw wealth into great masses. These masses
produce a power of *congregating* manufactures, and of making the
many work at them, for the *gain of a few*. The taxing government
finds great convenience in these congregations. It can lay its hand
easily upon a part of the produce; as ours does with so much effect.
But the land suffers greatly from this, and the country must finally
feel the fatal effects of it. The country people lose part of their natural
employment. The women and children, who ought to provide a great
part of the raiment, have nothing to do. . . . as the lords of the loom
have now a set of real slaves, by the means of whom they take away a
great part of the employment of the country-women and girls, these
must be kept by poor rates in whatever degree they lose employment
through the lords of the loom. One would think that nothing can be
much plainer than this; and yet you hear the *jolterheads* congratulating
one another upon the increase of Manchester, and such places! . . .

[In the vale of the Wiltshire Avon, 30 August 1826]   These mansions are all down now; and it is curious to see the former *walled
gardens* become *orchards*, together with other changes, all tending to
prove the gradual decay in all except what appertains merely to *the
land* as a thing of production for the distant market. But, indeed, the
people and the means of enjoyment must go away. They are *drawn*
away by the taxes and the paper-money. How are *twenty thousand
new houses* to be, all at once, building in the Wen, without people and
food and raiment going from this valley towards the Wen? It must
be so; and this unnatural, this dilapidating, this ruining and debasing
work must go on, until that which produces it be destroyed. . . .

[11 September 1826]   . . . I saw in one single farm-yard here more
food than enough for four times the inhabitants of the parish . . . but
while the poor creatures that raise the wheat and the barley and cheese
and the mutton and beef are living upon potatoes, an accursed *canal*
comes kindly through the parish to convey away the wheat and all
the good food to the tax-eaters and their attendants in the Wen!
What, then, is this 'an improvement?' Is a nation *richer* for the carrying

away of the food from those who raise it, and giving it to bayonet-men and others, who are assembled in great masses? . . . What! was it not better for the consumers of food to live near to the places where it was grown?

[22 October 1826] *Wens* have devoured market towns and villages . . .

[Near Worcester, 29 September 1826] The glove-trade is, like all others, slack from this last change in the value of money; but there is no horrible misery here, as at Manchester, Leeds, Glasgow, Paisley, and other Hell-Holes of 84 degrees of heat. There misery walks abroad in skin, bone and nakedness. There are no subscriptions wanted for Worcester . . . where manufacturing is mixed with agriculture, where the wife and daughters are at the needle, or the wheel, while the men and the boys are at plough, and where the manufacturing, of which one or two towns are the centres, is spread over the whole country round about, and particularly where it is, in very great part, performed by females in their *own homes*, and where the earnings come *in aid of the man's wages*; in such case the misery cannot be so great; and accordingly, while there is absolute destruction of life going on in the hell-holes, there is no *visible* misery at, or near, Worcester. . . .

Then this glove-manufacturing is not like that of cotton, a mere gambling concern, making baronets to-day and bankrupts to-morrow, and making those who do the work slaves. Here are no masses of people called together by a *bell*, and 'kept *to it*' by a driver; here are no 'patriots' who, while they keep Englishmen to it by fines, and almost by the scourge, in a heat of 84 degrees, are petitioning the parliament to 'give freedom' to the South Americans, who, as these 'patriots' have been informed, use a great quantity of *cottons*!

[31 January 1830] It was dark before we reached Sheffield; so that we saw the iron furnaces in all the horrible splendour of their ever-lasting blaze. Nothing can be conceived more grand or more terrific . . . Nature has placed the beds of iron and the beds of coal alongside of each other, and art has taught man to make one to operate upon the other . . . It is a surprising thing to behold; and it is impossible to behold it without being convinced that, whatever other nations may do with cotton and with wool, they will never equal England with regard to things made of iron and steel. . . . They call it black Sheffield, and black enough it is; but from this one town and its environs go nine-tenths of the knives that are used in the whole world . . . As to the land, viewed in the way of agriculture, it really does appear to be very little worth. . . . But this is all very proper: these coal-diggers, and iron-melters, and knife-makers, compel us to send the food to them, which, indeed, we do very cheerfully, in exchange for the produce of their rocks, and the wondrous works of their hands.

Note

1 The 1819 Act which restored the gold convertibility of paper-money had a deflationary effect on prices and economic activity.

8 The prevailing resort to towns, 1825

Extracts from Sir John Sinclair, *Analysis of the Statistical Account of Scotland*, (2 vols, Edinburgh, 1825), i, pp. 170–3.

John Sinclair (1754–1835, baronetcy 1786) inherited large estates in Caithness at an early age. Politician, agricultural improver, social statistician and would-be polymath, Sinclair was the first president of the government-sponsored Board of Agriculture in 1793 and organized the enquiry of which the results were published from 1791 to 1799 as the multi-volume *Statistical Account of Scotland*. His *Analysis* summarized the contributors' arguments against urbanization in Scotland but added its own defence of the development.

Depopulation in country districts, increase of towns, and encourage-ment given to manufacturing over agricultural industry, are subjects frequently discussed in the statistical volumes . . . In some instances the authors have perhaps gone too far in their objections to the new system; yet it is proper to give a general view of the arguments they make use of, in defence of a country, in preference to a town popula-tion.

It may be admitted, indeed, that where manufacturing families are scattered over a country, and where they have each a few acres of land, in the culture of which they are occasionally employed, a numerous and healthy population will be produced. But when numbers are cooped up, in ill-aired, low, damp houses, following

E

sedentary occupations, neither the parents, nor the children can have much vigour of constitution.

Few more interesting objects can engage the attention of a humane, patriotic, and enlightened statesman, than the question, Whether the increase of population *in towns* be a full compensation for its diminution in the country? . . . Is the *strength* and *security* of the state thereby augmented? Is the acquisition of numbers, and wealth, an equivalent for depravation of morals, and decay of public spirit? Is the *sum of happiness* in the great body of the people increased? Is a town life as favourable as a country one, to the culture of religious affections, and social virtues? Whether does a people, virtuous and religious, though wanting many temporal conveniences and accommodations of life, enjoy most happiness, or they who are less virtuous and religious, but possessed of better accommodations? . . .

Whether this revolution in the state of our country will prove a national advantage; and whether a servile, pallid, and sickly race, brought up in the confined air of cotton-mills, with few attachments, and not trained up in virtuous principles, will compensate for our having lost the sturdy sons of our plains and mountains, or will furnish as loyal and virtuous subjects, as we formerly possessed, are questions which it must be left to posterity fully to determine.

The internal welfare of the people at large, will be endangered and suffer in various ways, if a proper balance between agriculture and commerce be not . . . maintained. If . . . the bulk of our common people be drawn into cities and manufacturing towns, so that the country, whence come food and provisions for the whole community, are left with a scarcity of labourers in husbandry, farmers must then either pay extravagant wages, or be induced to diminish the quantity of cultivated land . . . In years unfavourable to the growth of corn, this decrease in its sowing will be sensibly felt. A loud cry of dearth soon comes from the manufacturing towns. . . . Perhaps, too, a manufacture unsuccessful, or not answering the expectations of its masters, breaks up. The disbanded workmen crowd into cities already in tumult, and increase the unhappy commotions.

The taste for enlarging and uniting farms, which seems to be on the increase throughout Scotland, . . . forces the people from the active, healthy employments of a country life, to take refuge in manufacturing towns and populous cities, which may literally be said to be the graves of the human species. It is accordingly observed, of towns in general, and of large manufacturing towns in particular, that the inhabitants are of a more sickly and delicate appearance, than their neighbours in the country. This may arise from the operation of various causes. From a sedentary life, which enervates and enfeebles the constitution; from impure and unwholesome air; and, above all, from habits of dissipation and profligacy. If it is from towns like these, that our armies must be supplied with recruits, it is easy to see, how ill fitted such men are defending the liberties and dearest rights of their fellow-citizens . . . .

Evils like these may not indeed be sensibly felt, for a considerable time: but though the operation may be slow, yet it will be certain; and they must be the means of accelerating national weakness and decline. In our ardour to extend manufactures and commerce, and to multiply the luxuries of life, we too readily forget, that human nature is liable to temptation, corruption, infirmity of body, and depravity of mind, more especially where great bodies are assembled; and that the prosperity, stability, and glory of nations, do not consist so much in *wealth*, as in their political, military, and personal character . . . and in the practice of those private and public virtues, which are alike conducive to the welfare and stability of kingdoms, and the improvement of the species.

By the change of system we have noticed, the breed of men is enervated, their morals are corrupted, and the strength of the state impaired . . . .

Under this new system, there will be an increase of inhabitants in Scotland; but the question is, will population increase most in well-peopled country parishes, or in crowded towns? In all infectious distempers, as fevers, small-pox, measles, hooping cough, the danger to children is greatest in towns; while their sickly looks show, that the country is preferable. . . . But how can the prevailing resort to towns be prevented, when the present taste is, to raze or suffer almost every house to go to decay, that is not conducive to the benefit of a farm?

These alarming representations, however, are confined to particular districts; for it appears, that during the ten years between 1800–1 and 1810–11 the increase of the inhabitants of Scotland . . . stands thus:—

The inhabitants of towns had increased . . .   907,431
The inhabitants of the country had increased . . .   898,257

. . . it proves the necessity of making *general inquiries*, and not relying exclusively on the representations of a few districts peculiarly circumstanced.

Besides, emigration to towns is the great means, by which employment is found for an increasing population. When the reverse takes place, as in the south of Ireland, the consequence is poverty and distress; nor does it follow, because the town population increases, that the country population diminishes. The supernumerary hands, indeed, leave the country; but the greater variety of articles which the augmented town population requires, renders an increase in the number of country hands necessary, to supply the food, which the increased town population requires; consequently, the country population will keep increasing with that of the town.

Two   From the 1820s to 1848: Passion and partisanship

The fundamental disagreements between the Tory Southey and the Whig Macaulay heralded a period of often passionate controversy. Southey's *Sir Thomas More* (9) elaborated his criticisms of London and the industrial towns as dangers to political order and as concentrations, if not sources, of social evil. He advocated a system of 'municipal police' (including churches, schools and poor relief as well as improved law-enforcement) to control the city poor and ameliorate their social condition. Macaulay (10a), confident of progress, rejected Southey's pessimism, mocked his idealization of the historic countryside, and argued that the economic forces which were enlarging the cities were distributing wealth widely and reducing mortality. Above all he condemned the reliance on an 'omnipotent state' to improve urban conditions. His advocacy of parliamentary reform (10b) showed his readiness to accommodate the interests of urban property within the constitution.

The physician Kay (11), though politically a liberal, wanted to publicize, not deny, social evils like those a cholera outbreak had helped to expose in the worst quarters of Manchester. He advocated municipal regulation of public health, as well as improved police and popular education, but he denied that Manchester's problems were inherent in its condition as an industrial city and he insisted that parliament should not impede its industrial enterprise, the tendencies of which he believed to be beneficial. What the city needed, in his opinion, was environmental regulation but economic freedom. Hostility to the Corn Laws bulked even larger in the popular verse of Ebenezer Elliott (12) who celebrated the technological and economic achievement of the industrial city and its promotion of political liberty. The nonconformist minister and Whiggish historian Vaughan (16) provided a more sophisticated version of the argument. Fearful of an assault on urban interests by the recently-formed Conservative government, Vaughan saw throughout history a continuing struggle between the enlightened civilization of cities and the feudalistic obscurantism of the lords of the soil. For him the city represented progress and liberty—intellectual, religious and political—and of its ultimate triumph he had little doubt. Despite his commitment to the Anti-Corn Law League and to Lancashire industrialism, Cooke Taylor (15) was less confident of the virtues of the city. Fearful of the city masses in a period of Chartism and union troubles, he advocated and anticipated a retreat by the cotton industry from cities like Manchester to rural factory settlements where the enlightened paternalism of the mill-owners would provide social discipline for their workers and make parliamentary interference with capitalist enterprise unnecessary.

Manchester, the exemplar of industrial cities, also dominated Mrs. Gaskell's novel *Mary Barton* (23). Conscious of the extent of squalor, destitution and discontent, and uncertain of the effect on the populace of the move from countryside to city, she could only trust in the ultimate benevolence of providence and hope for the reconciliation of classes through Christian feeling. Dickens's outlook had been equally bleak in *The Old Curiosity Shop* (13), a novel Wordsworthian in its pastoralism and its identification of the city with social atomization and spiritual perversion. By the time he wrote *Dombey* (22), however, Dickens had come to see the railways and the associated urban developments as tokens of progress and, now seeing the city as something to improve rather than to flee, he called for action to remedy the physical and moral debasement to be found in parts of London.

One influence upon Dickens was the public health movement for which Chadwick's *Sanitary Report* (14) provided a manifesto. Far from hostile to the economic interests identified with the cities, Chadwick catalogued the insalubrities of the large towns, where mortality was generally higher than in the countryside, but insisted that such conditions, which were anyway not exclusive to the cities, were remediable. Sanitary regulation would, he promised, alleviate the evils of which the cities' critics complained. The insistence on the city's adaptability to social needs encouraged criticism of specific circumstances but optimism about the long-term evolution of the cities.

Though not quite a pessimist, the High Church clergyman Boone (18) expressed many of the fears and reservations of Tory Anglicans about the cities. He saw the city as primarily a religious problem and insisted that its redemption had to come primarily by religious means, above all by the instrumentality of the Established Church. The Scot Carlyle (17) fitted conventional categories less easily.

Troubled by the plight of the poor and scornful of theories of competitive individualism, he nevertheless admired the energy and enterprise of the business classes, whom he regarded as an aristocracy of talent and merit fitter than the landowning classes to rule society. The city was the reservoir of social evil, rather than the source of it, and embodied the heroic energies which, properly directed, could regenerate society. The unconventional Tory Disraeli was similarly ambivalent. *Coningsby* (19) celebrated the ingenuity and enterprise of Manchester and the imaginative power and scope of the great city, but *Sybil* (21) attacked the notion of social individualism and characterized the city as 'aggregation without association'. The advocates of the economics of competitive individualism generally admired the city, especially the industrial city; their opponents usually condemned it. Carlyle and Disraeli, exhilarated by the cities but anxious for social cohesion which seemed to be threatened by unbridled individualism, cut across normal alignments, as did Cooke Taylor with his readiness to abandon the city in order to save capitalist industrialism.

The German socialist Engels (20) had some ground in common with the native critics. Hostile to the new industrialism and its ideological justifications, he believed that city society was dividing increasingly into extremes of wealth and poverty and that the growth of class consciousness among the city workers portended insurrection. The difference was that he accepted the necessity of such a stage of social evolution and welcomed the prospect of a revolution of the masses. In his indifference too to the possibilities of pragmatic social reform in the cities he was untypical of the way British opinion was moving in the 1840s.

9   Defective order, 1829

Extracts from Robert Southey, *Sir Thomas More: or, Colloquies on
the Progress and Prospects of Society* (2 vols, 1829), colloquies iii, iv, v
and xv.

Now influential as a theorist of conservatism, Robert Southey
elaborated his views on social change (see documents 3 and 5 above)
in his *Colloquies*, written in the form of conversations between one
Montesinos and the ghost of Sir Thomas More. With feudalistic
paternalism no longer practicable, Southey looked instead to
government to discipline urban society and ameliorate its condition.
The rational intervention of governmental agencies was to prevent
the violent revolt which the fragmentation of society in the cities
and manufacturing towns seemed to threaten. See document 10a
for Macaulay's critical reply to Southey.

Sir Thomas More: The importation of that scourge [the plague] is
as possible now as it was in former times: and were it once imported,
do you suppose it would rage with less violence among the crowded
population of your metropolis, than it did before the fire . . . ? On
the contrary, its ravages would be more general and more tremendous,
for it would inevitably be carried everywhere. Your provincial
towns have doubled and trebled in size; and in London itself, great
part of the population is as much crowded as it was then, and the space
which is covered with houses is increased at least fourfold. What if
the sweating-sickness . . . were to show itself again? Can any cause be
assigned why it is not as likely to break out in the nineteenth century
as in the fifteenth? What if your manufactures . . . were to generate
for you new physical plagues, as they have already produced a moral
pestilence unknown to all preceding ages? What if the small-pox . . .
should have assumed a new and more formidable character . . . ?
Visitations of this kind are in the order of nature and providence.
Physically considered, the likelihood of their recurrence becomes every
year more probable than the last; and looking to the moral govern-

ment of the world, was there ever a time when the sins of this kingdom
called more cryingly for chastisement?

. . . perhaps it will be found that the evil [of criminals] is at this time
more widely extended, more intimately connected with the constitution of society, like a chronic and organic disease, and therefore more
difficult of cure. Like other vermin they are numerous in proportion
as they find shelter; and for this species of noxious beast large towns
and manufacturing districts afford better cover than the forest or the
waste. The fault lies in your institutions, which in the time of the Saxons
were better adapted to maintain security and order than they are now.
. . . Every person had his place. There was a system of superintendence
everywhere, civil as well as religious. . . . None were wild, unless
they ran wild wilfully, and in defiance of control. None were beneath
the notice of the priest, nor placed out of the possible reach of his
instruction and his care. But how large a part of your population are
like the dogs at Lisbon and Constantinople, unowned, unbroken to
any useful purpose, subsisting by chance or by prey, living in filth,
mischief, and wretchedness, a nuisance to the community while they
live, and dying miserably at last! This evil had its beginning in my
days; it is now approaching fast to its consummation.

. . . When that [feudal order] also went into decay, municipal
police did not supply its place. Church discipline then fell into disuse;
clerical influence was lost; and the consequence now is, that in a country
where one part of the community enjoys the highest advantages of
civilisation . . . there is among the lower classes a mass of ignorance,
vice, and wretchedness, which no generous heart can contemplate
without grief, and which, when the other signs of the times are considered, may reasonably excite alarm for the fabric of society that rests
upon such a base. It resembles the tower in your own vision, its beautiful
summit elevated above all other buildings, the foundations placed
upon the sand, and mouldering. . . . . . Look at the populace of London,
and ask yourself what security there is that the same blind fury which
broke out in your childhood against the Roman Catholics may
not be excited against the government, in one of those opportunities
which accident is perpetually offering . . . .

Montesinos: It is an observation of Mercier's, that despotism loves
large cities. The remark was made with reference to Paris only a little
while before the French Revolution! But . . . he might have found
sufficient proof that insubordination and anarchy like them quite as
well.

Sir Thomas More: London is the heart of your commercial system, but it is also the hot-bed of corruption. It is at once the centre of wealth and the sink of misery; the seat of intellect and empire: and yet a wilderness wherein they, who live like wild beasts upon their fellow-creatures, find prey and cover. Other wild beasts have long since been extirpated . . . Man, and man alone, is permitted to run wild. . . . ignorance and misery and vice are allowed to grow, and blossom, and seed, not on the waste alone, but in the very garden and pleasure-ground of society and civilisation. . . .

. . . the inefficacious punishment of guilt is less to be deplored and less to be condemned than the total omission of all means for preventing it. Many thousands in your metropolis rise every morning without knowing how they are to subsist during the day, or many of them where they are to lay their heads at night. All men . . . know that wickedness leads to misery; but many . . . have yet to learn that misery is almost as often the cause of wickedness.

Montesinos: There are many who know this, but believe that it is not in the power of human institutions to prevent this misery. They see the effect, but regard the causes as inseparable from the condition of human nature.

Sir Thomas More: As surely as God is good, so surely there is no such thing as necessary evil. . . . Moral evils are of your own making, and undoubtedly the greater part of them may be prevented; . . . if any are lost for want of care and culture, there is a sin of omission in the society to which they belong.

. . . Ask yourself whether the wretched creatures of whom we are discoursing are not abandoned to their fate without the slightest attempt to rescue them from it? . . . Not a winter passes in which some poor wretch does not actually die of cold and hunger in the streets of London! . . . these things happen, to the disgrace of the age and country, and to the opprobrium of humanity, for want of police and order! . . .

Montesinos: . . . It is only in a huge overgrown city that such cases could possibly occur.

Sir Thomas More: The extent of a metropolis ought to produce no such consequences. Whatever be the size of a bee-hive or an ant-hill, the same perfect order is observed in it.

Montesinos: That is because bees and ants act under the guidance of unerring instinct.

Sir Thomas More: As if instinct were a superior faculty to reason! . . . It is for reason to observe and profit by the examples which instinct affords it.

Montesinos: . . . The consequences of defective order are indeed frightful, whether we regard the physical or the moral evils which are produced.

Sir Thomas More: And not less frightful when the political evils are contemplated. . . . you have spirits among you who are labouring day and night to stir up a *bellum servile*, an insurrection like that of Wat Tyler, of the Jacquerie, and of the peasants war in Germany. There is no provocation for this . . . but there are misery and ignorance and desperate wickedness to work upon, which the want of order has produced. Think for a moment what London, nay, what the whole kingdom would be, were your Catalines to succeed in exciting as general an insurrection as that which was raised by one madman in your childhood! Imagine the infatuated and infuriated wretches, whom not Spitalfields, St. Giles's, and Pimlico alone, but all the lanes and alleys and cellars of the metropolis would pour out—a frightful population, whose multitudes, when gathered together, might almost exceed belief! The streets of London would appear to teem with them, like the land of Egypt with its plagues of frogs: and the lava floods from a volcano would be less destructive than the hordes whom your great cities and manufacturing districts would vomit forth! . . .

. . . There is a fourth danger, the growth of your manufacturing system. . . . You have a great and increasing population, exposed at all times by the fluctuations of trade to suffer the greatest privations in the midst of a rich and luxurious society, under little or no restraint from religious principle, and if not absolutely disaffected to the institutions of the country, certainly not attached to them: a class of men aware of their numbers and of their strength; experienced in all the details of combination; improvident when they are in receipt of good wages, yet feeling themselves injured when those wages, during some failure of demand, are so lowered as no longer to afford the means of comfortable subsistence; and directing against the country their resentment and indignation for the evils which have been brought upon them by competition and the spirit of rivalry in trade. They have among them intelligent heads and daring minds; and you have already seen how perilously they may be wrought upon by seditious journalists and seditious orators in a time of distress.

10   The natural progress of society, 1830–1

Extracts from (*a*) the unsigned article [T. B. Macaulay], 'Southey's Colloquies on Society' in *Edinburgh Review*, 50, January 1830, pp. 528ff. (*b*) Macaulay's speech for parliamentary reform in the House of Commons on 2 March 1831. The text used is that in *Speeches of the Rt.Hon. T. B. Macaulay, M.P. Corrected by Himself* (1854).

Thomas Babington Macaulay (1800–59; peerage 1857), author and politician, was the son of a London merchant. Educated at Cambridge, he associated himself with the attitudes and traditions of aristocratic Whiggery at a time when it was making political alliance with the radicalism of the large towns. In the *Edinburgh Review* he replied to Southey's strictures upon the cities and economic change, and he supported parliamentary reform to give increased representation to the large towns.

---

a.

It is in the same manner that Mr. Southey appears to have formed his opinion of the manufacturing system. There is nothing which he hates so bitterly. It is, according to him, a system more tyrannical than that of the feudal ages—a system of actual servitude,—a system which destroys the bodies and degrades the minds of those who are engaged in it. . . .

   Mr. Southey does not bring forward a single fact in support of these views, and, as it seems to us, there are facts which lead to a very different conclusion. In the first place, the poor-rate is very decidedly lower in the manufacturing than in the agricultural districts. . . . the amount of parish relief required by the labourers in the different counties of England, is almost exactly in inverse proportion to the degree in which the manufacturing system has been introduced into those counties. The returns for the years ending in March 1825, and in March 1828, are now before us. In the former year, we find the poor-rate highest in Sussex,—about 20*s* to every inhabitant. Then come Buckinghamshire, Essex, Suffolk, Bedfordshire, Huntingdonshire,

Kent, and Norfolk. In all these the rate is above 15*s* a head. . . . But in the West Riding of Yorkshire, it is as low as 5*s*; and when we come to Lancashire, we find it at 4*s*.,—one-fifth of what it is in Sussex. The returns of the year ending in March 1828, are a little, and but a little, more unfavourable to the manufacturing districts. Lancashire, even in that season of distress, required a smaller poor-rate than any other district . . . These facts seem to indicate that the manufacturer is both in a more comfortable and in a less dependent situation than the agricultural labourer.

As to the effect of the manufacturing system on the bodily health, we must beg leave to estimate it by . . . the proportion of births and deaths. We know that, during the growth of this atrocious system— this new misery,—(we use the phrases of Mr. Southey)— . . . there has been a great diminution of mortality—and that this diminution has been greater in the manufacturing towns than anywhere else. The mortality still is, as it always was, greater in towns than in the country. But the difference has diminished in an extraordinary degree. There is the best reason to believe, that the annual mortality of Manchester, about the middle of the last century, was one in twenty-eight. It is now reckoned at one in forty-five. In Glasgow and Leeds a similar improvement has taken place. Nay, the rate of mortality in those three great capitals of the manufacturing districts, is now considerably less than it was fifty years ago over England and Wales taken together— open country and all. We might with some plausibility maintain, that the people live longer because they are better fed, better lodged, better clothed, and better attended in sickness; and that these improvements are owing to that increase in national wealth which the manufacturing system has produced.

Much more might be said on this subject. But to what end? It is not from bills of mortality and statistical tables that Mr. Southey has learned his political creed. He cannot stoop to study the history of the system which he abuses—to strike the balance between the good and evil which it has produced—to compare district with district, or generation with generation. . . .

. . . The fact is, that Mr. Southey's proposition is opposed to all history, and to the phenomena which surround us on every side. England is the richest country in Europe, the most commercial, and the most manufacturing. Russia and Poland are the poorest countries in Europe. They have scarcely any trade, and none but the rudest manufactures. Is wealth more diffused in Russia and Poland than in England? There are individuals in Russia and Poland, whose incomes are probably equal to those of our richest countrymen. . . . But are there as many fortunes of five thousand a-year, or of one thousand a-year? There are parishes in England, which contain more people of between five hundred and three thousand pounds a-year, than could be found in all the dominions of the Emperor Nicholas. The neat and commodious houses which have been built in London and its vicinity, for people of this class, within the last thirty years, would of themselves form a city larger than the capitals of some European kingdoms. And this is the state of society in which the great proprietors have devoured the smaller!

The cure which Mr. Southey thinks that he has discovered is worthy of the sagacity which he has shown in detecting the evil. The calamities arising from the collection of wealth in the hands of a few capitalists are to be remedied by collecting it in the hands of one great capitalist, who has no conceivable motive to use it better than other capitalists,— the all-devouring state.

It is not strange that, differing so widely from Mr. Southey as to the past progress of society, we should differ from him also as to its possible destiny. . . . We rely on the natural tendency of the human intellect to truth, and on the natural tendency of society to improvement. We know no well-authenticated instance of a people which has decidedly retrograded in civilisation and prosperity, except from the influence of violent and terrible calamities . . . .

History is full of the signs of this natural progress of society. We see in almost every part of the annals of mankind how the industry of individuals, struggling up against wars, taxes, famines, conflagrations, mischievous prohibitions, and more mischievous protections, creates faster than governments can squander, and repairs whatever invaders can destroy. We see the capital of nations increasing, and all the arts of life approaching nearer and nearer to perfection, in spite of the grossest corruption and the wildest profusion on the part of rulers.

b.

. . . We talk of the wisdom of our ancestors: and in one respect at least they were wiser than we. They legislated for their own times. They looked at the England which was before them . . . they would have been amazed indeed if they had foreseen, that a city of more than a hundred thousand inhabitants would be left without Representatives in the nineteenth century, merely because it stood on ground which, in the thirteenth century, had been occupied by a few huts. They framed a representative system, which . . . was well adapted to the state of England in their time. But a great revolution took place. The character of the old corporations changed. New forms of property came into existence. New portions of society rose into importance. ... Towns shrank into villages. Villages swelled into cities larger than the London of the Plantagenets. Unhappily, while the natural growth of society went on, the artificial polity continued unchanged. The ancient form of the representation remained; and. . . the spirit departed. Then came that pressure almost to bursting, the new wine in the old bottles, the new society under the old institutions. It is now time for us to pay a decent, a rational, a manly reverence to our ancestors, not by superstitiously adhering to what they, in other circumstances, did, but by doing what they, in our circumstances, would have done. All history is full of revolutions, produced by causes similar to those which are now operating in England. A portion of the community which had been of no account expands and becomes strong. It demands a place in the system, suited, not to its former weakness, but to its present power. If this is granted, all is well. If this is refused, then comes the struggle between the young energy of one class and the ancient privileges of another. . . . Such . . . is the struggle which the middle classes in England are maintaining against an aristocracy of mere locality, against an aristocracy the principle of which is to invest a hundred potwallopers in one place, or the owner of a ruined hovel in another, with powers which are withheld from cities renowned to the furthest ends of the earth, for the marvels of their wealth and of their industry.

11   Accidental evils and municipal regulation, 1832

Extracts from J. P. Kay, *The Moral and Physical Condition of the Working Classes employed in the Cotton Manufacture in Manchester* (2nd edn, 1832), pp. 8–15, 76–80 and 111–112.

James Kay (later Sir James Kay-Shuttleworth; 1804–77), a Lancastrian educated at Edinburgh University, later became secretary of the Privy Council Committee on Education and promoted the expansion and improvement of popular education with government financial assistance. In 1832 he was a physician in Manchester and his pamphlet, occasioned by a cholera epidemic, was written partly from personal experience and observation. Though he was anxious to publicize and improve the social condition of the poor, Kay's work was largely an extenuation of the factory system, the manufacturers and even of the city of Manchester itself. An advocate of legislation to permit municipal sanitary-regulation, he insisted that Parliament should not interfere with the cotton manufacture itself.

No event is more calculated painfully to excite the public mind, than the invasion of pestilence, and since it cannot be regarded as an isolated calamity, but prevails in consequence of, and in proportion to the existence of others,—no other can be so well calculated to unmask the deformity of evils which have preyed upon the energies of the community. He whose duty it is to follow the steps of this messenger of death, must descend to the abodes of poverty, must frequent the close alleys, the crowded courts, the over peopled habitations of wretchedness, where pauperism and disease congregate round the source of social discontent and political disorder, in the centre of our large towns, and behold with alarm, in the hot-bed of pestilence, ills that fester in secret, at the very heart of society.

That these evils should have been overlooked by the aristocracy of the country, cannot excite surprise. Very few of their order reside in, or near our large provincial towns. . . .Their parks are not often traversed by those who are capable of being the exponents of the evils endured by the working classes of large towns, and the hoarse voice of popular discontent disturbs not the Arcadian stillness of the scene. ... What wonder then, that the miseries of the people have been solemnly denied in both houses of parliament—that popular tumults have been attributed ... to the instigation of unprincipled leaders. ... The public welfare will be most powerfully promoted by every event, which exposes the condition of the people to the gentry of England.

... the enlightened manufacturers of the country, acutely sensitive to the miseries of large masses of the operative body, are to be ranked amongst the foremost advocates of every measure which can remove the pressure of the public burdens from the people, and the most active promoters of every plan which can conduce to their physical improvement, or their moral elevation. ...

You must perceive how the constant presence of this new danger will eventually affect the public mind. Boards of Health ... will become permanent organized centres of medical police, where municipal powers will be directed by scientific men, to the removal of those agencies which most powerfully depress the physical condition of the inhabitants. But I chiefly depend on the strong impression made upon *the public mind*, when I confidently expect that the singular energy of this restless era will be directed to promote, not only by general enactment, but by individual exertion, every scheme devised for the moral elevation of the working classes. .... I have carefully avoided instituting any comparison between the state of the labouring classes of Manchester, and that of those in other large manufacturing towns. I am not without the hope that similar enquiries will be undertaken elsewhere; and if they become general, the first object of this work will be accomplished. Were such investigations conducted ... Manchester might be very favourably compared with many large towns. The improvements which are constantly projected here, are carried on with an energy which shows that the inhabitants of Manchester, as they are second to none in the successful application of science to the arts—in foreign enterprise—and in wealth—so are they determined, in the future, to yield the palm to none in the perfection of their municipal regulations—the number of their institutions for the spread of knowledge and the advancement of science—in the stability of their civic economy, and the ornaments of their social state.

The evils here unreservedly exposed, so far from being the necessary consequences of the manufacturing system, have a remote and accidental origin, and might, by judicious management, be entirely removed. Nor do they flow from any single source: and especially in the present state of trade, the hours of labour cannot be materially diminished, without occasioning the most serious commercial embarrassment. This pamphlet chiefly exhibits a frightful picture of the effects of injudicious legislation. The evils of restricted commerce [by the Corn Laws] affect not the capitalist alone: for the working classes are reserved the bitterest dregs of the poisoned chalice. . . .

Visiting Manchester, the metropolis of the commercial system, a stranger regards with wonder the ingenuity and comprehensive capacity, which, in the short space of half a century, have here established the staple manufacture of this kingdom. He beholds with astonishment the establishments of its merchants—monuments to fertile genius and successful design:—the masses of capital which have been accumulated . . . and the restless but sagacious spirit which has made every part of the known world the scene of their enterprise. The sudden creation of the mighty system of commercial organization which covers this county, and stretches its arms to the most distant seas, attests the power and the dignity of man. . . .

When he turns from the great capitalists, he contemplates the fearful strength only of that multitude of the labouring population, which lies like a slumbering giant at their feet. He has heard of the turbulent riots of the people—of machine breaking—of the secret and sullen organization which has suddenly lit the torch of incendiarism, or well nigh uplifted the arm of rebellion in the land. He remembers that political desperadoes have ever loved to tempt this population to the hazards of the swindling game of revolution, and have scarcely failed. In the midst of so much opulence, however, he has disbelieved the cry of need.

Believing that the natural tendency of unrestricted commerce, (unchecked by the prevailing want of education, and the incentives afforded by imperfect laws to improvidence and vice,) is to develop the energies of society, to increase the comforts and luxuries of life, and to elevate *the physical condition* of every member of the social body, we have exposed . . . the conditions of the lower orders connected with the manufactures of this town, because we conceive that the evils affecting them result *from foreign and accidental causes*. A system, which promotes the advance of civilization, and diffuses it over the world . . . cannot be inconsistent with the happiness of the *great mass of the people*. There are men who believe that the labouring classes are condemned for ever, by an inexorable fate, to the unmitigated curse of toil, scarcely rewarded by the bare necessaries of existence, and often visited by the horrors of hunger and disease—that the heritage of ignorance, labour, and misery is entailed upon them as an eternal doom. Such an opinion might appear to receive a gloomy confirmation . . . only from the history of uncivilized races, and of feudal institutions. No modern Rousseau now rhapsodises on the happiness of the state of nature. Moral and physical degradation are inseparable from barbarism. . . .

Civilization, to which feudality is inimical, but which is most powerfully promoted by commerce, surrounds man with innumerable inventions. It has thus a constant tendency to multiply, without limit, the comforts of existence, and that by an amount of labour, at all times undergoing an indefinite diminution. . . . The cultivation of the faculties, the extension of knowledge, the improvement of the arts, enable man to extend his dominion over matter . . . .

The evils affecting the working classes, *so far from being the necessary results of the commercial system, furnish evidence of a disease which impairs its energies, if it does not threaten its vitality.*

The increase of the manufacturing establishments, and the consequent colonization of the district, have been exceedingly more rapid than the growth of its civic institutions. The eager antagonization of commercial enterprise, has absorbed the attention and concentrated the energies of every member of the community. In this strife, the remote influence of arrangements has sometimes been neglected, not from the want of humanity, but from the pressure of occupation, and the deficiency of time. Thus, some years ago, the internal arrangements of mills (now so much improved) . . . were such as to be extremely objectionable. The same cause has, we think, chiefly occasioned the want of police regulations to prevent the gross neglect of the streets and houses of the poor.

The great and sudden fluctuations to which trade is liable, are often the sources of severe embarrassment. Sometimes the demand for labour diminishes, and its price consequently falls in a corresponding ratio. On the other hand, the existing population has often been totally inadequate to the required production; and capitalists have eagerly invited a supply of labour from . . . the sister kingdom. The colonization of the Irish was thus first encouraged; and has proved one chief source of the demoralization, and consequent physical depression of the people.

The operative population constitutes one of the most important elements in society, and when numerically considered, the magnitude of its interests and the extent of its power assume such vast proportions, that the folly which neglects them is allied to madness. If the higher classes are unwilling to diffuse intelligence among the lower, those exist who are ever ready to take advantage of their ignorance; if they will seek their confidence, others will excite their distrust; if they will not endeavour to promote domestic comfort, virtue, and knowledge among them, their misery, vice, and prejudice will prove volcanic elements, by whose explosive violence the structure of society may be destroyed. The principles developed in this Pamphlet . . . may be unwittingly supposed to have relation to that locality [Manchester] alone. The object of the author will, however, be grossly misunderstood, if it be conceived, that he is desirous of placing in individual prominence defects . . . in the social constitution of his own town. He believes the evils here depicted to be incident, in a much larger degree, to many other great cities, and the means of cure here indicated to be equally capable of application there. His object is simply to offer to the public *an example* of what he conceives to be too generally the state of the working classes, throughout the kingdom, and to illustrate by *specific instances*, evils everywhere requiring the immediate inter-ference of legislative authority.

12   Parts of Nature's plan, 1840

Extracts from 'Steam at Sheffield' in Ebenezer Elliott, *Poetical Works* (1840).

Ebenezer Elliott (1781–1849), the Corn-Law poet, was born near Rotherham, son of a radical Dissenter in the iron trade, which he pursued himself in Sheffield from 1821 to 1842. He blamed the Corn Laws for his own setbacks through the vagaries of the trade cycle, and his verse attacked the Corn Laws and the landed interest and praised the earnest industriousness and mechanical ingenuity of the industrial cities.

> Well, gaze thou on the hills, and hedge-side flowers!
> But blind old Andrew will with me repair
> To yonder massive pile, where useful powers,
> Toiling unconsciously, aloud declare
> That man, too, and his works, are grand and fair.
> . . .

Ill it becomes thee, with ungrateful sneer,
The trade-fed town and townsmen to dispraise.
Why rail at Traffic's wheels, and crowded ways?
Trade makes thee rich; then . . . murmur not
Though Trade's black vapours ever round thee rise.
Trade makes thee sage; lo! thou read'st Locke and Scott!
While the poor rustic, beast-like, lives and dies,
Blind to the page of priceless mysteries!
'Fair is the bow that spans the shower,' thou say'st,
'But all unlovely, as an eyeless skull,
Is man's black workshop in the streeted waste.'
. . . shalt thou despair
To find, where man is found, the grand and fair?
Can'st thou love Nature, and not love the sound
Of cheerful labour? He who loathes the crew
To whose dark hands the toiling oar is bound,
Is dark of spirit, bilious as his hue,
And bread-tax-dyed in Tory lust's true blue.
'Thou lov'st the woods, the rocks, the quiet fields!'
But tell me, if thou can'st, enthusiast wan!
Why the broad town to thee no gladness yields?
If thou lov'st Nature sympathize with man;
For he and his are parts of Nature's plan.
. . .
And cannot the loud hammer, which supplies
Food for the blacksmith's rosy children, make
Sweet music to thy heart? . . .
. . . there is nobler beauty in the form
That welds the hissing steel, with ponderous blow;
Yea, there is majesty on that calm brow,
And in those eyes the light of thoughts divine!

Come, blind old Andrew Turner! link in mine
Thy time-tried arm, and cross the town with me;
For there are wonders mightier far than thine;
Watt! and his million-feeding enginery!
Steam-miracles of demi-deity!
Thou can'st not see, unnumber'd chimneys o'er,
From chimneys tall the smoky cloud aspire;
But thou can'st hear the unwearied crash and roar
Of iron powers, that, urged by restless fire,

Toil ceaseless, day and night, yet never tire,
Or say to greedy man, 'Thou dost amiss.'

Oh, there is glorious harmony in this
Tempestuous music of the giant, Steam,
Commingling growl, and roar, and stamp, and hiss,
With flame and darkness! Like a Cyclop's dream,
It stuns our wondering souls, that start and scream
With joy and terror . . . .
And, rolling wide his sightless eyes, he stands
Before this metal god, that yet shall chase
The tyrant idols of remotest lands,
Preach science to the desert, and efface
The barren curse from every pathless place
Where virtues have not yet atoned for crimes.
He loves the thunder of machinery!
It is beneficent thunder, though, at times,
Like heaven's red bolt, it lightens fatally.

. . . His sightless eyes
Brighten with generous pride, that man hath found
Redemption from the manacles which bound
His powers for many an age. A poor man's boy
Constructed these grand works! Lo! like the sun,
Shines knowledge now on all! He thinks with joy
Of that futurity which is begun—
Of that great victory which shall be won
By Truth o'er Falsehood; and already feels
Earth shaken by the conflict. . . .

. . . Upstart of Yesterday!
Thou doubler of the rent of every farm,
From John o'Groat's to Cornwall's farthest bay!
Engine of Watt! unrivall'd is thy sway.
Compared with thine, what is the tyrant's power?
His might destroys, while thine creates and saves.
Thy triumphs live and grow, like fruit and flower;
But his are writ in blood, and read on graves!
Let him yoke all his regimented slaves,
And bid them strive to wield thy tireless fly,
As thou canst wield it. Soon his baffled bands
Would yield to thee, despite his wrathful eye.

Lo! unto thee both Indies lift their hands!
Thy vapoury pulse is felt on farthest strands!
Thou tirest not, complainest not—though blind
As human pride (earth's lowest dust) art thou.
Child of pale thought! dread masterpiece of mind!
. . .

13   The miseries of Earth, 1840–1

Extracts from Charles Dickens, *The Old Curiosity Shop* (1840–1),
chapters 15 and 44–5.

Charles Dickens (1812–70), son of a government clerk, had achieved
popular success as a writer with *The Pickwick Papers* after early
struggles in London. In *The Old Curiosity Shop* Dickens displayed
a Wordsworthian Arcadianism and a marked antipathy to cities
where he saw the alienation of the individual and the perversion
of the human spirit. The plot centred on the flight of Little Nell
and her grandfather, ruined and persecuted, from London to the
countryside.

[Nell and her grandfather flee London] The two pilgrims . . . pursued
their way in silence. . . . All was so still at that early hour, that the few
pale people whom they met seemed as much unsuited to the scene,
as the sickly lamp which had been here and there left burning was
powerless and faint in the full glory of the sun.

Before they had penetrated very far into the labyrinth of men's
abodes which yet lay between them and the outskirts, this aspect
began to melt away, and noise and bustle to usurp its place. Some
straggling carts and coaches rumbling by, first broke the charm, then
others came, then others yet more active, then a crowd. The wonder
was at first to see a tradesman's window open, but it was a rare
thing soon to see one closed; then smoke rose slowly from the chimneys,
and sashes were thrown up to let in air, and doors were opened . . . .

This quarter passed, they came upon the haunts of commerce and great traffic, where many people were resorting, and business was already rife. The old man looked about him with a startled and bewildered gaze, for these were places that he hoped to shun. He pressed his finger on his lip, and drew the child along by narrow courts and winding ways, nor did he seem at ease until they had left it far behind, often casting a backward look towards it, murmuring that ruin and self-murder were crouching in every street, and would follow if they scented them; and that they could not fly too fast.

Again this quarter passed, they came upon a straggling neighbourhood, where the mean houses parcelled off in rooms, and windows patched with rags and paper, told of the populous poverty that sheltered there. The shops sold goods that only poverty could buy, and sellers and buyers were pinched and griped alike. Here were poor streets where faded gentility essayed with scanty space and shipwrecked means to make its last feeble stand, but tax-gatherer and creditor came there as elsewhere, and the poverty that yet faintly struggled was hardly less squalid and manifest than that which had long ago submitted and given up the game.

This was a wide track—for the humble followers of the camp of wealth pitch their tents around about it for many a mile—but its character was still the same. Damp rotten houses, many to let, many yet building, many half-built and mouldering away—lodgings, where it would be hard to tell which needed pity most, those who let or those who came to take—children, scantily fed and clothed, spread over every street, and sprawling in the dust—scolding mothers, stamping their slipshod feet with noisy threats upon the pavement—shabby fathers, hurrying with dispirited looks to the occupations which brought them 'daily bread' and little more—mangling-women, washerwomen, cobblers, tailors, chandlers, driving their trades in parlours and kitchens and back rooms and garrets, and sometimes all of them under the same roof—brick-fields, skirting gardens paled with staves of old casks, or timber pillaged from houses burnt down and blackened and blistered by the flames—mounds of dock-weed, nettles, coarse grass and oyster-shells, heaped in rank confusion—small Dissenting chapels to teach, with no lack of illustration, the miseries of Earth, and plenty of new churches, erected with a little superfluous wealth, to show the way to Heaven.

At length these streets, becoming more straggling yet, dwindled and dwindled away, until there were only small garden patches bordering the road, with many a summer house innocent of paint and built of old timber or some fragments of a boat . . . To these

succeeded pert cottages, two and two with plots of ground in front ...
Then came the public-house, freshly painted in green and white,
with tea-gardens and a bowling-green ... then fields; and then some
houses, one by one, of goodly size with lawns ... Then came a turn-
pike; then fields again with trees and hay-stacks; then a hill; and on
top of that the traveller might stop, and—looking back at old Saint
Paul's looming through the smoke, its cross peeping above the cloud
(if the day were clear), and glittering in the sun; and casting his eyes
upon the Babel out of which it grew until he traced it down to the
furthest outposts of the invading army of bricks and mortar whose
station lay for the present nearly at his feet—might feel at last that
he was clear of London.

The freshness of the day, the singing of the birds, the beauty of
the waving grass, the deep green leaves, the wild flowers, and the
thousand exquisite scents and sounds that floated in the air,—deep
joys to most of us, but most of all to those whose life is in a crowd
or who live solitarily in great cities as in the bucket of a human
well,—sunk into their breasts and made them glad. The child had
repeated her artless prayers once that morning ... but as she felt all
this, they rose to her lips again. The old man took off his hat—he
had no memory for the words—but he said amen, and that they
were very good.

[They reach Birmingham] The throng of people hurried by, in
two opposite streams, with no symptom of cessation or exhaustion;
intent upon their own affairs; and undisturbed in their business
speculations, by the roar of carts and waggons laden with clashing
wares, the slipping of horses' feet upon the wet and greasy pavement ...
the jostling of the more impatient passengers, and all the noise and
tumult of a crowded street in the high tide of its occupation: while
the two poor strangers, stunned and bewildered by the hurry they
beheld but had no part in, looked mournfully on; feeling amidst the
crowd a solitude which has no parallel but in the thirst of the shipwrecked mariner, who, tossed to and fro upon the billows of a mighty
ocean, his red eyes blinded by looking on the water which hems
him in on every side, has not one drop to cool his burning tongue.

Evening came on. They were still wandering up and down, with
fewer people about them, but the same sense of solitude, in their own
breasts, and the same indifference from all around. The lights in the
streets and shops made them feel yet more desolate, for with their
help, night and darkness seemed to come on faster. Shivering with the

cold and damp, ill in body, and sick to death at heart, the child needed her utmost firmness and resolution even to creep along.

Why had they ever come to this noisy town, when there were peaceful country places, in which, at least, they might have hungered and thirsted with less suffering than in its squalid strife! They were but an atom, here, in a mountain heap of misery, the very sight of which increased their hopelessness and suffering.

In all their journeying, they had never longed so ardently, they had never so pined and wearied, for the freedom of pure air and open country, as now. No, not even on that memorable morning, when, deserting their old home, they abandoned themselves to the mercies of a strange world . . . not even then, had they yearned for the fresh solitudes of wood, hillside, and field, as now; when the noise and dirt and vapour of the great manufacturing town, reeking with lean misery and hungry wretchedness, hemmed them on every side, and seemed to shut out hope, and render escape impossible.

'Two days and nights!' thought the child. 'He said two days and nights we should have to spend among such scenes as these. Oh! if we live to reach the country once again, if we get clear of these dreadful places, though it is only to lie down and die, with what a grateful heart I shall thank God for so much mercy!'

14   Removable circumstances, 1842

Extracts from Edwin Chadwick, *Report on the Sanitary Condition of the Labouring Population of Great Britain* (1842), pp. 4–5, 15, 37, 44, 113–14, 127–34, 167–8, 203 and 370–1.

Edwin Chadwick (1800–1890), civil servant and social reformer, was secretary to the Poor Law Board in 1842. Trained as a lawyer and formerly assistant to the Utilitarian philosopher Bentham, Chadwick had taken a leading part in framing and administering the 1834 Poor Law Act. He became increasingly interested in the health problems of towns and cities, which cholera had publicized, and his official report of 1842 argued for the provision of water supply and sewers and for the appointment of local officers of health in order to reduce mortality and improve health. Though it documented the insalubrious conditions in the cities, it stressed that such conditions were neither a prerogative of towns nor inherent in them. The message was that the cities were improvable and many of their evils remediable.

The first extracts present the subjects of the enquiry in their general condition under the operation of several causes, yet almost all will be found to point to one particular, namely, atmospheric impurity, occasioned by means within the control of legislation, as the main cause of the ravages of epidemic, endemic, and contagious diseases among the community, and as aggravating most other diseases. The subsequent extracts from the sanitary reports from different places will show that the impurity and its evil consequences are greater or less in different places, according as there is more or less sufficient drainage of houses, streets, roads, and land, combined with more or less sufficient means of cleansing and removing solid refuse and impurities, by available supplies of water for the purpose. . . .

The following extracts will serve to show, in the language chiefly of eye-witnesses, the varied forms in which disease attendant on removable circumstances appears from one end of the island to the other amidst the population of rural villages, and of the smaller towns, as well as amidst the population of the commercial cities and the most thronged of the manufacturing districts—in which last pestilence is frequently supposed to have its chief and almost exclusive residence.

The report from Mr. Hodgson and the physicians of the town of Birmingham will be considered a valuable public document, as exhibiting the effect of drainage produced by a peculiarly fortunate situation. The houses, of which I requested drawings, are on the whole built upon an improved plan. This town, it will be seen, is distinguished apparently by an immunity from fever, and the general health of the population is high, although the occupations are such as are elsewhere deemed prejudicial to health.

Between a town population similarly situated in general condition, one part inhabiting streets which are unpaved, and another inhabiting streets that are paved, a general difference of health is observed. The town of Portsmouth is built upon a low portion of the marshy island of Portsea. It was formerly subject to intermittent fever, but since the town was paved, in 1769, it was noticed . . . that this disorder no longer prevailed; whilst Kilsea and the other parts of the island retained the aguish disposition until 1793, when a drainage was made which subdued its force.

The discipline of the army has advanced beyond the civic economy of the towns. . . .

The towns whose population never change their encampment, have no such care, and whilst the houses, streets, courts, lanes, and streams, are polluted and rendered pestilential, the civic officers have generally contented themselves with the most barbarous expedients, or sit still amidst the pollution, with the resignation of Turkish fatalists, under the supposed destiny of the prevalent ignorance, sloth, and filth.

Whilst such neglects are visited by the scourge of a regularly recurring pestilence and ravages of death more severe than a war, it may be confidently stated that the exercise of attention, care, and industry, directed by science in their removal, will not only be attended by exemptions from the pains of the visitation, but with exemptions from pecuniary burdens, and with promise even of the profits of increased production from the community.

. . . if there were a regular system of periodical inspection of the places of work or places of large assemblage, it would be attended with great advantage to the lower orders . . . .

One most important result of such investigations would be to disabuse the popular mind of much prejudice against particular branches of industry arising from the belief that causes of ill health really *accidental* and removable, and sometimes unconnected, are *essentials* to the employment itself. By pointing out the real causes, warning will be given for their avoidance, and indications extended for the application of more certain remedies. . . . A working person of any of the classes whose condition I have described, presenting himself with the symptoms of a consumption, the medical man has no means of detecting *the* one of many causes by which it may have been occasioned . . . unless the medical investigator had himself the means of observing the different personal condition of the different sets of persons following the same occupation in town and in country, it is highly probable that the evidence that the disease is not essential to the occupation would escape him. Thus, between different sets of workmen who work at the same descriptions of work during the same hours, and in the same town, but in well or in ill-ventilated factories, a marked difference in the personal condition and general health of the work-people has been perceived. Great differences are perceptible in the general personal condition of persons working during the same hours in cotton-mills in town, and in cotton-mills in rural districts, where they have not only a purer atmosphere, but commonly larger and more commodious places of abode.

It would require much time and various opportunities of observation to attempt to make an exact analysis of the combined causes, and an estimate of the effect of each separate cause which operate to produce the masses of moral and physical wretchedness met with in the investigation of the condition of the lowest population. But it became evident, in the progress of the inquiry, that several separate circumstances had each its separate moral as well as physical influence. Thus tenements of inferior construction had manifestly an injurious operation on the moral as well as on the sanitary condition, independently of any overcrowding. For example, it appears to be matter of common observation, in the instance of migrant families of workpeople who are obliged to occupy inferior tenements, that their habits soon become 'of a piece' with the dwelling. . . .

Here, then, we have from the one agent, a close and polluted atmosphere, two different sets of effects; the one set here noticed engendering improvidence, expense, and waste,—the other, the depressing effects of external and internal miasma on the nervous system, tending to incite the habitual use of ardent spirits; both tending to precipitate this population into disease and misery. . . .

No education as yet commonly given appears to have availed

against such demoralizing circumstances as those described; but cases of moral improvement of a population, by cleansing, draining, and the improvement of the internal and external conditions of the dwellings, of which instances will be presented, are more numerous and decided . . . The most experienced public officers acquainted with the condition of the inferior population of the towns would agree in giving the first place in efficiency and importance to the removal of what may be termed the physical barriers to improvement, and that as against such barriers moral agencies have but a remote chance of success.

An impression is often prevalent that a heavy mortality is an unavoidable condition of all large towns, and of a town population in general. It has, however, been shown that groups of cottages on a high hill, exposed to the most salubrious breezes when cleanliness is neglected, are often the nests of fever and disease, as intense as the most crowded districts. The mortuary returns of particular districts (in the essentials of drainage, cleansing, and ventilation, to which it is practicable to make other districts approximate . . .) prove that a high degree of mortality does not invariably belong to the population of all towns, and probably not necessarily to any, even where the population is engaged in manufactures. The proportion of deaths appears in some of the suburbs of the metropolis (as at Hackney), and of Manchester and Leeds, to be lower than amongst the highest classes in two of the agricultural counties.

The facts indicated will suffice to show the importance of the moral and political considerations, viz., that the noxious physical agencies depress the health and bodily condition of the population, and act as obstacles to education and to moral culture; that in abridging the duration of the adult life of the working classes they check the growth of productive skill, and abridge the amount of social experience and steady moral habits in the community; that they substitute for a population that accumulates and preserves instruction and is steadily progressive, a population that is young, inexperienced, ignorant, credulous, irritable, passionate, and dangerous, having a perpetual tendency to moral as well as physical deterioration.

The primary and most important measures, and at the same time the most practicable, and within the recognized province of public administration, are drainage, the removal of all refuse of habitations, streets, and roads, and the improvement of the supplies of water.

. . . for the general promotion of the means necessary to prevent disease, that it would be good economy to appoint a district medical officer independent of private practice, and with the securities of special qualifications and responsibilities to initiate sanitary measures and reclaim the execution of the law.

That by the combinations of all these arrangements, it is probable that the full ensurable period of life indicated by the Swedish tables; that is, an increase of 13 years at least, may be extended to the whole of the labouring classes.

That the attainment of these and the other collateral advantages . . . are within the power of the legislature, and are dependent mainly on the securities taken for the application of practical science, skill, and economy in the direction of local public works.

And that the removal of noxious physical circumstances, and the promotion of civic, household, and personal cleanliness, are necessary to the improvement of the moral condition of the population . . . .

15 Not a fair specimen, 1842

Extracts from W. Cooke Taylor, *Notes of a Tour in the Manufacturing Districts of Lancashire: in a series of Letters to his Grace the Archbishop of Dublin* (2nd edn, 1842), pp. 1–15, 140–1, 163–5 and 291–3.

William Cooke Taylor (1800–49), son of an Ulster manufacturer, established himself in London as a political and historical writer. A Whig in politics, he had become a devotee of free-trade ideas and a propagandist for the Anti-Corn Law League, the organization of the Lancashire cotton interest. His *Notes of a Tour*, published when Chartism, the League, the movement for factory legislation and a trade slump were attracting attention to industrial Lancashire, provided a defence of the factory system and attacked the Corn Laws for impeding trade expansion.

I well remember the effect produced on me by my earliest view of Manchester, when I looked upon the town for the first time . . . and saw the forest of chimneys pouring forth volumes of steam and smoke, forming an inky canopy which seemed to embrace and involve the entire place. I felt I was in the presence of those two mighty and mysterious agencies, fire and water . . . and I felt eager to discover how their powers could be employed to the uttermost, and the perils of their ascendency at the same time be averted. Sure I was that such physical agencies, developed before me to a startling extent, must exercise a most important influence over the social, the intellectual, and the moral condition of the community; and I resolved to study their effects in order to discover whether they were productive of good or evil . . . Years have passed away since that morning, but repeated visits to Manchester have not weakened the effects of that first impression. . . .

Like most strangers, I formed at the first an unfavourable opinion of Manchester and the Factory system, because I estimated both by an inapplicable standard,—by the results of previous reading and experience. A second error was that I was disposed to regard factories as modes of social existence placed upon their trial,—to be retained if they were found worthy, and to be rejected if they were proved to be injurious. . . . A great step was gained when I comprehended that the subject I proposed to examine was an 'established innovation.'

. . . . It would be absurd to speak of Factories as mere abstractions, and consider them apart from the manufacturing population: —that population is a stern reality, and cannot be neglected with impunity. As a stranger passes through the masses of human beings which have been accumulated round the mills and print-works in this and the neighbouring towns, he cannot contemplate these 'crowded hives' without feelings of anxiety and apprehension almost amounting to dismay. The population, like the system to which it belongs, is NEW; but it is hourly increasing in breadth and strength. It is an aggregate of masses, our conceptions of which clothe themselves in terms that express something portentous and fearful. We speak not of them indeed as of sudden convulsions, tempestuous seas, or furious hurricanes, but as of the slow rising and gradual swelling of an ocean which must, at some future and no distant time, bear all the elements of society aloft upon its bosom, and float them—Heaven knows whither. There are mighty energies slumbering in those masses: had our ancestors witnessed the assemblage of such a multitude as is poured forth every evening from the mills of Union Street, magistrates would have assembled, special constables would have been sworn, the riot act read, the military called out, and most probably some fatal collision would have taken place. The crowd now scarcely attracts the notice of a passing policeman, but it is, nevertheless, a crowd, and therefore susceptible of the passions which may animate a multitude.

The most striking phenomenon of the Factory system is, the amount of population which it has suddenly accumulated on certain points; there has been long a continuous influx of operatives into the manufacturing districts from other parts of Britain; these men have very speedily laid aside all their old habits and associations, to assume those of the mass in which they are mingled. The manufacturing population is not new in its formation alone: it is new in its habits of thought and action, which have been formed by the circumstances of its condition, with little instruction, and less guidance, from external sources. It may be matter of question whether the circumstances surrounding the manufacturing labourer are better or worse than those belonging to the agricultural condition, but there can be no doubt that the former are preferred by the operative. In the present severe pressure of commercial distress . . . these men submit to the pressure of hunger, and all its attendant sufferings, with an iron endurance which nothing can bend, rather than be carried back to an agricultural district. . . . The Factory system is, therefore, preferred to the more usual conditions of labour by the population which it employs, and this at once ensures its permanence as a formative element of society, and at the same time renders its influence directly efficacious on character.

. . . Contrary to general belief, experience has shown me that Manchester does not afford a fair specimen of the factory population in any of the conditions of its existence, and that the outward aspect of the place affords a very imperfect test of the state of trade in South Lancashire. . . . there is always, and must necessarily be, considerable distress in a place where there is a large demand for untrained labour. Though the factories require skilled labour, yet there are many occupations connected with the commerce of cotton which only demand the exertion of brute strength . . . This demand for untrained labour is not so great as in Liverpool, nor could Manchester exhibit anything so low in the social scale as the dock-population of that port; still the demand exists to a considerable extent, and is mainly, if not entirely, supplied by immigrants from Ireland, Wales, Scotland, and the English agricultural counties. In consequence of the rapidity of the growth of manufactures in Manchester, the increase of population very rapidly outstripped the means of accommodation; even the factory operatives are badly lodged; and the dwellings of the class below them are the most wretched that can be conceived. This is particularly the case in the township of Manchester: its narrow streets, its courts and cellars, have been abandoned to the poorest grade of all. There they live, hidden from the view of the higher ranks by piles of stores, mills, warehouses, and manufacturing establishments, less known to their

G

wealthy neighbours,—who reside chiefly in the open spaces of Cheetham, Broughton, and Chorlton,—than the inhabitants of New Zealand or Kamtschatka.

Your Grace is aware that to some extent Dublin is similarly divided into the city of the rich and the city of the poor; but . . . the smoke-nuisance drives everybody from the township of Manchester who can possibly find means of renting a house elsewhere. These conditions necessarily produce an unhealthy condition of society, both physically and morally. I find that in the township of Manchester the rate of mortality is so high as 1 in 30; and . . . this rate indicates a very large amount of misery and suffering arising from causes purely physical.

Another evil of fearful magnitude arises from this separation of Manchester into districts in which relative poverty and wealth form the demarkation of the frontiers. The rich lose sight of the poor, or only recognise them when attention is forced to their existence by their appearance as vagrants, mendicants, or delinquents. It is a very common error to attribute to the factories the evils which really arise from an immigrating and non-factory population . . . I took some pains to ascertain the character of this immigrating population, and I found it such as to account, in a very great degree, for the high rate of mortality and the low condition of morals in the township of Manchester. It appeared that peasants inadequate to the fatigues of rural toil frequently come into the towns with the hope of finding some light employment suited to their feeble strength, and that persons whose character is blighted in the country seek to escape notice in the crowd of the town. Having conversed with many of these persons, and also made inquiries from the guardians of the poor and the administrators of public charities, I am persuaded that Manchester must long continue to present an appearance of great destitution and delinquency which does not belong to the town itself, but arises from a class of immigrants and passengers.

. . . When perturbating causes of such enormous amount are in operation, it is sufficiently obvious that the condition of Manchester would afford a very erroneous test of the influence of factories on a population.

The factory system had, and . . . has, a tendency within itself to correct many of the evils to which I have directed your Lordship's attention. Before the progress of manufacturing industry met the severe interruption from which it now suffers, it was daily becoming what might perhaps be termed *Sporadic*; new mills, instead of being crowded together in streets, were chiefly erected in villages or in suburbs, affording employers opportunities of coming frequently into personal communication with their workpeople, and exercising a healthy control over their domestic habits and private morals. They could join in instituting circulating libraries, societies for mutual instruction, and for enjoying little concerts of vocal and instrumental music. Such conduct has been exhibited in the establishments of the Greggs, the Ashworths, the Ashtons, the Whiteheads, and many others. Nor can there be a reasonable doubt that, if manufacturing industry had continued prosperous, this system would have been greatly strengthened and extended. A healthy spirit of emulation has long existed among the proprietors of rural mills and print-works: they were not less proud of the comforts and respectable appearance of their operatives than a nobleman is of his palace or demesne. The place in which I am is a proof of the great social benefit which arises from the management I have described: in everything that tends to promote intellectual acquisition the operatives in a well-managed country mill are fully on an equality with their brethren in Manchester; in the means for preserving health, cleanliness, and morality, they are decidely superior.

. . . I devoted the morning to a further examination of the social economy of a country mill, and I am confirmed in my conviction that in no place does labour exist under such favourable conditions. The interest of the proprietor in the health, morals, and prosperity of those he employs is obvious and immediate; most are connected with him in the double relation of workmen and of tenants . . . These circumstances also compel many country manufacturers to go on working their mills at a disadvantage in seasons of commercial distress; because if they stopped, they would have to endure a double loss . . . As a necessary consequence, there is a more patriarchal relation between master and man in the country than can possibly exist in large towns. I repeat . . . that the geographical limits of non-intercourse established in Manchester are the greatest of the special evils connected with that town.

The isolation of classes in England has gone far to divide us into nations as distinct as the Normans and the Saxons . . . Ardwick knows less about Ancoats that it does about China, and feels more interested in the condition of New Zealand than of Little Ireland. . . .

Nowhere can a more perfect contrast to this isolation be found than in Turton, Egerton, Hyde, and most indeed of the country mills which I have visited: there the employer knows the employed and is known by them; an affectionate sense of mutual dependence and mutual interest is created equally advantageous to both parties; the factory displays to a great extent the relations of a family, and the operatives regard themselves as members of one common household. . . .

[A clergyman] . . . has proclaimed from the pulpit the astounding discovery that the extension of manufactures is in some way or other a contravention of the moral purposes of Providence in the government of this world. . . . The reasons for this extraordinary discovery, so far as any reasons can be discovered . . . are the increased demoralization of a population when it is collected into a limited locality, and the greater difficulty of attending to the spiritual wants of a large flock than a small one . . . . Now, is it at all a proved fact that a rural population is more virtuous, moral, and orderly than a town population? I know that such a notion is a very general prejudice—a remnant of the old infidel fallacy, started as a novelty, though it is as old as the hills, by Rousseau in the last century, that the life of the savage is more natural, and therefore more virtuous, than that of the civilised man. But our concern is with facts: those which best illustrate the subject . . . certainly give the balance of morality to the towns. . . .

But we are further to consider how much of the immorality of dense masses of population is to be attributed to manufactures. In the name of common sense, what would they be without the manufactures? I have shown . . . that a very small portion indeed of the delinquency of Manchester can be traced to the factory population . . . I can show by indisputable facts that factories have a decidedly moral tendency. Take the examples of Hyde, Turton, Hollymount, and other manufacturing villages. . . .

16   The spirit of the age, 1843

Extracts from R. Vaughan, *The Age of Great Cities: or, Modern Civilization viewed in its relation to Intelligence, Morals, and Religion* (2nd edn, 1843), pp. 1–8, 77–8, 90–3, 108–9, 116–29, 146–51, and 275–82.

Robert Vaughan (1795–1868) was a Congregational minister and historical writer. From 1835 to 1843 he was professor of history at University College, London, which was patronized by Whig and Liberal politicians. *The Age of Great Cities*, a spirited reply to Tory charges against the cities, provided a defence acceptable both to cosmopolitan Whiggery and to the Liberal nonconformity of the provinces.

Our age is pre-eminently the age of great cities. Babylon and Thebes, Carthage and Rome, were great cities, but the world has never been so covered with cities as at the present time, and society generally has never been so leavened with the spirit natural to cities. In Europe, this fact has assumed its present magnitude by slow degrees. In the meantime, the old state of things, which the progress of commercial enterprise, and its attendant civilization, have done so much to disturb, has profited by the change, and has become stronger, in some respects, by means of the great social revolution which has seemed to threaten it with extinction. If the baron be not so military as formerly, he is more opulent. If his lands are not often so extended, they are more cultivated and more valuable.... But he is no longer alone as the possessor of power. The power which has changed the form of his own power ... has become a rival; and while not unwilling that his social position should be improved by such means, he is by no means willing that any portion of his old pretensions should become subject from this cause to new questionings. ... Hence, while greatly enriched and elevated by the change which is coming fast over all human affairs, the class of persons adverted to are resolutely opposed to some of its most natural tendencies, being much concerned that its influence should

prove favourable to the strength of the privileged, and equally concerned that it should not prove favourable to the strength of the
people.

In no part of Europe is this struggle between the feudal and the civic,
as generally represented by the landlord class and the mercantile class,
so pervading, so organized, or so determined, as among ourselves. In
no other land is there a commercial power embodying so fully the
spirit of the age in this respect; and in no protestant country beside is
there an aristocracy or an established church retaining so much of the
form and spirit of remote times. . . . The elements of social life which
tend necessarily to collision, are nowhere so powerful, nowhere so
nearly balanced . . . .

. . . The power of the commercial interest has never been so great
in the history of this country as at the present moment. But, at the same
time, its exigencies have never been so great, its dangers never so
imminent . . . The danger in respect of the things of the past has
thickened, and the fear and resentment of all the parties concerned to
perpetuate such things have increased in the same proportion.

Hence the time has come, in which some men do not scruple to
speak of great cities as the great evil of the age. It is not deemed too
much to say, that the accident, or revolution, which should diminish
everything commercial and civic, so as to place the military and the
feudal in its old undisturbed ascendancy, would be a change fraught
with more good than with evil. . . . According to some discoveries in
social philosophy which have been recently made, every great city
should be regarded as an unsightly 'wen,' and not as a healthy or
natural portion of the body politic. Its speedy disappearance, either by
dispersion, or by almost any other means, so far from being a matter
to be deplored, should be an object of desire. . . .

Were the error in relation to the social influence of great cities, to
which reference has been made, an error confined in its influence to
the science of politics, I should have readily left it . . . to the sagacity
of politicians. But it extends—and the men who broach it mean that
it should extend—far beyond the circle of mere politics. It bears
immediately upon everything belonging to our most important
interests as a people. If left to its natural course it would be fatal, not
only to all secular freedom, but especially to those purer morals, and
to that higher order of intelligence, which the abettors of such opinions
expect us to regard as matters taken under their peculiar patronage. Its
true tendency must be to bring back the rudeness of a feudal age.
Its natural effect must be, not only to place all religious liberty under

a rigorous proscription, but to supersede religion itself, by substituting the priestly arts of a debasing superstition in its place. . . .

Nothing is further from my intention than any attempt to conceal, or to extenuate, the evils which exist in our great cities, and which have always had their place in connexion with such forms of civilization. The ignorance, the immorality, and the irreligion which grow up in such associations I shall . . . endeavour to make prominent, in in the hope of . . . calling a wiser, and a more Christian attention, to questions concerning the remedies which may be best provided against such evils. But my claim is, that I may be permitted to look to the good belonging to such a state of society, as well as to its evil; and that I may be allowed to institute a fair comparison between this state of things . . . and that other state of things which some men would recall from the past, and substitute in its room. . . .

. . . the strength of Protestantism is a strength on the side of industry, of human improvement, and of the civilization which leads to the formation of great cities. Such cities may be regarded with misgiving . . . But they exist as the result of causes which are manifestly the work of a divine hand. We have our Babylons from the same will of providence that has given to us our Bibles. Our purer Christianity and our great cities are results from the same cause. The genius of Protestantism is the genius of all pacific and manly enterprise. It is in its nature that it should give to the civic spirit this ascendency over the military. So long, also, as it exists, it must exist as a potent agency in favour of the higher culture of cities, as compared with the lower culture of provinces. It is itself from God, and this living impulse in favour of all social elevation which is inseparable from it, is also from him. The present course of things, accordingly, is not to be thrust back or impeded. . . .

. . . Yes—cities, and their resources, must soon become, in a greater degree than ever, the acknowledged wealth and power of nations. Philosophers are beginning to see this; cabinets are obliged to act upon it; and monarchs cannot conceal from themselves that it will be to their interest to conform to this new current in human affairs. Thus the feudal temper, which rested its dominion upon the sword, is giving place to the spirit of a civilization which aims at dominion by means of intelligence, industry, order, law, and liberty. It will not be upon the sovereign and his nobles . . . that the states of Europe in the future will depend for the means of safety. As nations come to abound in great cities, they learn to become their own defenders, and their own rulers.

In forwarding these great moral results, science is lending her
influence in many powerful forms. The new and speedy communication which will soon be completed between all great cities in every
nation of Europe, will necessarily tend to swell the larger towns into
still greater magnitude, and to diminish the weight of many smaller
places, as well as of the rural population generally in social affairs.
Everywhere we trace this disposition to converge upon great points.
It avails nothing to complain of this tendency as novel, inconsiderate,
hazardous. The pressure toward such an issue is irresistible, nor do we
see the slightest prospect of its ceasing to be so.

. . . the danger of great states in the future will be from within
more than from without. . . . The great demand made upon the
wisdom, upon the virtue,—ay, and upon the courage, too, of modern
nations, will be to adjust, in the best manner, the relative claims of the
several classes making up their own respective communities. The one
thing needful in their history will be a good domestic policy. In the
absence of that good, their greatest foes will be those of their own
household.

This increase in the magnitude and power of cities . . . is nowhere
more conspicuous than in Great Britain. In France, during a long period,
all political power had its centre and home in Paris. . . . But this state of
things did not obtain to the same degree in England, especially after
the accession of the house of Stuart. The national strength was manifestly a more diffused and independent strength, pervading in a great
degree all the towns and cities of the land. Since that time, this fact in
our social progress has become more and more prominent. Birmingham, Manchester, Liverpool, all may be said to have been created since
that day. Our country has become emphatically a land of great cities.
Our metropolis has become such as the world has not seen. Our
leading towns in the provinces equal the capitals of ordinary kingdoms.
Whatever, therefore, of good or evil may pertain to the character
of modern civilization, must pertain in an eminent degree to Great
Britain, so that if any nation is to be lost or saved by the character of
its great cities, our own is that nation. . . .

. . . Regarding great cities in their relation to physical science, we may
safely speak of this branch of intelligence as deriving all its higher
culture, if not its existence, from the ingenuities which are natural to
men in such associations. Cities are at once the great effect, and the
great cause, of progress in this department of knowledge. The monuments of Thebes and Persepolis, of Athens and Rome, are as so many
mutilated treatises on the science of the ancients. . . . Cities which can

hardly be said to have had a literature at all, have risen to extraordinary magnificence purely as the effect of science. . . .

Every region that has become the home of such cities has become the home of an improved agriculture. This has resulted in part from the wealth of the cities; but still more from their mechanical and scientific skill. In this manner it has often been reserved to cities to convert the desert into a garden, and to give to the richer soils of the earth the aspect of a paradise. . . . The owners of land, accordingly, have always had a deep interest in the prosperity of cities; and when such persons begin to regard cities with jealousy, . . . they become chargeable with the baseness of ingratitude, or with the madness of self-destruction. . . .

. . . science is . . . the parent and the offspring of cities, first creating them, and then nourished by them. . . .

. . . If the influence of great cities on the progress of natural science is thus manifest, their tendency to foster just and enlightened views in relation to political science is no less obvious. Every municipal body must have its local regulations, and its local functionaries to carry them into effect. As those regulations have respect to the common interest, it is natural that they should be the result of something like common deliberation, and common consent. If it be reasonable that laws relating to the common interest should seem to emanate from the common will, it is further reasonable that the common will should reserve to itself the power of choosing its own executive.

In this manner a popular character naturally attaches to municipal law and municipal authority. Every such community is constantly under influences which dispose it to imbibe the spirit, and to take up the forms of a commonwealth. In proportion as a nation becomes a nation of towns and cities, this spirit, and these forms, are likely to become more prevalent and more fixed. Cities are states upon a small scale, and are of necessity schools in relation to the policy most in harmony with the genius of a people. Political knowledge never diffused itself more wholesomely among a people, than when it results, in this manner, slowly and steadily, from circumstances and experience; and when its principles are to be brought out upon a large scale, by men who have worked them successfully on a smaller scale.

. . . In this manner, then, the principles of self-government have ascended from the borough to the senate, from the councilmen of the city to the councilmen of the nation. Such is the natural course of things. The more the principles of self-government are acted upon in the parish, the town, the great city, and the district, the more men will be interested in the affairs of their country generally, the more competent will they be to judge of the manner in which the business of their country should be conducted, and the more probable will it be that statesmen will regulate their course by principles that will abide the severest scrutiny. . . .

. . . it must not be forgotten, that with all the faults of an ill-regulated citizenship, men would possess few opinions worth contending about, and still less freedom of opinion, were there no cities. Political science, taking in the great moral questions belonging to good government, finds its birthplace in cities, and in its birthplace only will it be found to make hopeful advances towards maturity. Its aim should be to discountenance tyranny in every form—the tyranny of opinion, no less than the tyranny of law, or of the sword. Its object is the good of all, and it should know how to respect the opinions of all. . . . We see its faults, but . . . . we do not make choice of subjection to the much greater social evils which must belong to the condition of the people who do not build cities. Our aim is not to commend barbarism, but to improve civilization . . . .

. . . Every man of discernment must have observed that apart from any technical or direct means of instruction, there is much in the nearer, the more constant, and more varied association, into which men are brought by means of great cities, which tends necessarily to impart greater knowledge, acuteness, and power to the mind, than would have been realized by the same persons if placed in the comparative isolation of a rural parish. As we pass from the town to the country, from the crowd to the comparative solitude, we soon become sensible to another kind of diminution than that which meets the eye. It is soon perceptible that men are losers in intelligence, in proportion as they are losers in the habit of association. In the population of a village, we see a small circle of persons, and little variety of occupation. . . . The dull have little chance of being roused to shrewdness; and those who are not dull, possess little inducement to bestow their attention on anything deserving the name of mental cultivation.

. . . As men congregate in large numbers, it is inevitable that the strong should act as an impetus upon the weak. In other respects, also, the pressure of numbers is necessarily on the side of intelligence. It is a mistake to suppose that minds of the same class possess no more power collectively than they possess separately. Supposing the same degree of capability to belong to them all, its combinations will be more or less different in each, and the consequent modification of the view taken by each in relation to any given subject, must contribute to form an aggregate intelligence, which will be of much greater variety and compass than would have pertained to any separate mind. It is this which gives so much weight to public opinion. . . .

. . . Civil freedom, then, is the result mainly of civic association, and it is in the nature of such freedom to contribute . . . both to intelligence and virtue. In no connexion is the nature of this freedom so conspicuously exhibited as in the liberty of the press. . . . But let our great cities disappear, and the freedom of the press, and nearly the whole system of liberty of which that freedom is a part, must also disappear. This system has approached toward maturity only as the old relation between the vassal and his lord, and the subsequent relation between the subject and his sovereign, have given place to the more instructed relationship between the citizen and the community. It is to man as a citizen that we owe this liberty of utterance; and it is from him that the men who do not dwell in cities have learnt to avail themselves of a freedom which it would not have been in the nature of their habits, and still less within the power of their circumstances, to have originated. . . .

. . . The tendency of the great facts which characterize modern civilization in regard to the social relations, is an extended subject. In some views, the moral results proceeding from this cause may not be pleasing. But we must look to the feeling which this change has served to generate, as well as to that which it has tended to efface or impair. The relations subsisting between master and servant, landlord and tenant, employer and employed, are no longer the same, either in fact or feeling. The permanence attaching to these relations in more feudal times is hardly discoverable in these later days. Every such connexion seems to partake of the uncertain and the transient, and is wanting accordingly in the feeling which could not fail to result from old recollections, and from a stronger sense of mutual service, interest and expectation.

But this change is the natural effect of that greater degree of social independence, and of that nearer approach toward equality, which characterizes modern society, and which brings its good along with its evil. In proportion as society is graduated into classes, men think more about their class than about the community. Protection, and favour, and even sympathy, may descend from those who are above to those who are beneath, but it is still as from the high to the low. It is not the more full, manly, and moral sentiment which has place between equals. . . .

. . . If the chivalrous devotion induced by the conventionalism of feudal times is gone, something of the sense of moral obligation proper to much wiser times has come. If we are bound less strongly to the men immediately about us, we are bound more strongly to man as everywhere. . . .

17   Contravening supply-and-demand, 1843–50

Extracts from (a) Thomas Carlyle, *Past and Present* (1843), books iii, 15, and iv, 4; (b) Thomas Carlyle, *Latter-day Pamphlets* (1850), no. 1, 'The Present Time'.

Thomas Carlyle (1795–1881), the son of a Dumfriesshire mason, was educated at Edinburgh University and was once destined for the Kirk. Moving to London, he made his name as a publicist of the 'condition of England' question, especially by his attacks on *laissez-faire* economics and what he saw as mammon-worship. Unlike most of the enemies of political economy, however, he admired the heroic energies which could 'build cities, conquer waste worlds', and he saw the industrial entrepreneurs as a genuine aristocracy of talent which ought to govern society in place of the decadent landed aristocracy and turn its talents and energies to bettering the condition of the poor. He was thus ambivalent towards the cities, critical of conditions of destitution and squalor, but ready to see immense potentialities within urban society for improvement.

a.

. . . Is not this still a World? Spinning Cotton under Arkwright and Adam Smith; founding Cities by the Fountain of Juturna, on the Janiculum Mount; tilling Canaan under Prophet Samuel and Psalmist David, man is ever man; the missionary of unseen Powers; and great and victorious, while he continues true to his mission; mean, miserable, foiled, and at last annihilated and trodden out of sight and memory, when he proves untrue. Brother, thou art a Man, I think; thou art not a mere building Beaver, or two-legged Cotton-Spider; thou hast verily a Soul in thee, asphyxied or otherwise! Sooty Manchester,—it too is built on the infinite Abysses; overspanned by the skyey Firmaments; and there is birth in it, and death in it;—and it is every whit as wonderful, as fearful, unimaginable, as the oldest Salem or Prophetic City. Go or stand, in what time, in what place we will, are there not immensities, Eternities over us, around us, in us. . . .

. . . all men are beginning to see, that Legislative interference, and interferences not a few are indispensable; that as a lawless anarchy of supply-and-demand, on market-wages alone, this province of things cannot longer be left. . . .

Again, are not Sanitary Regulations possible for a Legislature? The old Romans had their Aediles; who would, I think, in direct contravention to supply-and-demand, have rigorously seen rammed up into total abolition many a foul cellar in our Southwarks, Saint-Gileses, and dark poison-lanes; saying sternly, 'Shall a Roman man dwell there?' The Legislature, at whatever cost of consequences, would have had to answer, 'God forbid!'—The Legislature, even as it is now, could order all dingy Manufacturing Towns to cease from their soot and darkness; to let-in the blessed sunlight; the blue of Heaven, and become clear and clean; to burn their coal-smoke, namely, and to make flame of it. Baths, free air, a wholesome temperature, ceilings twenty feet high, might be ordained, by Act of Parliament, in all establishments licensed as Mills. There are such Mills already extant;—honour to the builders of them! The Legislature can say to others: Go ye and do likewise; better if you can.

Every toiling Manchester, its smoke and soot all burnt, ought it not, among so many world-wide conquests, to have a hundred acres or so of free greenfield, with trees on it, conquered, for its little children to disport in; for its all-conquering workers to take a breath of twilight air in? You would say so! A willing Legislature could say so with effect. A willing Legislature could say very many things! And to whatsoever 'vested interest,' or suchlike, stood up, gainsaying merely, 'I shall lose profits,'—the willing Legislature would answer, 'Yes, but my sons and daughters will gain health, and life, and a soul.' . . .

b.

. . . what a world have we made of it, with our fierce Mammon-worships, and our benevolent philanderings, and idle godless nonsenses of one kind and another! Supply-and-demand, Leave-it-alone, Voluntary Principle, Time will mend it:—till British industrial existence seems fast becoming one huge hideous poison-swamp of reeking pestilence physical and moral; a hideous *living* Golgotha of souls and bodies buried alive; such a Curtius' gulf, communicating with the Nether Deeps, as the Sun never saw till now. These scenes . . . ought to excite unspeakable reflections in every mind. Thirty-thousand outcast Needlewomen working themselves swiftly to death; three-million Paupers rotting in forced idleness, *helping* said Needlewomen to die: these are but items in the sad ledger of despair.

Thirty-thousand wretched women, sunk in that putrefying well of abominations; they have oozed-in upon London, from the universal Stygian quagmire of British industrial life; are accumulated in the *well* of the concern, to that extent. British charity is smitten to the heart, at the laying-bare of such a scene; passionately undertakes, by enormous subscription of money, or by other enormous effort, to redress that individual horror; as I and all men hope it may. But, alas, what next? This general well and cesspool once baled clean out today, will begin before night to fill itself anew. The universal Stygian quagmire is still there; opulent in women ready to be ruined, and in men ready. Towards the same sad cesspool will these waste currents of human ruin ooze and gravitate as heretofore; except in draining the universal quagmire itself there is no remedy. 'And for that, what is the method?' cry many in an angry manner. To whom, for the present, I answer only, 'Not "emancipation," it would seem, my friends; not the cutting-loose of human ties, something far the reverse of that!'

18 A peculiar need of Christianity, 1844

Extracts from J. S. Boone, *The Need of Christianity to Cities: a sermon . . .* (1844), pp. 10ff.

James Shergold Boone (1799–1859), a High Churchman and a popular preacher, was minister of St John's Church, Paddington, from 1832. This sermon was preached in 1844 in aid of the Metropolis Churches Fund which Bishop Blomfield had established in 1836 to provide additional churches and clergymen for London. Despite its rhetoric, it was not unfairly representative of the Tory Anglican analysis of the cities and of the case being made for church extensions in London and the large towns.

. . . we have to consider the need of religion to great cities, and the infinite mischief of its absence. Here the difficulty is to decide in which shape the argument is the stronger; whether as drawn from reason and human nature, or as drawn from all history and all actual observation.

The proof is in both ways abundant, that the atmosphere of cities is essentially a worldly atmosphere; that the life of cities is essentially a worldly life . . . there is much in all cities which must be uncongenial with a vital and pure Christianity.

The country, with its pure serenity—oh, how unlike the hot thick breath of towns—of itself inspires some feeling of religion. The country has always soothing and sacred influences; it can always instil a hallowed calm, and a spirit of reverence, into the mind and heart of man, save where his mind and heart are utterly vitiated, and we might also say, brutalized. . . . The contemplation of nature, as every one has said and felt, leads up the soul to the contemplation of the God of nature. But how is it in cities? In cities, the case is reversed. In cities, we are always tempted to stop with man, and the works of man. The influences of cities . . . always tend to put God out of sight, and to puff men up with pride in themselves and their own doings, with self-complacency and self-elation. All that we see around us is artificial, and in some sense human. All speaks of this life, rather than of the life to come. All is confined and close, even in its vastness; no open expanse, no solemn harmonies, to bid our minds expatiate into the infinite and the eternal. . . . They, too, who having been long accustomed to some sequestered farm, to some remote village or hamlet, are suddenly thrown into the streets of an enormous city, will recoil, even as they wonder; and while they behold much to awaken their admiration, will behold more which must strike them as unnatural and unhealthy, and which must shock their moral feeling.

The streets, indeed, of large cities have oftentimes presented to a Christian eye, by day, and still more by night, a truly awful spectacle. And the causes are only too obvious. The very extent of edifices, and the very collection of vast masses of human beings into one spot, humanity remaining what is it, must be fraught into moral infection. . . . Cities are the centres and theatres of human ambition, human cupidity, human pleasure. On the one side, the appetites, the passions, the carnal corruptions of man are forced, as in a hot-bed, into a rank and foul luxuriance, and countless evils, which would have elsewhere a feeble and difficult existence, are struck out into activity and warmth, by their mere contact with each other. On the other side, many restraints and safeguards are weakened, or even withdrawn. Amidst these teeming multitudes, a man is too often led to persuade himself that he can live with impunity according to the worst 'devices of his own evil heart:' . . . He lives, at least, with a diminished sense of responsibility, whether to God or to his fellow-creatures. God is almost effaced from his remembrance; and, as to his fellow-creatures, he, a mere unit, a single individual, among thousands and hundreds of thousands, passes . . . unmarked in the crowd. His good actions, he thinks, are lost; his bad actions, he thinks, are unnoticed. Unless he violates and even outrages the common decencies of life, he is almost safe from reprobation; while contagious example, with the ordinary tone of conversation and sentiment, helps to blunt his perceptions of right and wrong, and lull his conscience into lethargy. . . . He stands in the all-pervading presence of opportunity and temptation; and he finds a hundred facilities for the perpetration and concealment of crime.

True at the top, these remarks are also true at the bottom of the social scale. Whatever realities may occur, sadly to disturb our dreams of pastoral contentment and rural virtue, our peasantry, in the agricultural districts, are betrayed into vice, not so much by the scenes which surround them, as by some hardships or delusions of the moment, or by some wrong bias within themselves. But in cities, there is a complication of evils; external forces co-operate with inward desires, in tainting, defiling, poisoning the character; in at once sharpening and perverting the intellect, and producing that crooked cleverness, the opposite and worst enemy of wisdom, which only renders its possessors more dextrous in sin and self-deception.

The mischiefs, moreover, to which the community at large is liable, are scarcely less signal than the incitements to private immorality. As cities swell to a prodigious magnitude, all mutual acquaintance between the different classes of their inhabitants becomes well-nigh impossible. They are estranged from each other; while the extremes of society, nevertheless, are flung together in startling contrast, opulence and mendicancy, gorgeousness and rags, luxurious splendour, and squalid penury: in front, wealth, glitter, and magnificence; close behind them, the loathsome clusters of filth, sordidness, and hunger. Nor in vast cities have those persons ever been wanting, whose business it is, and whose delight, to set these various orders against each other in enmity and antagonism, aggravating misconceptions by distrust, and embittering estrangement into antipathy: so that the same persons who might have been united, in smaller circles, by the golden cords of courtesy, sympathy, and reciprocal good offices, are, in cities, too often alienated and kept aloof by jealousy, suspicion, hatred, and fear.

. . . consider, honestly and seriously, with yourselves, *what London now is* . . . Still so immense a wilderness of streets and edifices, with all the wants and passions of its dense multitude heaving and fermenting in the midst of it, is . . . a contemplation, which should awaken in our minds serious apprehensions and misgivings, . . . which must suggest the doubt, whether the extension of cities may not be inordinately great, and whether some acknowledged advantages, secured by concentration within their walls, and unattainable by men in a state of insulation, may not oftentimes be purchased at a fatal price. . . . For the conclusion is forced upon us, that unless the utmost care be taken physically and morally, great cities are great evils. We cannot, perhaps, diminish the size of cities, or even prevent their increase. . . . But we can all evince a Christian anxiety to arrest the spread of that worst canker which afflicts them, through the only means by which it can ever be arrested. We must at least draw the inevitable inference, that, as religion is a necessity everywhere, it is a tenfold necessity in a city such as ours . . . that, as there is an infinite need of Christianity for men as men, so there is even a peculiar need of Christianity for men as the inhabitants of cities.

It is only hard to determine for what age or class, in such a city as

London, religion is needed *most:* whether for the old, or for the young; whether for the man, or for the woman, or for the child; whether for those rich, who are surrounded by so many allurements and seductions, inflating them with an arrogant selfishness, and an effeminate vanity . . . or for those in the middle position, who are so immersed in the occupations of this busy mart, and so tempted to make gain their god; or for those poor, who taught to look with a rankling eye on their superiors in station, and who are thronging, crushing, trampling upon each other, in the straitness of circumstances.

. . . And say, my brethren, do not the annals of modern Europe admonish us, what havoc can be made in the virtue and repose of *nations* by the populace of a city made practically atheists by the long and supercilious neglect of those above them; goaded by want, solicited by appetite, inflamed and exasperated by infidel demagogues, with nothing, or almost nothing, to sweeten and gladden existence . . . to give them hope, to teach them patience and self-government, to cheer them under their life of labour and privations, to soothe them in their fierce struggles with themselves and with the world? The same causes will produce the same effects; they will, without question, increase the number of those regarded by the politician as the '*dangerous classes*,' who are to be watched and repressed; regarded by the Christian philanthropist as the '*unhappy classes*,' who are to be reclaimed and reformed . . . And what wonder is it, then, if we have been emphatically told by our Diocesan . . . . 'unless something be done to afford spiritual instruction there will be spread throughout the land a spirit of anarchy which will shake the whole frame-work of society; that a more urgent appeal must be made, and that, if it fails, we must look for the decay and downfall of everything we hold sacred.'

For can you dream that any other instrumentality, besides religion, could be sufficient for resisting or rectifying these fearful evils . . . ? Would you trust to law, or police, or military force; to prisons, and penitentiaries, and penal colonies? . . . Would you trust to municipal arrangements for the better construction and regulation of streets and dwelling-houses; or to enlightened systems of policy and commerce giving hope of more constant employment, higher wages, better food; or to the spread of education and intelligence . . . ? . . . such things are most useful as auxiliaries and adjuncts to religion; but . . . they can never be accepted as its substitutes. They are, after all, but external and superficial; they appertain, at most, to matters of decency and order, not to a holy discipline of the heart. . . . Whenever we would improve the condition of the people, the great thing is to improve the people themselves; to make them susceptible of the application of other improvements. . . . In other words, the only radical reform for man is religion. . . . so that it would be better to live in a desert in the midst of wild beasts, than in a proud city, with two millions of inhabitants, stripped of the . . . influences of Christianity.

. . . London is not only a gigantic city but an imperial city . . . the metropolis and capital of all the British dominions. It, therefore, gives, in a great measure, a tone and character to the whole empire. It is the centre, to which and from which the lines are radiating, which connect it with every point in the circumference: it is the heart to which and from which the life-blood circulates through every artery and vein of the entire body. . . . Not only it increases and stretches out its colossal dimensions at a rate perhaps unparalled, and, year after year, absorbs fresh districts into itself; but through the modern and more rapid modes of transit, communication, and intercourse, the whole country is more approximated to it, more linked with it, more affected by its direct influences, and by the example which it sets. . . . let London once become thoroughly irreligious, and there will come a dry rot into the whole fabric of our greatness. . . .

. . . That any supply of churches and clergymen will do all that is required—and do it all at once—we are very far from saying; but . . . this provision will effect more without anything else, than all else without this provision. . . . the institutions and charities always annexed to a Christian Church will accelerate or ripen all other improvements: will set men at work upon them: will make them certain . . . . For a church brings with itself all other forms of good: it becomes a centre of all benevolent designs: it excites and calls into action those unwearied persons . . . who will discover, visit, and relieve, physical and temporal, as well as mental and moral necessities: who will carry their benignant assault against idleness, improvidence, callousness, drunkenness, all the pernicious habits, which first impoverish the labouring classes, and then make poverty worse than poor: who, in a word, will attend, in every way, to the public health and the sanitary condition of the people. . . .

19   The type of some great idea, 1844

Extracts from Benjamin Disraeli, *Coningsby, or the New Generation* (1844), book iii, ch. 1; iv, 1 and 2; ix, 4.

Benjamin Disraeli (1804–81), the future Conservative prime minister, was a backbench M.P. in 1844. Of Jewish race, he was more notable as a novelist, a Bohemian and a member of the 'Young England' group of Tory romantics than as a serious politician. Though Disraeli was critical of the social theories of the economists, his young aristocratic hero in *Coningsby* found imaginative inspiration in the great city, especially in the power and achievement of industrial Manchester.

[Coningsby meets the mysterious stranger Sidonia] 'Ah! but the Mediterranean!' exclaimed Coningsby. 'What would I not give to see Athens!'

'I have seen it,' said the stranger, slightly shrugging his shoulders; 'and more wonderful things. Phantoms and spectres! The age of ruins is past. Have you seen Manchester?' . . .

. . . A great city, whose image dwells in the memory of man, is the type of some great idea. Rome represents conquest; faith hovers over the towers of Jerusalem; and Athens embodies the pre-eminent quality of the antique world, art.

In modern ages, commerce has created London; while manners . . . have long found a supreme capital in the airy and bright-minded city of the Seine.

What art was to the ancient world, science is to the modern; the distinctive faculty. In the minds of men the useful has succeeded to the beautiful. Instead of the city of the Violet Crown, a Lancashire village has expanded into a mighty region of factories and warehouses. Yet, rightly understood, Manchester is as great a human exploit as Athens.

The inhabitants, indeed, are not so impressed with their idiosyncrasy as the countrymen of Pericles and Phidias. They do not fully comprehend the position which they occupy. It is the philosopher alone who can conceive the grandeur of Manchester, and the immensity of its future. There are yet great truths to tell, if we had either the courage to announce or the temper to receive them. . . .

. . . [Coningsby arrives in Manchester] He had travelled the whole day through the great district of labour, his mind excited by strange sights and at length wearied by their multiplication. He had passed over the plains where iron and coal superseded turf and corn, dingy as the entrance to Hades, and flaming with furnaces, and he was now among illuminated factories, with more windows than Italian palaces, and smoking chimneys taller than Egyptian obelisks. Alone in the great metropolis of machinery itself, sitting down in a solitary coffee-room glaring with gas, with no appetite, a whirling head, and not a plan or purpose for the morrow, why was he there? Because a being, whose name even was unknown to him, had . . . told him that the age of ruins was past.

. . . Even his bedroom was lit by gas. Wonderful city! . . . He opened the window. The summer air was sweet, even in this land of smoke and toil. He feels a sensation such as in Lisbon or Lima precedes an earthquake. The house appears to quiver. It is a sympathetic affection occasioned by a steam-engine in a neighbouring factory.

. . . He saw all; they were kind and hospitable to the young stranger, whose thought, and earnestness, and gentle manners attracted them. One recommended him to another; all tried to aid and assist him. He entered chambers vaster than are told of in Arabian fable, and peopled with inhabitants more wondrous than Afrite or Peri. For there he beheld, in long-continued ranks, those mysterious forms full of existence without life that perform with facility, and in an instant, what man can fulfil only with difficulty and in days. A machine is a slave that neither brings nor bears degradation; it is a being endowed with the greatest degree of energy, and acting under the greatest degree of excitement, yet free at the same time from all passion and emotion. It is, therefore, not only a slave, but a supernatural slave. And why should one say that the machine does not live? It breathes, for its breath forms the atmosphere of some towns. It moves with more regularity than man. And has it not a voice? . . .

Nor should the weaving-room be forgotten, where a thousand or fifteen hundred girls may be observed in their coral necklaces . . . some pretty, some pert, some graceful and jocund, some absorbed in their occupations; a little serious some, few sad. And the cotton you have observed in its rude state, that you have seen the silent spinner change into thread, and the bustling weaver convert into cloth, you may now watch as in a moment it is tinted with beautiful colours, or printed with fanciful patterns. And yet the mystery of mysteries is to view machines making machines, a spectacle that fills the mind with curious, and even awful speculation.

From early morn to the late twilight, our Coningsby for several days devoted himself to the comprehension of Manchester. It was to him a new world, pregnant with new ideas and suggestive of new trains of thought and feeling. In this unprecedented partnership between capital and science, working on a spot which Nature had indicated as the fitting theatre of their exploits, he beheld a great source of the wealth of nations which had been reserved for these times, and he perceived that this wealth was rapidly developing classes whose power was imperfectly recognized in the constitutional scheme, and whose duties in the social system seemed altogether omitted. Young as he was, the bent of his mind and the inquisitive spirit of the times had sufficiently prepared him, not indeed to grapple with these questions, but to be sensible of their existence, and to ponder.

... 'But after all,' said Coningsby, with animation, 'it is the machinery without any interposition of manual power that overwhelms me. It haunts me in my dreams,' continued Coningsby; 'I see cities peopled with machines. Certainly Manchester is the most wonderful city of modern times!' ...

...[Disinherited and broken in spirit, Coningsby has to make his way as a lawyer in London] The day passed in a dark trance rather than in a reverie. Nothing rose to his consciousness. He was like a particle of chaos; at the best, a glimmering entity of some shadowy Hades. Towards evening the wind changed, the fog dispersed, there came a clear starry night, brisk and bright. Coningsby roused himself, dressed, and wrapping his cloak around him, sallied forth. Once more in the mighty streets, surrounded by millions, his petty griefs and personal fortunes assumed their proper position. Well had Sidonia taught him, view everything in its relation to the rest. 'Tis the secret of all wisdom. Here was the mightiest of modern cities; the rival even of the most celebrated of the ancient. Whether he inherited or forfeited fortunes, what was it to the passing throng? They would not share his splendour, or his luxury, or his comfort. But a word from his lip, a thought from his brain, expressed at the right time, at the right place, might turn their hearts, might influence their passions, might change their opinions, might affect their destiny. Nothing is great but the personal. As civilization advances, the accidents of life become each day less important. The power of man, his greatness and his glory, depend upon essential qualities. Brains every day become more precious than blood. You must give men new ideas, you must teach them new words, you must modify their manners, you must change their laws, you must root out prejudices, subvert convictions, if you wish to be great. Greatness no longer depends on rentals, the world is too rich; nor on pedigrees, the world is too knowing.

'The greatness of this city destroys my misery,' said Coningsby, 'and my genius shall conquer its greatness!'

This conviction of power in the midst of despair was a revelation of intrinsic strength. It is indeed the test of a creative spirit. From that moment all petty fears for an ordinary future quitted him. He felt that he must be prepared for great sacrifices, for infinite suffering . . . but the dawn would break, and the hour arrive, when the welcome morning hymn of his success and his fame would sound and be re-echoed.

He returned to his rooms; calm, resolute. He slept the deep sleep of a man void of anxiety, that has neither hope nor fear to haunt his visions, but is prepared to rise on the morrow collected for the great human struggle.

20   The social war, 1845

Extracts from Friedrich Engels, *The Condition of the Working-Class in England in 1844* (1845), introduction and chapters 1, 2 and 5. (The translation from the original German by F. K. Wischnewetsky, first published in New York in 1887 and in England in 1892.)

Friedrich Engels (1820–95), the son of a German textile manufacturer and later Marx's collaborator as a theorist of communist revolution, visited England in 1842–4 to study the cotton industry in Manchester. *The Condition of the Working-Class*, which drew on contemporary accounts of city conditions, condemned the consequences and tendencies of capitalist industrialism and anticipated a rising of the urban proletariat. Though written for continental consumption and untypical of English attitudes in some respects, it remains an interesting gloss upon the contemporary argument about cities in England.

Such . . . is the history of English industrial development in the past sixty years, a history which has no counterpart in the annals of humanity. Sixty, eighty years ago, England was a country like every other, with small towns, few and simple industries, and a thin but *proportionally* large agricultural population. Today it is a country like *no* other; with a capital of two and a half million inhabitants; with vast manufacturing cities; with an industry that supplies the world and produces almost everything by means of the most complex machinery; with an industrious, intelligent, dense population, of which two-thirds are employed in trade and commerce, and composed of classes wholly different; forming, in fact, with other customs and other needs, a different nation from the England of those days. The industrial revolution is of the same importance for England as the political revolution for France . . . and the difference between England in 1760 and in 1844 is at least as great as that between France, under the *ancien régime* and during the revolution of July. But the mightiest result of this industrial transformation is the English proletariat.

The centralising tendency of manufacture does not, however, stop here. Population becomes centralised just as capital does; and, very naturally, since the human being, the worker, is regarded in manufacture simply as a piece of capital for the use of which the manufacturer pays interest under the name of wages. A manufacturing establishment requires many workers employed together in a single building, living near each other and forming a village of themselves in the case of a good-sized factory. They have needs for satisfying which other people are necessary; handicraftsmen, shoemakers, tailors, bakers, carpenters, stonemasons, settle at hand. The inhabitants of the village, especially the younger generation, accustom themselves to factory work, grow skilful in it, and when the first mill can no longer employ them all, wages fall, and the immigration of fresh manufacturers is the consequence. So the village grows into a small town, and the small town into a large one. The greater the town, the greater its advantages. It offers roads, railroads, canals; the choice of skilled labour increases constantly, new establishments can be built more cheaply because of the competition among builders and machinists who are at hand, than in remote country districts, whither timber, machinery, builders, and operatives must be brought; it offers a market to which buyers crowd, and direct communication with the markets supplying raw material or demanding finished goods. Hence the marvellously rapid growth of the great manufacturing towns . . . the centralising tendency of manufacture continues in full force, and every new factory built in the country bears in it the germ of a manufacturing town. If it were possible for this mad rush of manufacture to go on at this rate for another century, every manufacturing district of England would be one great manufacturing town, and Manchester and Liverpool would meet at Warrington or Newton; for in commerce, too, this centralisation of the population works in precisely the same way, and hence it is that one or two great harbours, such as Hull and Liverpool, Bristol, and London, monopolise almost the whole maritime commerce of Great Britain.

Since commerce and manufacture attain their most complete development in these great towns, their influence upon the proletariat is also most clearly observable here. Here the centralisation of property has reached the highest point; here the morals and customs of the good old times are most completely obliterated; here it has gone so far that the name Merry Old England conveys no meaning. . . . Hence, too, there exist here only a rich and a poor class, for the lower middle-class vanishes more completely with every passing day.

Thus the class formerly most stable has become the most restless one. . . .

But in these towns the proletarians are the infinite majority, and how they fare, what influence the great town exercises upon them, we have now to investigate. . . .

. . . A town, such as London, where a man may wander for hours together without reaching the beginning of the end, without meeting the slightest hint which could lead to the inference that there is open country within reach, is a strange thing. This colossal centralisation, this heaping together of two and a half millions of human beings at one point, has multiplied the power of this two and a half millions a hundredfold; has raised London to the commercial capital of the world, created the giant docks and assembled the thousand vessels that continually cover the Thames. . . .

But the sacrifices which all this has cost become apparent later. After roaming the streets of the capital a day or two, making headway with difficulty through the human turmoil and the endless lines of vehicles, after visiting the slums of the metropolis, one realises for the first time that these Londoners have been forced to sacrifice the best qualities of their human nature, to bring to pass all the marvels of civilisation which crowd their city; that a hundred powers which slumbered within them have remained inactive, have been suppressed in order that a few might be developed more fully and multiply through union with those of others. The very turmoil of the streets has something repulsive, something against which human nature rebels. The hundreds of thousands of all classes and ranks crowding past each other, are they not all human beings with the same qualities and powers, and with the same interest in being happy? And have they not, in the end, to seek happiness in the same way, by the same means? And still they crowd by one another as though they had nothing in common, nothing to do with one another, and their only agreement is the tacit one, that each keep to his own side of the pavement, so as not to delay the opposing streams of the crowd, while it occurs to no man to honour another with so much as a glance. The brutal indifference, the unfeeling isolation of each in his private interest becomes the more repellant and offensive, the more these individuals are crowded together, within a limited space. And, however much one may be aware that this isolation of the individual, this narrow self-seeking is the fundamental principle of our society everywhere, it is nowhere so shamelessly barefaced, so self-conscious as just here in the crowding of the great city. The dissolution of mankind into nomads, of which each one has a separate principle, the world of atoms, is here carried to its utmost extreme.

Hence it comes, too, that the social war, the war of each against all, is here openly declared . . . each exploits the other, and the end of it all is, that the stronger treads the weaker under foot, and that the powerful few, the capitalists, seize everything for themselves, while to the weak many, the poor, scarcely a bare existence remains.

What is true of London, is true of Manchester, Birmingham, Leeds, is true of all great towns. Everywhere barbarous indifference, hard egotism on one hand, and nameless misery on the other, everywhere social warfare, every man's house in a state of siege, everywhere reciprocal plundering under the protection of the law, and all so shameless, so openly avowed that one shrinks before the consequences of our social state as they manifest themselves here undisguised, and can only wonder that the whole crazy fabric still hangs together.

Since capital, the direct or indirect control of the means of subsistence and production, is the weapon with which this social warfare is carried on, it is clear that all the disadvantages of such a state must fall upon the poor. For him no man has the slightest concern. Cast into the whirlpool, he must struggle through as well as he can. . . .

. . . The great towns are chiefly inhabited by working people, since in the best case there is one bourgeois for two workers, often for three, here and there for four; these workers have no property whatsoever of their own, and live wholly upon wages, which usually go from hand to mouth. Society, composed wholly of atoms, does not trouble itself about them; leaves them to care for themselves and their families, yet supplies them no means of doing this in an efficient and permanent way. Every working-man, even the best, is therefore constantly exposed to loss of work and food, that is to death by starvation, and many perish in this way. The dwellings of the workers are everywhere badly planned, badly built, and kept in the worst condition, badly ventilated, damp, and unwholesome. The inhabitants are confined to the smallest possible space, and at least one family usually sleeps in each room. The interior arrangement of the dwellings is poverty-stricken in various degrees, down to the utter absence of even the most necessary furniture. The clothing of the workers, too, is generally scanty, and that of great multitudes is in rags. The food is in general, bad; often almost unfit for use, and in many cases, at least at times, insufficient in quantity, so that, in extreme cases, death by starvation results. Thus the working-class of the great cities offers a graduated scale of conditions of life, in the best cases a temporarily

endurable existence for hard work and good wages, . . . in the worst
cases, bitter want, reaching even homelessness and death by starvation.
The average is much nearer the worst case than the best. . . .

. . . And when all these conditions have engendered vast demoralisation
among the workers, a new influence is added to the old, to spread
this degradation more widely and carry it to the extremest point.
This influence is the centralisation of the population. The writers of
the English bourgeoisie are crying murder at the demoralising tendency
of the great cities, like perverted Jeremiahs, they sing dirges, not over
the destruction, but the growth of the cities. . . . And this is natural,
for the propertied class has too direct an interest in the other conditions
which tend to destroy the worker body and soul. If they should admit
that 'poverty, insecurity, overwork, forced work, are the chief
ruinous influences', they would have to draw the conclusion, 'then
let us give the poor property, guarantee their subsistence, make laws
against overwork,' and this the bourgeoisie dare not formulate. But
the great cities have grown up so spontaneously, the population has
moved into them so wholly of its own motion, and the inference
that manufacture and the middle-class which profits from it alone
have created the cities is so remote, that it is all extremely convenient
for the ruling class to ascribe all the evil to this apparently unavoidable
source; whereas the great cities really only secure a more rapid and
certain development for evils already existing in the germ. . . .

. . . And our bourgeois is perfectly justified in his fears. If the
centralisation of population stimulates and develops the property-
holding class, it forces the development of the workers yet more
rapidly. The workers begin to feel as a class, as a whole; they begin
to perceive that, though feeble as individuals, they form a power
united; their separation from the bourgeoisie, the development of
views peculiar to the workers and corresponding to their position in
life, is fostered, the consciousness of oppression awakens, and the
workers attain social and political importance. The great cities are
the birthplaces of labour movements; in them the workers first began
to reflect upon their own condition, and to struggle against it; in
them the opposition between proletariat and bourgeoisie first made
itself manifest; from them proceeded the Trades-Unions, Chartism,
and Socialism. The great cities have transformed the disease of the
social body, which appears in chronic form in the country, into an
acute one, and so made manifest its real nature and the means of
curing it. Without the great cities and their forcing influence upon
the popular intelligence, the working-class would be far less advanced

than it is. Moreover, they have destroyed the last remnant of the patriarchal relation between working-men and employers, a result to which manufacture on a large scale has contributed by multiplying the employés dependent upon a single employer. The bourgeoisie deplores all this, it is true, and has good reason to do so; for, under the old conditions, the bourgeois was comparatively secure against a revolt on the part of his hands. . . . Only when estranged from his employer, when convinced that the sole bond between employer and employé is the bond of pecuniary profit, when the sentimental bond between them, which stood not the slightest test, had wholly fallen away, then only did the worker begin to recognise his own interests and develop independently; then only did he cease to be the slave of the bourgeoisie in his thoughts, feelings, and the expression of his will. And to this end manufacture on a grand scale and in great cities has most largely contributed.

21 Aggregation without association, 1845

An extract from Benjamin Disraeli, *Sybil, or the Two Nations* (1845), book ii, chapter 5.

In *Sybil*, Disraeli painted a much darker picture of the industrial towns and districts than in *Coningsby* published the previous year. (See document 19) With the Chartist troubles as the setting, the novel emphasized problems of destitution, public health and social conflict and expounded the tenets of 'Young England' Toryism.

[At a ruined abbey the young aristocrat Egremont meets a stranger who regrets the sixteenth-century dissolution of the monasteries] 'You lament the old faith,' said Egremont, in a tone of respect.

'I am not viewing the question as one of faith,' said the stranger. '. . . you had no right to deprive men of their property, and property moreover which, under their administration, so mainly contributed to the welfare of the community.'

'As for community,' said a voice which proceeded neither from Egremont nor the stranger, 'with the monasteries expired the only type that we ever had in England of such an intercourse. There is no community in England; there is aggregation, but aggregation under circumstances which make it rather a dissociating than a uniting principle.'

... 'You also lament the dissolution of these bodies,' said Egremont.

'There is so much to lament in the world in which we live,' said the younger of the strangers, 'that I can spare no pang for the past.'

'Yet you approve of the principle of their society; you prefer it, you say, to our existing life.'

'Yes; I prefer association to gregariousness.'

'That is a distinction,' said Egremont, musingly.

'It is a community of purpose that constitutes society,' continued the younger stranger; 'without that, men may be drawn into contiguity, but they still continue virtually isolated.'

'And is that their condition in cities?'

'It is their condition everywhere; but in cities that condition is aggravated. A density of population implies a severer struggle for existence, and a consequent repulsion of elements brought into too close contact. In great cities men are brought together by the desire of gain. They are not in a state of co-operation, but of isolation, as to the making of fortunes; and for all the rest they are careless of neighbours. Christianity teaches us to love our neighbour as ourself; modern society acknowledges no neighbour.'

'Well, we live in strange times,' said Egremont ...

'When the infant begins to walk, it also thinks that it lives in strange times,' said his companion.

'Your inference?' asked Egremont.

'That society, still in its infancy, is beginning to feel its way.'

... 'Well, society may be in its infancy,' said Egremont, ... 'but, say what you like, our Queen reigns over the greatest nation that ever existed.'

'Which nation?' asked the younger stranger, 'for she reigns over two. ... Two nations; between whom there is no intercourse and no sympathy: who are as ignorant of each other's habits, thoughts, and feelings, as if they were dwellers in different zones, or inhabitants of different planets; who are formed by a different breeding, are fed by a different food, are ordered by different manners, and are not governed by the same laws.'

'You speak of—' said Egremont, hesitatingly.

'THE RICH AND THE POOR.'

22   Always towards the town, 1846-8

Extracts from Charles Dickens, *Dombey and Son* (1848), chapters 15, 33 and 47.

Dombey, which appeared in serial form in 1846-8, showed Dickens's attitudes changed since *The Old Curiosity Shop*. (See document 13) Now critical of the romanticization of country life and of the past, Dickens recognized the inevitability of London's growth and welcomed the developments connected with the railways, though he also demanded the improvement of the city districts which harboured physical and moral pestilence.

[Two characters try to locate a low neighbourhood in Camden Town] There was no such place as Staggs's Gardens. It had vanished from the earth. Where the old rotten summer-houses once had stood, palaces now reared their heads, and granite columns of gigantic girth opened a vista to the railway world beyond. The miserable waste ground, where the refuse-matter had been heaped of yore, was swallowed up and gone; and in its frowsy stead were tiers of warehouses, crammed with rich goods and costly merchandise. The old by-streets now swarmed with passengers and vehicles of every kind; the new streets that had stopped disheartened in the mud and waggon-ruts, formed towns within themselves, originating wholesome comforts and conveniences belonging to themselves, and never tried nor thought of until they sprung into existence. Bridges that had led to nothing, led to villas, gardens, churches, healthy public walks. The carcasses of houses, and beginnings of new thoroughfares, had started off upon the line at steam's own speed, and shot away into the country in a monster train.

As to the neighbourhood which had hesitated to acknowledge the railroad in its struggling days, that had grown wise and penitent, as any Christian might in such a case, and now boasted of its powerful and prosperous relation. There were railway patterns in its drapers' shops, and railway journals in the windows of its newsmen. There were railway hotels, coffee-houses, lodging-houses, boarding-houses; railway plans, maps, views, wrappers, bottles, sandwich-boxes, and time-tables; railway hackney-coach and cabstands; railway omnibuses, railway streets and buildings, railway hangers-on and parasites, and flatterers out of all calculation. There was even railway time observed in clocks, as if the sun itself had given in. . . .

To and from the heart of this great change, all day and night, throbbing currents rushed and returned, incessantly like its life's blood. Crowds of people and mountains of goods, departing and arriving scores upon scores of times in every four-and-twenty hours, produced a fermentation in the place that was always in action. The very houses seemed disposed to pack up and take trips. Wonderful Members of Parliament, who, little more than twenty years before, had made themselves merry with the wild railroad theories of engineers, and given them the liveliest rubs in cross-examination, went down into the north with their watches in their hands, and sent on messages before by the electric telegraph to say that they were coming. Night and day the conquering engines rumbled at their distant work, or, advancing smoothly to their journey's end, and gliding like tame dragons into the allotted corners grooved out to the inch for their reception, stood bubbling and trembling there, making the walls quake, as if they were dilating with the secret knowledge of great powers yet unsuspected in them, and strong purposes not yet achieved.

[Harriet Carker lives on the northern fringes of London] She often looked with compassion, at such a time, upon the stragglers who came wandering into London, by the great highway hard by, and who, footsore and weary, and gazing fearfully at the huge town before them, as if foreboding that their misery there would be but as a drop of water in the sea, or as a grain of sea-sand on the shore, went shrinking on, cowering before the angry weather, and looking as if the very elements rejected them. Day after day, such travellers crept past, but always, as she thought, in one direction—always towards the town. Swallowed up in one phase or other of its immensity, towards which they seemed impelled by a desperate fascination, they never returned. Food for the hospitals, the churchyards, the prisons, the river, fever, madness, vice, and death,—they passed on to the monster, roaring in the distance, and were lost.

Alas! are there so few things in the world, about us, most unnatural, and yet most natural in being so! Hear the magistrate or judge admonish the unnatural outcasts of society; unnatural in brutal habits, unnatural in want of decency, unnatural in losing and confounding all distinctions between good and evil; unnatural in ignorance, in vice, in recklessness, in contumacy, in mind, in looks, in everything. But follow the good clergyman or doctor, who, with his life imperilled at every breath he draws, goes down into their dens, lying within the echoes of our carriage-wheels and daily tread upon the pavement stones. Look round upon the world of odious sights—millions of immortal creatures have no other world on earth—at the lightest mention of which humanity revolts, and dainty delicacy living in the next street, stops her ears, and lisps 'I don't believe it!' Breathe the polluted air, foul with every impurity that is poisonous to health and life; and have every sense, conferred upon our race for its delight and happiness, offended, sickened and disgusted, and made a channel by which misery and death alone can enter. Vainly attempt to think of any simple plant, or flower, or wholesome weed, that, set in this foetid bed, could have its natural growth, or put its little leaves forth to the sun as GOD designed it. And then, calling up some ghastly child, with stunted form and wicked face, hold forth on its unnatural sinfulness, and lament its being, so early, far away from Heaven—but think a little of its having been conceived, and born and bred, in Hell!

Those who study the physical sciences, and bring them to bear upon the health of Man, tell us that if the noxious particles that rise from vitiated air were palpable to the sight, we should see them lowering in a dense black cloud above such haunts, and rolling slowly on to corrupt the better portions of a town. But if the moral pestilence that rises with them, and, in the eternal laws of outraged Nature, is inseparable from them, could be made discernible too, how terrible the revelation! Then should we see depravity, impiety, drunkenness, theft, murder, and a long train of nameless sins against the natural affections and repulsions of mankind, overhanging the devoted spots, and creeping on, to blight the innocent and spread contagion among the pure. Then should we see how the same poisoned fountains that flow into our hospitals and lazar-houses, inundate the gaols, and make the convict-ships swim deep, and roll across the seas, and overrun vast continents with crime. Then should we stand appalled to know, that where we generate disease to strike our children down and entail itself on unborn generations, there also we breed, by the same certain process, infancy that knows no innocence, youth without modesty or shame, maturity that is mature in nothing but in suffering and guilt, blasted old age that is a scandal on the form we bear. Unnatural humanity! When we shall gather grapes from thorns, and figs from

I

thistles; when fields of grain shall spring up from the offal in the bye-ways of our wicked cities, and roses bloom in the fat churchyards that they cherish; then we may look for natural humanity and find it growing from such seed.

Oh for a good spirit who would take the house-tops off, . . . and show a Christian people what dark shapes issue from amidst their homes, to swell the retinue of the Destroying Angel as he moves forth among them! For only one night's view of the pale phantoms rising from the scenes of our too-long neglect; and from the thick and sullen air where Vice and Fever propagate together, raining the tremendous social retributions which are ever pouring down, and ever coming thicker! Bright and blest the morn that should rise on such a night; for men, delayed no more by stumbling-blocks, of their own making, which are but specks of dust upon the path between them and eternity, would then apply themselves, like creatures of one common origin, owning one duty to the Father of one family, and tending to one common end, to make the world a better place!

Not the less bright and blest would that day be for rousing some who never have looked out upon the world of human life around them, to a knowledge of their own relation to it, and for making them acquainted with a perversion of nature in their own contracted sympathies and estimates; as great, and yet as natural in its development when once begun, as the lowest degradation known.

23   Rabid politics, 1848

Extracts from Mrs Gaskell, *Mary Barton* (1848), chapters 6 and 8.

Elizabeth Gaskell (1810–65), the novelist, was the wife of a Unitarian
minister in Manchester. *Mary Barton*, the novel which established
her literary reputation, was written in the middle-1840s and
published anonymously. Set in Manchester, the capital of the
Lancashire cotton industry, during the years of economic depression
and Chartist agitation around 1840, it gave a predominantly bleak
picture of the industrial city and its problems, particularly those of
class conflict and individual alienation, while accepting the
inevitability of urbanization and industrialization.

On the way Wilson said Davenport was a good fellow, though too
much of a Methodee; that his children were too young to work,
but not too young to be cold and hungry; that they had sunk lower
and lower, and pawned thing after thing, and that now they lived
in a cellar in Berry Street . . . Barton growled inarticulate words of
no benevolent import to a large class of mankind, and so they went
along till they arrived in Berry Street. It was unpaved; and down the
middle a gutter forced its way, every now and then forming pools in
the holes with which the street abounded. . . . As they passed, women
from their doors tossed household slops of *every* description into the
gutter; they ran into the next pool, which overflowed and stagnated.
Heaps of ashes were the stepping-stones . . . Our friends were not
dainty, but even they picked their way till they got to some steps
leading down into a small area, where a person standing would have
his head about one foot below the level of the street, and might at
the same time, without the least motion of his body, touch the window
of the cellar and the damp muddy wall right opposite. You went down
one step even from the foul area into the cellar in which a family of
human beings lived. It was very dark inside. The window-panes
were many of them broken and stuffed with rags . . . The smell was
so foetid as almost to knock the two men down. Quickly recovering

themselves, as those inured to such things do, they began to penetrate the thick darkness of the place, and to see three or four little children rolling on the damp, nay wet, brick floor, through which the stagnant, filthy moisture of the street oozed up; the fire-place was empty and black; the wife sat on her husband's chair, and cried in the dank loneliness.

. . . 'The fever' was (as it usually is in Manchester), of a low, putrid, typhoid kind; brought on by miserable living, filthy neighbourhood, and great depression of mind and body. It is virulent, malignant, and highly infectious. But the poor are fatalists with regard to infection; and well for them it is so, for in their crowded dwellings no invalid can be isolated. . . .

. . . But could no doctor be had? In all probability no; the next day an infirmary order might be begged, but meanwhile the only medical advice they could have must be from a druggist's. So Barton . . . set out to find a shop in London Road.

It is a pretty sight to walk through a street with lighted shops; the gas is so brilliant, the display of goods so much more vividly shown than by day, and of all shops a druggist's looks the most like the tales of our childhood . . . No such associations had Barton; yet he felt the contrast between the well-filled, well-lighted shops and the dim gloomy cellar, and it made him moody that such contrasts should exist. They are the mysterious problem of life to more than him. He wondered if any in all the hurrying crowd, had come from such a house of mourning. He thought they all looked joyous, and he was angry with them. But he could not, you cannot, read the lot of those who daily pass you by in the street. How do you know the wild romances of their lives; the trials, the temptations they are even now enduring, resisting, sinking under? You may be elbowed one instant by the girl desperate in her abandonment, laughing in mad merriment with her outward gesture, while her soul is longing for the rest of the dead, and bringing itself to think of the cold-flowing river as the only mercy of God remaining to her here. You may pass the criminal, meditating crimes at which you will shudder tomorrow as you read them. You may push against one, humble and unnoticed, the last upon earth, who in Heaven will for ever be in the immediate light of God's countenance. Errands of mercy—errands of sin—did you ever think where all the thousands of people you daily meet are bound? Barton's was an errand of mercy; but the thoughts of his heart were touched by sin, by bitter hatred of the happy, whom he, for the time, confounded with the selfish. . . .

. . . For three years past, trade had been getting worse and worse, and the price of provisions higher and higher. This disparity between the amount of the earnings of the working classes, and the price of their food, occasioned in more cases than could well be imagined, disease and death. Whole families went through a gradual starvation. They only wanted a Dante to record their suffering. And yet even his words would fall short of the awful truth; they could only present an outline of the tremendous facts of the destitution that surrounded thousands upon thousands in the terrible years 1839, 1840, and 1841. Even philanthropists who had studied the subject, were forced to own themselves perplexed in the endeavour to ascertain the real cause of the misery; the whole matter was of so complicated a nature, that it became next to impossible to understand it thoroughly. It need excite no surprise then to learn than a bad feeling between workingmen and the upper classes became very strong in this season of privation. The indigence and sufferings of the operatives induced a suspicion in the minds of many of them, that their legislators, their magistrates, their employers, and even the ministers of religion, were, in general, their oppressors and enemies; and were in league for their prostration and enthralment. The most deplorable and enduring evil which arose out of the period of commercial depression . . . was this feeling of alienation between the different classes of society. It is so impossible to describe . . . the state of distress which prevailed in the town at that time, that I will not attempt it; and yet I think again that surely, in a Christian land, it was not known even so feebly as words could tell it, or the more happy and fortunate would have thronged with their sympathy and their aid. In many instances the sufferers wept first, and then they cursed. Their vindictive feelings exhibited themselves in rabid politics. And when I hear, as I have heard, of the sufferings and privations of the poor . . . of parents sitting in their clothes by the fireside during the whole night for seven weeks together, in order that their only bed and bedding might be reserved for the use of their large family . . . —of others being compelled to fast for days together, uncheered by any hope of better fortune, living, moreover, or rather starving, in a crowded garret, or damp cellar, and gradually sinking under the pressure of want and despair into a premature grave; and when this has been confirmed by the evidence of their care-worn looks, their excited feelings, and their desolate homes,—can I wonder that many of them, in such times of misery and destitution, spoke and acted with ferocious precipitation?

Three   From 1848 to the 1880s: Acceptance and optimism

By the late 1840s an acceptance of the cities, even of their further growth, and a faith in social progress were becoming more general. Ruskin (24) acknowledged the inevitability of further urbanization and, having discovered the mediaeval city, sought the aesthetic and spiritual redemption of the modern city through the art and architecture of the Gothic revival. Arnold (26) accepted the cities as a necessary stage in human progress even though he preferred to contemplate the higher things to follow. With the industrial towns now more settled in their prosperity and social stability Mrs Gaskell, cured of her earlier fears, put a positive case in *North and South* (29) for the creativity and purposefulness of industrial civilization and, on balance, preferred it to the rural society of southern England. The Anglican clergyman Kingsley, an environmentalist in his analysis of social evils, moved towards optimism too. *Alton Locke* (25), inspired by the last Chartist agitation, rejected Arcadian nostalgia but condemned the irresponsibility of the wealthy and the effects of economic competition in the cities and demanded remedial action. His lecture in 1857 (31) painted a brighter picture. He now counted the blessings of progress and business enterprise, and his vision of the environmental transformation of the cities had become more grandiose. Liberal M.P.s from the business classes sang the city's praises even more loudly. Cowen (37) boasted of the industrial city's economic and political achievements, and Chamberlain (35) aspired to a civic dignity and grandeur for Birmingham that would rival the great cities of the past. He attached more importance to the activism of municipal government than Cowen did, but they both believed that the liberal democracy of the cities would and should come to dominate national politics, even to fertilize the barrenness of rural society.

Some of the city's admirers saw the need for further improvement, especially for the raising of the condition of the poorest classes, but they were confident that the necessary means were ready to hand. They relied on sanitary improvement and municipal regulation; on the beneficial effects of economic expansion and business enterprise; on philanthropy and voluntary effort, especially by the religious denominations; and, above all, on self-help, for they saw economic individualism as the ethic of urban society. Enthusiasm for legislation and central government waned after the 1840s, except as they provided a framework for municipal action. Crime and punishment, however, were an accepted responsibility of central government, so that the criminologist Hill (27), detecting a deficiency of social control in the cities, could urge government action in education and juvenile reformation to check criminal tendencies. For the most part, however, as memories of political disorder and economic dislocation faded, the city was expected to provide the better future for itself. Mrs Gaskell's Thornton (29) scouted the idea of legislative interference and compulsion and voiced the provincial distrust of London government. Stanley (30), a Conservative grandee anxious to come to terms with commercial Lancashire, relied on municipal action and private initiative to effect social improvement and saw progress already being achieved. As with Chamberlain (35) later, civic pride was to be the mainspring of individual effort for the common good and to guide the city's business enterprise and energy towards civic and social improvement. By the 1870s Chamberlain was pushing 'local self-government' further along the road of municipal enterprise and activism, but even most critics of crude *laissez-faire* theories were anxious to keep social reform clear of the fields of legitimate economic enterprise. Stanley, now Earl of Derby (34), recognized that the population increase of the large cities made the problems of 'overcrowding' and working-class housing peculiarly intractable but insisted that matters should be left to the combination of philanthropy and private investment. As yet optimism prevailed. The public-health enthusiast Richardson (36) exemplified the mid-century preoccupation with mortality rates and the sanitary environment in depicting a model city of health. The extent to which existing cities fell short of the ideal did not prevent him from forecasting the eventual arrival of the sanitary Utopia.

There was, however, some criticism which amounted to a rejection of the cities and of the direction of their development. After the short-lived optimism of *Dombey*, Dickens in *Hard Times* (28) pilloried Coketown, a cardboard cut-out of an industrial town, meanly monotonous in its physical appearance and 'a muddle' in its social relations, as the embodiment of Utilitarian economics blind to the needs of human nature. His reaction against the materialism of urban society extended to London as well as to the factory towns, so that Dickens, the mid-century novelist who drew most on city life for inspiration and material, came to conform to Kingsley's dictum that the true literature of the city should call for its reformation and sing of its woes. Two other members of the artistic and literary world had just as little impact upon government and parliamentary politics. After the disorders connected with the passage of the Second Reform Act, Arnold (33), distrustful of urban democracy, turned against the Liberal exponents of a negative individualism who, blind to the portents of anarchy, did nothing for the material and intellectual elevation of the city masses. He argued, unusually for this period, that only the State, the potential embodiment of society's highest values, could bring political order, social amelioration and spiritual aspiration to the city. Ruskin (32), nourishing social ideals derived from his vision of the mediaeval craftsman, moved gradually towards a total rejection of the modern cities where he saw only physical and moral ugliness being produced by the forces of economic competition and capitalist industrialism. Eventually despairing of transforming urban society, he escaped to an involvement in schemes for founding small co-operative communities on the land.

24   The power of ancient architecture, 1849

Extracts from John Ruskin, *The Seven Lamps of Architecture* (1849),
chapters 3 and 6.

John Ruskin (1819–1900), the son of a wealthy London wine-
merchant, was educated at Oxford and made his name as an art
critic with *Modern Painters* (1843–60) and *The Stones of Venice* (1851–3),
the latter a loving exploration of the architecture of old Venice and
of the lost world of the mediaeval city craftsman. Hostile to modern
technology, economic theory and materialistic values, Ruskin
preached a regeneration of society through craftsmanship, religious
faith and moral aspiration. An early work, *The Seven Lamps*, proposed
the transformation and elevation of the modern city through a new
(or revived) code of artistic values and practice.

Until that street architecture of ours is bettered . . . I know not how
we can blame our architects for their feebleness in more important
work; their eyes are inured to narrowness and slightness; can we
expect them at a word to conceive and deal with breadth and solidity?
They ought not to live in our cities; there is that in their miserable
walls which bricks up to death men's imaginations, as surely as ever
perished foresworn nun. An architect should live as little in cities as a
painter. Send him to our hills, and let him study there what nature
understands by a buttress, and what by a dome. There was something
in the old power of architecture, which it had from the recluse more
than from the citizen. The buildings of which I have spoken with chief
praise, rose, indeed, out of the war of the piazza, and above the fury
of the populace: and Heaven forbid that for such cause we should ever
have to lay a larger stone, or rivet a firmer bar, in our England! But
we have other sources of power, in the imagery of our iron coasts
and azure hills; of power more pure, nor less serene, than that of the
hermit spirit which once lighted with white lines of cloisters the glades
of the Alpine pine, and raised into ordered spires the wild rocks of the

Norman sea; . . . and lifted, out of the populous city, grey cliffs of
lonely stone, into the midst of sailing birds and silent air. . . .

. . . I cannot but think it an evil sign of a people when their houses are
built to last for one generation only. . . . And I look upon those pitiful
concretions of lime and clay which spring up, in mildewed forward-
ness, out of the kneaded fields about our capital—upon those thin,
tottering, foundationless shells of splintered wood and imitated stone—
upon those gloomy rows of formalised minuteness, alike without
difference and without fellowship, as solitary as similar—not merely
with the careless disgust of an offended eye, not merely with sorrow
for a desecrated landscape, but with a painful foreboding that the roots
of our national greatness must be deeply cankered when they are thus
loosely struck in their native ground; that those comfortless and
unhonoured dwellings are the signs of a great and spreading spirit
of popular discontent; that they mark the time when every man's
aim is to be in some more elevated sphere than his natural one, and
every man's past life is his habitual scorn; when men build in the hope
of leaving the places they have built, and live in the hope of forgetting
the years that they have lived; when the comfort, the peace, the religion
of home have ceased to be felt; and the crowded tenements of a struggling and restless population differ only from the tents of the Arab or
the Gipsy by their less healthy openness to the air of heaven, and less
happy choice of their spot of earth; by their sacrifice of liberty without
the gain of rest, and of stability without the luxury of change. . . .

. . . A fair building is necessarily worth the ground it stands upon
. . . nor is any cause whatever valid as a ground for its destruction.
If ever valid, certainly not now, when the place both of the past and
future is too much usurped in our minds by the restless and discontented
present. The very quietness of nature is gradually withdrawn from us;
thousands who once in their necessarily prolonged travel were subjected to an influence, from the silent sky and slumbering fields, more
effectual than known or confessed, now bear with them even there the
ceaseless fever of their life; and along the iron veins that traverse the
frame of our country, beat and flow the fiery pulses of its exertions,
hotter and faster every hour. All vitality is concentrated through those
throbbing arteries into the central cities; the country is passed over like
a green sea by narrow bridges, and we are thrown back in continually
closer crowds upon the city gates. The only influence which can in any
wise *there* take the place of that of the woods and fields, is the power
of ancient Architecture. Do not part with it for the sake of the formal
square, or of the fenced and planted walk, nor of the goodly street nor

opened quay. The pride of a city is not in these. Leave them to the crowd; but remember that there will surely be some within the circuit of the disquieted walls who would ask for some other spots than these wherein to walk; for some other forms to meet their sight familiarly . . .

25   The poetry of London, 1850

Extracts from Charles Kingsley, *Alton Locke, Tailor and Poet* (1850), chapters 8 and 9.

Charles Kingsley (1819–75), novelist, social critic and Anglican clergyman, was rector of Eversley, Hampshire, from 1844. He became associated with the Christian Socialist group in London and he was impressed by the Chartist episode in London in 1848, a year of revolts on the continent. *Alton Locke*, a story of a working-class poet in London, centres on the events of 1848 and explores the related themes of poverty and popular radicalism.

[The artisan narrator, Alton Locke, writes poetry about Pacific islands, to the disgust of his Scottish mentor, Mackaye]

'What the deevil! is there no harlotry and idolatry here in England, that ye maun gang speering after it in the Cannibal Islands? Are ye gaun to be like they puir aristocrat bodies, that wad suner hear an Italian dog howl, than an English nightingale sing . . .? Coral Islands? Pacific? What do ye ken about Pacifics? Are ye a Cockney or a Cannibal Islander? . . . Whaur de ye live?'

'What do you mean, Mr. Mackaye?' asked I . . . .

'Mean—why, if God had meant ye to write aboot Pacifics, He'd ha' put ye there—and because He means ye to write aboot London town, He's put ye there—and gien ye an unco sharp taste o' the ways o't; and I'll gie ye anither. Come along wi' me.'

And he seized me by the arm, and hardly giving me time to put on my hat, marched me out into the streets, and away through Clare Market to St. Giles's.

It was a foul, chilly, foggy Saturday night. From the butchers' and greengrocers' shops the gas-lights flared and flickered, wild and ghastly, over haggard groups of slip-shod dirty women, bargaining for scraps of stale meat and frost-bitten vegetables, wrangling about short weight and bad quality. Fish-stalls and fruit-stalls lined the edge of the greasy pavement, sending up odours as foul as the language of sellers and buyers. Blood and sewer water crawled from under doors and out of spouts, and reeked down the gutters amid offal, animal and vegetable, in every stage of putrefaction. Foul vapours rose from cowsheds and slaughter-houses, and the doorways of undrained alleys, where the inhabitants carried the filth out on their shoes from the backyard into the court, and from the court up into the main street; while above, hanging like cliffs over the streets—those narrow, brawling torrents of filth, and poverty, and sin—the houses with their teeming load of life were piled up into the dingy, choking might. A ghastly, deafening, sickening sight it was. Go, scented Belgravian! and see what London is! and then go to the library which God has given thee—one often fears in vain—and see what science says this London might be!

'Ay,' he muttered to himself, as he strode along, 'sing awa; get yoursel' wi' child wi' pretty fancies and gran' words, like the rest o' the poets, and gang to hell for it.'

'To hell, Mr. Mackaye?'

'Ay, to a verra real hell, Alton Locke, laddie . . . the hell on earth o' being a flunkey, and a humbug, and a useless peacock, wasting God's gifts on you ain lusts and pleasures—and kenning it—and not being able to get oot o' it, for the chains o' vanity and self-indulgence. I've warned ye. Now look there—'

He stopped suddenly before the entrance of a miserable alley—

'Look! there's not a soul down that yard, but's either beggar, drunkard, thief, or warse. Write anent that! Say how you saw the mouth o' hell, and the twa pillars thereof at the entry—the pawn-broker's shop o' one side, and the gin palace at the other—twa monstrous deevils, eating up men, and women, and bairns, body and soul. Look at the jaws o' the monsters, how they open and open, and swallow in anither victim and anither. Write anent that.'

. . . 'Well—but—Mr. Mackaye, I know nothing about these poor creatures.'

'Then ye ought. What do ye ken anent the Pacific? Which is maist to your business?—thae bare-backed hizzies that play the harlot o' the other side o' the warld, or these—these thousands o' bare-backed hizzies that play the harlot o' your ain side—made out o' your ain flesh and blude? You a poet! True poetry, like true charity, my laddie, begins at hame. If ye'll be a poet at a', ye maun be a cockney poet; and while the cockneys be what they be, ye maun write, like Jeremiah of old, o' lamentation and mourning and woe, for the sins o' your people. Gin you want to learn the spirit o' a people's poet, down wi' your Bible and read thae auld Hebrew prophets . . . and gin ye'd learn the matter, just gang after your nose, and keep your eyes open, and ye'll no miss it.'

'But all this is so—so unpoetical.'

'Hech! Is there no the heeven above them there, and the hell beneath them? and God frowning, and the deevil grinning? No poetry there! Is no the verra idea of the classic tragedy defined to be, man conquered by circumstance? Canna ye see it there? And the verra idea of the modern tragedy, man conquering circumstance?—and I'll show you that, too—in mony a garret where no eye but the gude God's enters, to see the patience, and the fortitude, and the self-sacrifice, and luve stronger than death, that's shining in thae dark places o' the earth. Come wi' me, and see,'

. . .

'Poetic element? Yon lassie, rejoicing in her disfigurement and not here beauty—like the nuns of Peterborough in auld time—is there na poetry there? That puir lassie, dying on the bare boards, and seeing her Saviour in her dreams, is there na poetry there, callant? That ault body owre the fire, wi' her "an officer's dochter," is there na poetry there? That ither, prostituting hersel' to buy food for her freen—is there na poetry there?—tragedy . . . Ay, Shelley's gran'; always gran'; but Fact is grander—God and Satan are grander. All around ye, in every gin shop and costermonger's cellar, are God and Satan at death grips; every garret is a hail Paradise Lost or Paradise Regained; and will ye think it beneath ye to be the "People's Poet"?'

. . . I thought—I talked poetry to myself all day long. . . . I had taken Mackaye at his word. I had made up my mind that if I had any poetic power, I must do my duty therewith in that station of life to which it had pleased God to call me, and to look at everything simply and faithfully as a London artisan. To this, I suppose, is to be attributed the little geniality and originality for which the public have kindly praised my verses—a geniality which sprung, not from the atmosphere whence I drew, but from the honesty and single-mindedness with which, I hope, I laboured. Not from the atmosphere, indeed—that was ungenial enough; crime and poverty, all-devouring competition, and hopeless struggles against Mammon and Moloch, amid the roar of wheels, the ceaseless stream of pale, hard faces, intent on gain, or brooding over woe; amid endless prison walls of brick, beneath a lurid, crushing sky of smoke and mist. It was a dark, noisy, thunderous element that London life; a troubled sea that cannot rest, casting up mire and dirt; resonant of the clanking of chains, the grinding of remorseless machinery, the wail of lost spirits from the pit. And it did its work upon me; it gave a gloomy colouring, a glare as of some Dantean *Inferno*, to all my utterances. It did not excite me or make me fierce—I was much too inured to it—but it crushed and saddened me; it deepened in me that peculiar melancholy of intellectual youth, which Mr. Carlyle has christened . . . 'Werterism'; I battened on my own melancholy. I believed, I loved to believe, that every face I passed bore the traces of discontent as deep as was my own—and was I far wrong? Was I so far wrong either in the gloomy tone of my own poetry? Should not a London poet's work just now be to cry, like the Jew of old, about the walls of Jerusalem, 'Woe, woe to this city?' Is this a time to listen to the voices of singing men and singing women? . . . Is it not noteworthy, also, that it is in this vein that the London poets have always been greatest? Which of poor Hood's[1] lyrics have an equal chance of immortality with 'The Song of the Shirt' and 'The Bridge of Sighs,' rising, as they do, right out of the depths of that Inferno, sublime from their very simplicity? . . .

Note

1 Thomas Hood (1799–1845), the poet, whose 'Song of the Shirt' about sweated labour in London appeared in *Punch* in 1843.

26 The river of Time, 1852

'The Future', first printed in Matthew Arnold, *Empedocles on Etna, and Other Poems* (1852),

Matthew Arnold (1822–88), the poet and critic, was the son of Thomas Arnold, the headmaster of Rugby. Liberal in politics, he served as a government inspector of schools from 1851 to 1883. This early poem reveals a Whiggish condescension in accepting the cities as a necessary stage in human progress.

A Wanderer is man from his birth.
He was born in a ship
On the breast of the river of Time;
Brimming with wonder and joy
He spreads out his arms to the light,
Rivets his gaze on the banks of the stream.
As what he sees is, so have his thoughts been.
Whether he wakes,
Where the snowy mountainous pass,
Echoing the screams of the eagles,
Hems in its gorges the bed
Of the new-born clear-flowing stream;
Whether he first sees light
Where the river in gleaming rings
Sluggishly winds through the plain;
Whether in sound of the swallowing sea—
As is the world on the banks,
So is the mind of the man.

Vainly does each, as he glides,
Fable and dream
Of the lands which the river of Time
Had left ere he woke on its breast,
Or shall reach when his eyes have been closed.

Only the tract where he sails
He wots of; only the thoughts,
Raised by the objects he passes are his.

Who can see the green earth any more
As she was by the sources of Time.
Who imagines her fields as they lay
In the sunshine, unworn by the plough?
Who thinks as they then thought,
The tribes who then roam'd on her breast,
Her vigorous, primitive sons?

What girl
Now reads in her bosom as clear
As Rebekah read, when she sate
At eve by the palm-shaded well?
Who guards in her breast
As deep, as pellucid a spring
Of feeling, as tranquil, as sure?

What bard,
At the height of his vision, can deem
Of God, of the world, of the soul,
With a plainness as near,
As flashing as Moses felt
When he lay in the night by his flock
On the starlit Arabian waste?
Can rise and obey
The beck of the Spirit like him?

This tract which the river of Time
Now flows through with us, is the plain.
Gone is the calm of its earlier shore.
Border'd by cities and hoarse
With a thousand cries is its stream.
And we on its breast, our minds
Are confused as the cries which we hear,
Changing and shot as the sights which we see.

And we say that repose has fled
For ever the course of the river of Time.
That cities will crowd to its edge
In a blacker, incessanter line;

That the din will be more on its banks,
Denser the trade on its stream,
Flatter the plain where it flows,
Fiercer the sun overhead.
That never will those on its breast
See an ennobling sight,
Drink of the feeling of quiet again.

But what was before us we know not,
And we know not what shall succeed.

Haply, the river of Time—
As it grows, as the towns on its marge
Fling their wavering lights
On a wider, statelier stream—
May acquire, if not the calm
Of its early mountainous shore,
Yet a solemn peace of its own.

And the width of the waters, the hush
Of the grey expanse where he floats,
Freshening its current and spotted with foam
As it draws to the Ocean, may strike
Peace to the soul of the man on its breast—
As the pale waste widens around him,
As the banks fade dimmer away,
As the stars come out, and the night-wind
Brings up the stream
Murmurs and scents of the infinite sea.

27   Without natural police, 1852

Extracts from M. D. Hill's evidence in Parliamentary Papers, 1852, vii, *Report of the Select Committee on Criminal and Destitute Juveniles*, Minutes of Evidence, pp. 34–6.

Matthew Davenport Hill (1792–1872), brother of Rowland Hill, the postal reformer, was the first recorder of Birmingham from 1839 to 1865. A radical in politics and briefly a Liberal M.P., he became an acknowledged expert on crime and penal policy. Here Hill, examined by a House of Commons committee on juvenile crime, describes a breakdown of social control through the growth of the cities and advocates vigorous government action in a sphere where there were few ideological objections to it.

... It appears to me that juvenile crime results from the concurrent operation of a considerable number of causes. ... I will point to some that are in augmenting operation. Let me first draw the attention of the Committee to the augmenting magnitude of our towns, as containing within itself a great source of crime, both adult and juvenile. A century and a half ago ... there was scarcely a large town in the island, except London—when I use the term large town, I use it with reference to the subject under hand,—I mean where an inhabitant of the humbler classes is unknown to the majority of the inhabitants of that town; by a small town, I mean a town where ... every inhabitant is more or less known to the mass of the people of the town; ... in small towns there must be a sort of natural police, of a very wholesome kind, operating upon the conduct of each individual, who lives, as it were, under the public eye; but in a large town he lives, if he choose, in absolute obscurity, and we know that large towns are sought by way of refuge because of that obscurity, which to a certain extent gives impunity. Again, there is another cause, which ... I am disposed to consider very important, and that is the gradual separation of classes which takes place in towns by a custom which has gradually grown up, that every person who can afford it lives out of the town, and at a spot distant from his place of business. Now, this was not so formerly; it is a habit which has ... grown up within the last half century. The result of the old habit was, that rich and poor lived in proximity, and the superior classes exercised that species of silent but very efficient control over their neighbours to which I have already referred. They are now gone, and the consequence is, that large masses of population are gathered together without those wholesome influences which operated upon them when their congregation was more mixed; when they were divided, so to speak, by having persons of a different class of life better educated among them. Those two causes, namely, the magnitude of towns and the separation of classes, have acted concurrently, and the effect has been, that we find in very large towns which I am acquainted with, that in certain quarters there is a public opinion and a public standard of morals very different to what we are accustomed to, and very different to what we should desire to see. Then, the children who are born amongst those masses, grow up under that opinion, and make that standard of morals their own, and with them the best lad or the best man is he who can obtain subsistence, or satisfy the wants of life with the least labour, by begging or by stealing, and who shows the greatest dexterity in accomplishing his object, and the greatest wariness in escaping the penalities of the law, and, lastly, the greatest power of endurance and defiance when he comes under the lash of the law.

Do you ascribe any influence as a cause of crime to the state of the dwellings of many of the poor?—A very great influence indeed; it seems very difficult to imagine how it is possible that a dirty, unwholesome, ill-drained tenement, which is too small for purposes of decency, should contain respectable inhabitants (respectable in a moral sense); and I conceive that every improvement of a sanitary kind will have its operation in the diminution of crime. On the other hand, I am very much disposed to believe that any improvement in the moral desires and aspirations of the class inhabiting these houses will come in aid of sanitary measures ....

The character that seems to be common to all those classes appears to be that of moral destitution?—Exactly so; and that indicates the manner in which poverty works ... these children are liable to that moral destitution,—that want of training; and I wish emphatically to distinguish between training and what is usually called education, meaning thereby instruction in certain branches, reading, writing, and arithmetic, for instance, which, useful as they no doubt are, are of themselves ... very poor defences against criminality. It is training, moral, religious, and industrial, to which we are to look as the chief means of reformation.

28   Fact and fancy, 1854

Extracts from Charles Dickens, *Hard Times* (1854), book i, chapter 5; book ii, chapters 1 and 5.

Dickens's relative optimism about the city shown in *Dombey* (see document 22) did not last very long. Before writing *Hard Times*, his only major treatment of a northern industrial town, Dickens visited Preston, where a strike was in progress. In attacking what he took to be Utilitarian theories and attitudes, he depicted 'Coketown' as the embodiment of a materialism blind to human feelings and needs.

Coketown . . . was a triumph of fact; it had no greater taint of fancy in it than Mrs. Gradgrind herself. Let us strike the keynote, Coketown, before pursuing our tune.

It was a town of red brick, or of brick that would have been red if the smoke and ashes had allowed it; but as matters stood it was a town of unnatural red and black like the painted face of a savage.

It was a town of machinery and tall chimneys, out of which interminable serpents of smoke trailed themselves for ever and ever, and never got uncoiled.

It had a black canal in it, and a river that ran purple with ill-smelling dye, and vast piles of building full of windows where there was a rattling and a trembling all day long, and where the piston of the steam-engine worked monotonously up and down like the head of an elephant in a state of melancholy madness. It contained several large streets all very like one another, and many small streets still more like one another, inhabited by people equally like one another, who all went in and out at the same hours, with the same sound upon the same pavements, to do the same work, and to whom every day was the same as yesterday and tomorrow, and every year the counterpart of the last and the next.

These attributes of Coketown were in the main inseparable from the work by which it was sustained; against them were to be set off, comforts of life which found their way all over the world, and elegancies of life which made, we will not ask how much of the fine lady, who could scarcely bear to hear the place mentioned. The rest of its features were voluntary, and they were these.

You saw nothing in Coketown but what was severely workful. If the members of a religious persuasion built a chapel there—as the members of eighteen religious persuasions had done—they made it a pious warehouse of red brick, with sometimes (but this is only in highly ornamented examples) a bell in a birdcage on the top of it. . . . All the public inscriptions in the town were painted alike, in severe characters of black and white. The jail might have been the infirmary, the infirmary might have been the jail, the town-hall might have been either, or both, or anything else, for anything that appeared to the contrary in the graces of their construction. Fact, fact, fact, everywhere in the material aspect of the town; fact, fact, fact, everywhere in the immaterial. The M'Choakumchild school was all fact, and the school of design was all fact, and the relations between master and man were all fact, and everything was all fact between the lying-in hospital and the cemetery, and what you couldn't state in figures, or show to be purchasable in the cheapest market and saleable in the dearest, was not, and never should be, world without end, Amen.

A town so sacred to fact, and so triumphant in its assertion, of course got on well? Why no, not quite well. No? Dear me!

No. Coketown did not come out of its own furnaces, in all respects like gold that had stood the fire. First, the perplexing mystery of the place was, Who belonged to the eighteen denominations? Because, whoever did, the labouring people did not. It was very strange to walk through the streets on a Sunday morning, and note how few of *them* the barbarous jangling of bells that was driving the sick and nervous mad, called away from their own quarter, from their own close rooms, from the corners of their own streets . . . Then came the Teetotal Society, who complained that these same people *would* get drunk, and showed in tabular statements that they did get drunk. . . . Then came the chemist and druggist, with other tabular statements, showing that when they didn't get drunk, they took opium. Then came the experienced chaplain of the jail, with more tabular statements, . . . showing that the same people *would* resort to low haunts, hidden from the public eye, where they heard low singing and saw low dancing, and mayhap joined in it; . . . Then came Mr. Gradgrind and Mr. Bounderby, the two gentlemen at this present moment walking through Coketown, and both eminently practical, who could, on occasion, furnish more tabular statements derived from their own personal experience . . . from which it clearly appeared—in short, it was the only clear thing in the case—that these same people were a bad lot altogether, gentlemen; that do what you would for them they were never thankful for it, gentlemen; that they never knew what they wanted; that they lived upon the best, and bought fresh butter; and insisted on Mocha coffee, and rejected all but prime parts of meat, and yet were eternally dissatisfied and unmanageable. . . .

Is it possible, I wonder, that there was any analogy between the case of the Coketown population and the case of the little Gradgrinds? Surely, none of us in our sober senses and acquainted with figures, are to be told at this time of day, that one of the foremost elements in the existence of the Coketown working-people had been for years deliberately set at nought? That there was any Fancy in them demanding to be brought into healthy existence instead of struggling on in convulsions? That exactly in the ratio as they worked long and monotonously, the craving grew within them for some physical relief— some relaxation, encouraging good humour and good spirits, and giving them a vent—some recognised holiday though it were but for an honest dance to a stirring band of music—some occasional light pie in which even M'Choakumchild had no finger—which craving must and would be satisfied aright, or must and would inevitably go wrong, until the laws of the Creation were repealed? . . .

. . . A sunny midsummer day. There was such a thing sometimes, even in Coketown.

Seen from a distance in such weather, Coketown lay shrouded in a haze of its own, which appeared impervious to the sun's rays. You only knew the town was there, because you knew there could have been no such sulky blotch upon the prospect without a town. A blur of soot and smoke . . . a dense formless jumble, with sheets of cross light in it, that showed nothing but masses of darkness:— Coketown in the distance was suggestive of itself, though not a brick of it could be seen.

The wonder was, it was there at all. It had been ruined so often, that it was amazing how it had borne so many shocks. Surely there never was such fragile china-ware as that of which the millers of Coketown were made. . . . They were ruined, when they were required to send labouring children to school; they were ruined, when inspectors were appointed to look into their works; they were ruined, when such inspectors considered it doubtful whether they were quite justified in chopping people up with their machinery; they were utterly undone, when it was hinted that perhaps they need not always make quite so much smoke. Besides Mr. Bounderby's gold spoon which was generally received in Coketown, another prevalent fiction was very popular there. It took the form of a threat. Whenever a Coketowner felt he was ill-used—that is to say, whenever he was not left entirely alone, and it was proposed to hold him accountable for the consequences of any of his acts—he was sure to come out with the awful menace, that he would 'sooner pitch his property into the Atlantic.' This had terrified the Home Secretary within an inch of his life, on several occasions.

However, the Coketowners were so patriotic after all, that they never had pitched their property into the Atlantic yet, but, on the contrary, had been kind enough to take mighty good care of it. So there it was, in the haze yonder; and it increased and multiplied.

The streets were hot and dusty on the summer day ... Stokers emerged from low underground doorways into factory yards, and sat on steps, and posts, and palings, wiping their swarthy visages, and contemplating coals. The whole town seemed to be frying in oil. There was a stifling smell of hot oil everywhere. The steam-engines shone with it, the dresses of the Hands were soiled with it, the mills throughout the many stories oozed and trickled it. The atmosphere of those Fairy palaces was like the breath of the simoom: and their inhabitants, wasting with heat, toiled languidly in the desert. But no temperature made the melancholy mad elephants more mad or more sane. Their wearisome heads went up and down at the same rate, in hot weather and cold, wet weather and dry, fair weather and foul. The measured motion of their shadows on the walls was the substitute Coketown had to show for the shadows of rustling woods; while, for the summer hum of insects, it could offer, all the year round, from the dawn of Monday to the night of Saturday, the whirr of shafts and wheels.

... the mills, and the courts and alleys, baked at a fierce heat. Down upon the river that was black and thick with dye, some Coketown boys who were at large—a rare sight there—rowed a crazy boat ... while every dip of an oar stirred up vile smells. But the sun itself, however beneficent generally, was less kind to Coketown than hard frost, and rarely looked intently into any of its closer regions without engendering more death than life. So does the eye of Heaven itself become an evil eye, when incapable or sordid hands are interposed between it and the things it looks upon to bless.

[Stephen Blackpool, an honest mill-hand, confronts Bounderby, his employer] 'What,' repeated Mr. Bounderby, folding his arms, 'do you people, in a general way, complain of?'

Stephen looked at him with some little irresolution for a moment, and then seemed to make up his mind.

'Sir, I were never good at showing o't, though I ha' had'n my share in feeling o't. 'Deed we are in a muddle, sir. Look round town—so rich as 'tis—and see the numbers o' people as has been broughten into being heer, fur to weave, an to card, an to piece out a livin', aw the same one way, somehows, twixt their cradles and their graves. Look how we live, and wheer we live, an in what numbers, an by what chances, and wi' what sameness; and look how the mills is awlus a goin, and how they never works us no higher to ony dis'ant object— ceptin awlus, Death. Look how you considers of us, and writes of us, and talks of us, and goes up wi' yor deputations to Secretaries o' State 'bout us, and how yo are awlus right, and how we are awlus wrong, and never had'n no reason in us sin ever we were born. Look how this ha' growen an growen, sir, bigger an bigger, broader an broader, harder an harder, fro year to year, fro generation unto generation. Who can look on't, sir, and fairly tell a man 'tis not a muddle?'

... 'Sir, I canna, wi' my little learning an my common way, tell the genelman what will better aw this ... but I can tell him what I know will never do't. The strong hand will never do't. Vict'ry and triumph will never do't. Agreeing fur to mak one side unnat'rally awlus and for ever right, and toother side unnat'rally and for ever wrong, will never, never do't. Nor yet lettin alone will never do't. Let thousands upon thousands alone, aw leading the like lives and aw faw'en into the like muddle, and they will be as one, and yo will be as anoother, wi' a black unpassable world betwixt yo, just as long or short a time as sitch-like misery can last. Not drawin nigh to fok, wi' kindness and patience an cheery ways ... will never do't till th' Sun turns t'ice. Most o' aw, rating 'em as so much Power, and reg'latin 'em as if they was figures in a soom, or machines: wi'out loves and likens, wi'out memories and inclinations, wi'out souls to weary and souls to hope—when aw goes quiet, draggin on wi' em as if they'd nowt o' th' kind, and when aw goes onquiet, reproachin 'em for their want o' sitch humanly feelins in their dealins wi' yo—this will never do't, sir, till God's work is onmade.'

29   Proud of belonging to a town, 1854-5

Extracts from Mrs. Gaskell, *North and South* (1855), chapters 10, 37 and 40.

In *North and South*, which followed *Hard Times* as a serial in Dickens's *Household Words* in 1854-5, Elizabeth Gaskell returned to the subject and the scene of *Mary Barton* (see document 32), with Manchester now disguised as 'Milton'. Though still critical of some of its features, she had now become more confident of industrial civilization. *North and South* put a positive case for the industrial city and its entrepreneurial energy and compared them favourably with the very different society of southern England.

[Thornton, the manufacturer, was] occupied in explaining to Mr. Hale the magnificent power, yet delicate adjustment of the might of the steam-hammer, which was recalling to Mr. Hale some of the wonderful stories of subservient genii in the Arabian Nights. . . .

'And this imagination, this practical realization of a gigantic thought, came out of one man's brain in our good town. That very man has it within him to mount, step by step, on each wonder he achieves to higher marvels still. . . . we have many among us who, if he were gone, could spring into the breach and carry on the war which compels, and shall compel, all material power to yield to science.'

'Your boast reminds me of the old lines—

"I've a hundred captains in England," he said,
       "As good as ever was he." '

At her father's quotation Margaret looked suddenly up, with inquiring wonder in her eyes. How in the world had they got from cog-wheels to Chevy Chase?

'It is no boast of mine,' replied Mr. Thornton; 'it is plain matter-of-fact. I won't deny that I am proud of belonging to a town—or perhaps I should rather say a district—the necessities of which give birth to such grandeur of conception. I would rather be a man toiling, suffering —nay, failing and successless—here, than lead a dull prosperous life in the old worn grooves of what you call more aristocratic society down in the South, with their slow days of careless ease. One may be clogged with honey and unable to rise and fly.' ...

...[Higgins, an unemployed cotton-worker, tells the Hales of his plan to migrate to the agricultural South] 'Miss there ... has often talked grand o' the South, and the ways down there. Now I dunnot know how far off it is, but I've been thinking if I could get 'em down theer, where food is cheap and wages good, and all the folk, rich and poor, master and man, friendly like; yo' could, may be, help me to work. I'm not forty-five, and I've a deal o' strength in me, measter.'

'But what kind of work could you do, my man?'

'Well, I reckon I could spade a bit—'

'And for that,' said Margaret, stepping forwards, 'for anything you could do, Higgins, with the best will in the world, you would, may be, get nine shillings a week; may be ten, at the outside. Food is much the same as here, except that you might have a little garden—'

'The childer could work at that,' said he. 'I'm sick o' Milton anyways, and Milton is sick o' me.'

'You must not go the the South,' said Margaret, 'for all that. You could not stand it. You would have to be out in all weathers. It would kill you with rheumatism. The mere bodily work at your time of life would break you down. The fare is far different to what you have been accustomed to.'

'I'se nought particular about my meat,' said he, as if offended.

'But you've reckoned on having butcher's meat once a day, if you're in work; pay for that out of your ten shillings, and keep those poor children if you can. I owe it to you—since it's my way of talking that has set you off on this idea—to put it all clear before you. You would not bear the dulness of the life; you don't know what it is; it would eat you away like rust. Those who have lived there all their lives, are used to soaking in the stagnant waters. They labour on, from day to day, in the great solitude of steaming fields—never speaking or lifting up their poor, bent, downcast heads. The hard spadework robs their brain of life; the sameness of their toil deadens their imagination: they don't care to meet to talk over thoughts and speculations, even of the weakest, wildest kind, after their work is done; they go home brutishly tired, poor creatures! caring for nothing but food and rest. You could not stir them up into any companionship, which you get in a town as plentiful as the air you breathe, whether it be good or bad ... you of all men are not one to bear a life among such labourers. What would be peace to them, would be eternal fretting to you. ...

'... And men theer mun have their families to keep ... God help 'em!' said he ... suddenly renouncing the idea, '... God help 'em! North an' South have each getten their own troubles. If work's sure and steady theer, labour's paid at starvation prices; while here we'n rucks o' money coming in one quarter, and ne'er a farthing th' next. For sure, th' world is in a confusion that passes me or any other man to understand ....'

[Bell, fellow of an Oxford college, boasts of Oxford's superiority to Milton] ... 'I should like to be the representative of Oxford, with its beauty and its learning, and its proud old history.... Ah! I wish I could show you our High Street—our Radcliffe Square. I am leaving out our colleges, just as I give Mr. Thornton leave to omit his factories in speaking of the charms of Milton....'

Mr. Thornton was annoyed more than he ought to have been at all that Mr. Bell was saying.... he was galled enough to attempt to defend what was never meant to be seriously attacked.

'I don't set up Milton as a model of a town.'

'Not in architecture?' slyly asked Mr. Bell.

'No! We've been too busy to attend to mere outward appearances.'

'Don't say *mere* outward appearances,' said Mr. Hale, gently. 'They impress us all, from childhood upward—every day of our life.'

'Wait a little while,' said Mr. Thornton. 'Remember, we are of a different race from the Greeks, to whom beauty was everything, and to whom Mr. Bell might speak of a life of leisure and serene enjoyment, much of which entered in through their outward senses. I don't mean to despise them, any more than I would ape them. But I belong to Teutonic blood; it is little mingled in this part of England to what it is in others; we retain much of their language; we retain more of their spirit; we do not look upon life as a time for enjoyment, but as a time for action and exertion. Our glory and our beauty arise out of our inward strength, which makes us victorious over material resistance, and over greater difficulties still. We are Teutonic up here in Darkshire in another way. We hate to have laws made for us at a distance. We wish people would allow us to right ourselves, instead of continually meddling, with their imperfect legislation. We stand up for self-government, and oppose centralization.... If we do not reverence the past as you do in Oxford, it is because we want something which can apply to the present more directly. It is fine when the study of the past leads to a prophecy of the future. But to men groping in new circumstances, it would be finer if the words of experience could direct us how to act in what concerns us most intimately and immediately; which is full of difficulties that must be encountered; and upon the mode in which they are met and conquered—not merely pushed aside for the time—depends our future. Out of the wisdom of the past, help us over the present. But no! People can speak of Utopia much more easily than of the next day's duty; and yet when that duty is all done by others, who so ready to cry, "Fie, for shame!"'

30   Energy and public spirit, 1855

Extracts from Lord Stanley's speech at Bolton in October 1855, printed in *Speeches and Addresses of Edward Henry XVth Earl of Derby* (2 vols, 1894), ed. T. H. Sanderson and E. S. Roscoe, i, pp. 7–12.

Edward Henry Stanley (1826–93), son of the Conservative leader, the 14th Earl of Derby, was educated at Arnold's Rugby and Trinity, Cambridge. M.P. for King's Lynn from 1848, he became identified with the reformist wing of the Conservatives and suspected of sympathy with Cobdenite liberalism. Keenly interested in the 'condition of England' question and particularly in the towns and cities of industrial Lancashire, his family's county, Stanley was ready to see their virtues and qualities while looking for social improvement under the lead of the local employers.

. . . I will say that in these Lancashire towns—in these great industrial communities throughout that entire district which acknowledges Manchester as its centre—which may be almost regarded as one continuous town, and which, so regarded, exceeds in population and productive power London itself—there exists a more vigorous healthy life than among any other portion, be it what it may, of English society. Life is more earnest—industry more intense—thought more free: mere externals and conventionalities occupy a smaller share of men's time and thoughts. It is not amongst you an honour and a distinction to be idle; you not only admit, but practically act upon and enforce, the truth that, whoever . . . lives disengaged from any active pursuit, is thereby wronging his own nature—leaving undeveloped the best of its faculties, and failing to fulfil those obligations which we all owe to the society of which we are members.

Whatever faults there are in the social system of these districts... are due in great part to the very energy and activity which have made Lancashire what it is, and to the extreme rapidity with which material and commerical progress had advanced.... I mean that notwith-standing great and laudable efforts on the part of individuals, aided by the sympathy and approval of all, not quite enough has yet been done in Lancashire—I say yet, and I lay emphasis on the word, for much is doing now—for the common social benefit of all classes, and particu-larly for that of the less wealthy classes.

There are some institutions—there are some public works, which no well-ordered town of any magnitude ought to be without, but which there has scarcely been leisure fully to attend to in these localities, where that which fifty years ago was a village is now a city. In the first place, no town should be without accommodation, in some place of worship, for as many of its inhabitants as can reasonably be expected to attend.... Again, there ought to be room in your schools for every child between the ages of five and fifteen; and not only room, but some effort made... by organisation among the wealthy, to get the children sent; and, still more, there should be a constant local vigilance and superintendence to see that the teaching is good in quality as well as sufficient in quantity. Thirdly... it is wrong that thirty thousand—fifty thousand—or sixty thousand, as here—even in some places one hundred thousand human beings, should be cooped up in one spot without something in the nature of a park or public gardens, in which children and boys may have their outdoor amusements, and grown men and women take exercise and breathe the air of heaven as little obscured by smoke as may be. In this particular Manchester has set a good example; Liverpool, I am told, means to do the same; and Preston has made up its mind not to be left far behind. Fourthly, you require a free public rate-supported library, in a central position, with means of distributing and circulating its books within convenient distances, and on a scale commensurate with the wants of the town in which it is set up. In this respect... there is no deficiency here. And it is within my personal knowledge that the energy and public spirit displayed in Bolton have operated, and are now operating, on at least two of the other neighbouring towns. Fifth in the list of requirements I place public baths and washhouses.... Sixthly, you require places of amusement—of recreation and refreshment— for working men. ... I mean places such as news-rooms and refreshment-rooms combined in one, with a few books accessible—a kind of poor man's club, where he may find all the comforts of a public house without its attendant evils . . . I believe no more effectual rival to the public-house can be set up, and no heavier blow inflicted upon that which I am afraid is our national vice—intemperance. Lastly . . . no urban community can be complete—can be furnished with all these appliances of civilisation which the habits of the times and country require—which does not contain some institution for the promotion of adult learning. . . .

If in every Lancashire town . . . these various wants were supplied—if the same spirit were everywhere exhibited which has dictated these vast and costly improvements on which the authorities of this town are even now engaged, we should not see . . . side by side with the most wonderful results of inventive talent and the most assiduous display of industry, signs of neglect in many common matters affecting domestic comfort. Streets crowded every evening with operatives, who lounge there literally because they have no other place to resort to, except the public-house or the comfortless lodging—dirty, untaught children swarming about the ground below—and a gin-shop or beer-shop at every corner. Now I know there are circumstances in our mode of life in this part of England which have a peculiar tendency to destroy or weaken—at least among one class—all local attachments. I allude especially to that continual movement of the population—that influx and efflux which is constantly taking place, dependent upon commercial success or failure—the extent of which is hardly known or regarded. For instance, I look for Bolton in the census of 1851, and find that, of 61,000 inhabitants there set down, only 36,000 were returned as born in the town itself; 16,000 more as born within the limits of the county, but not in the town; while 9,000 were strangers altogether. That is a state of things not favourable to local patriotism. But . . . the capitalists of this town, and of others similarly situated, know both their duty and their interest far too well to ignore that moral tie—that tie of common interest and common prosperity, which inevitably results from, and is inseparably connected with, the bond of pecuniary connection.

We live in a new age; the conditions of society are changed; there is no longer a recognised dependence of man upon man—a recognised claim to obedience on the one hand, and to protection on the other. Those days have passed away, and it is vain and idle, even were it desirable, to think of restoring them. But one risk, one danger to which we are now exposed in that higher social state upon which

England is entering, is that of carrying into social science the idea, the maxim, which economically is true, but true only in the strict economical sense—namely, that the relations of employer and employed—of the poor and of the wealthy—can be regulated only by the principle of supply and demand. That is not morally true, and never can be; and our present state in regard to that question is merely one of transition—one which will last only until the relations of mankind under the altered circumstances of this century are better understood.

Do not imagine . . . that I wish to reproach manufacturing employers with any indifference to the welfare of the multitudes among whom they live. I know that it is far otherwise. I have seen it in a hundred instances; and, if a comparison were drawn between the state of the manufacturing and agricultural population, I apprehend there is little doubt which would have the advantage. I speak not in reproach, but in envy—in envy of the advantages enjoyed by those who can deal with a large and intelligent population concentrated within a narrow space. In rural districts, do what you will, it is not easy to set up a club, a school, a library, an institute, on any but the smallest scale—distances are too great—population is too sparse—there is not the same habit of acting in concert—a thousand obstacles exist of which you fortunately know nothing here. Therefore, all that I contend for is, not that little has been done, but that there exists an opportunity, of which I am sure advantage will be taken, of doing more.

31   Treating the causes, 1857

Extracts from Charles Kingsley, 'Great Cities and their Influence for Good and Evil' (a lecture delivered at Bristol in 1857), in *Sanitary and Social Lectures and Essays* (1880), pp. 187ff.

With the easing of political tension and agitation after the 1840s, Charles Kingsley, now established as a writer and public figure, became more confident about the cities than he had been in writing *Alton Locke*. (See document 25.) His lecture to the Social Science Association at Bristol, where as a boy he had seen the devastation caused by the riots of 1831, revealed his growing admiration for the cities and his novel scheme for improving the residential conditions of the poorer classes.

. . . It required many years—years, too, of personal intercourse with the poor—to explain to me the true meaning of what I saw here in October twenty-seven years ago, and to learn a part of that lesson which God taught to others thereby. And one part at least of that lesson was this: That the social state of a city depends directly on its moral state, and . . . that the moral state of a city depends— . . . to an extent as yet uncalculated, and perhaps incalculable—on the physical state of that city; on the food, water, air, and lodging of its inhabitants.

But that lesson, and others connected with it, was learnt, and learnt well, by hundreds. From the sad catastrophe I date the rise of that interest in Social Science; that desire for some nobler, more methodic, more permanent benevolence than that which stops at mere almsgiving and charity-schools. The dangerous classes began to be recognised as an awful fact which must be faced; and faced, not by repression, but by improvement. . . .

. . . if the population of a great city have got into a socially diseased state, it matters little what shock may have caused it to explode. Politics may in one case, fanaticism in another, national hatred in a third, hunger in a fourth . . . inflame a whole population to madness and civil war. Our business is not with the nature of the igniting spark, but of the powder which is ignited.

I will not . . . go as far as some who say that 'A great city is a great evil.' We cannot say that Bristol was in 1830, or is now, a great evil. It represents so much realised wealth; and that, again, so much employment for thousands. It represents so much commerce; so much knowledge of foreign lands; so much distribution of their products; so much science, employed about that distribution.

And it is undeniable, that as yet we have had no means of rapid and cheap distribution of goods, whether imports or manufactures, save by this crowding of human beings into great cities, for the more easy dispatch of business. Whether we shall devise other means hereafter is a question of which I shall speak presently. Meanwhile, no man is to be blamed for the existence, hardly even for the evils, of great cities. The process of their growth has been very simple. They have gathered themselves round abbeys and castles, for the sake of protection; round courts, for the sake of law; round ports, for the sake of commerce; round coal mines, for the sake of manufacture. Before the existence of railroads, penny-posts, electric telegraphs, men were compelled to be as close as possible to each other, in order to work together.

. . . [The plague epidemics in the mediaeval cities] showed that the crowded city life can bring out human nobleness as well as human baseness; that to be crushed into contact with their fellow-men, forced at least the loftier and tender souls to know their fellow-men, and therefore to care for them, to love them, to die for them. Yes—from one temptation the city life is free, to which the country life is sadly exposed—that isolation which, self-contented and self-helping, forgets in its surly independence that man is his brother's keeper. . . .

. . . When we examine into the ultimate cause of a dangerous class; into the one property common to all its members, whether thieves, beggars, profligates, or the merely pauperised—we find it to be this loss of self-respect. . . . And whatever may be the fate of virtuous parents, children brought up in dens of physical and moral filth cannot retrieve self-respect. They sink, they must sink, into a life on a level with the sights, sounds, aye, the very smells, which surround them. . . .

. . . reformatories, ragged schools, even hospitals and asylums, treat only the symptoms, not the actual causes, of the disease; . . . the causes are only to be touched by improving the simple physical conditions of the class; by abolishing foul air, foul water, foul lodging, over-crowded dwellings, in which morality is difficult and common decency impossible.

There is a class, again, above all these, which is doubtless the most important of all . . . the capitalist, small and great, from the shopkeeper to the merchant prince.

Heaven forbid that I should speak of them with aught but respect. There are few figures, indeed, in the world on which I look with higher satisfaction than on the British merchant; the man whose ships are on a hundred seas; who sends comfort and prosperity to tribes whom he never saw, and honourably enriches himself by enriching others. There is something to me chivalrous, even kingly, in the merchant life; and there were men in Bristol of old—as I doubt not there are now—who nobly fulfilled that ideal. I cannot forget that Bristol was the nurse of America; that more than two hundred years ago, the daring and genius of Bristol converted yonder narrow stream into a mighty artery, down which flowed the young life-blood of that great Transatlantic nation destined to be hereafter, I believe, the greatest which the world ever saw. Yes—were I asked to sum up in one sentence the good of great cities, I would point first to Bristol, and then to the United States, and say, That is what great cities can do. By concentrating in one place, and upon one subject, men, genius, information, and wealth, they can conquer new-found lands by arts instead of arms; they can beget new nations; and replenish and subdue the earth from pole to pole. . . .

. . . I assure you that, after years of thought, I see no other remedy for the worst evils of city life. . . . if you cannot bring the country into the city, the city must go into the country.

Do not fancy me a dreamer dealing with impossible ideals. I know well what cannot be done; fair and grand as it would be, if it were done, a model city is impossible in England. We have here no Eastern despotism. . . . The great value of land, the enormous amount of vested interests, the necessity of keeping to ancient sites around which labour, as in Manchester, or commerce, as in Bristol, has clustered itself on account of natural advantages, all these things make any attempts to rebuild in cities impossible. But they will cause us at last, I believe, to build better things than cities. They will issue in a complete interpenetration of city and of country, a complete fusion of their different modes of life, and a combination of the advantages of both, such as no country in the world has ever seen. We shall have, I believe and trust, ere another generation has past, model lodging-houses springing up, not in the heart of the town, but on the hills around it; and those will be—economy, as well as science and good government, will compel them to be—not ill-built rows of undrained cottages, each rented for awhile, and then left to run into squalidity and disrepair, but huge blocks of building, each with its common eating-house, bar, baths, washhouses, reading-room, common conveniences of every kind, where, in free and pure country air, the workman will enjoy comforts which our own grandfathers could not command, and at a lower price than that which he now pays for such accommodation as I should be ashamed to give to my own horse; while from these great blocks of building, branch lines will convey the men to or from their work by railroad, without loss of time, labour, or health.

Then the city will become what it ought to be; the workshop, and not the dwelling-house, of a mighty and healthy people. The old foul alleys, as they become gradually depopulated, will be replaced by fresh warehouses, fresh public buildings; and the city, in spite of its smoke and dirt, will become a place on which the workman will look down with pride and joy, because it will be to him no longer a prison and a poison-trap, but merely a place for honest labour.

... [Such improvements] will pay directly and at once, in the saving of poor-rates. They will pay by exterminating epidemics, and numberless chronic forms of disease which now render thousands burdens on the public purse; consumers, instead of producers of wealth. They will pay by gradually absorbing the dangerous classes; and removing from temptation and degradation a generation yet unborn. They will pay in the increased content, cheerfulness, which comes with health in increased goodwill of employed towards employers. They will pay by putting the masses into a state fit for education. They will pay, too, ... by the increased physical strength and hardihood of the town populations. For it is from the city, rather than from the country, that our armies must mainly be recruited. . . . the townsman actually makes a better soldier than the countryman. He is a shrewder, more active, more self-helping man; give him but the chances of maintaining the same physical strength and health as the countryman, and he will support the honour of the British arms as gallantly as the Highlander or the Connaughtman, and restore the days when the invincible prentice-boys of London carried terror into the heart of foreign lands. In all ages, in all times, whether for war or for peace, it will pay. The true wealth of a nation is the health of her masses.

32   The Goddess of Getting-on, 1865–9

Extracts from John Ruskin, *The Crown of Wild Olive* (1st edn 1866; 4th edn 1873), chapters 1, 2 and 4.

Ruskin, now despairing of elevating society by artistic theory and practice (see document 24), had launched a frontal attack on the doctrines of political economy and the economic forces which they justified in *Unto this last* in 1862. Rejecting materialistic and acquisitive values, he demanded an altered economic organization on lines suggested by his admiration for the skilled and independent craftsman of the middle ages. The contemporary city, standing for the machine-technology and large-scale capitalism which he loathed, was a particular object of scorn, and with the foundation of the Guild of St George in 1871 he attempted to create rustic settlements as alternatives to city life.

[A lecture delivered at the Working Men's Institute, Camberwell, in 1865] The first of all English games is making money. That is an all-absorbing game; and we knock each other down oftener in playing at that, than at football, or any other roughest sport: and it is absolutely without purpose; no one who engages heartily in that game ever knows why. Ask a great money-maker what he wants to do with his money,—he never knows. He doesn't make it to do anything with it. He gets it only that he *may* get it. . . . Just as, at cricket, you get more runs. There's no use in the runs, but to get more of them than other people is the game. And there's no use in the money, but to get more of it than other people is the game. So all that great foul city of London there,—rattling, growling, smoking, stinking,—a ghastly heap of fermenting brickwork, pouring out poison at every pore,—you fancy it is a city of work? Not a street of it! It is a great city of play; very nasty play, and very hard play, but still play. It is only Lord's cricket-ground without the turf:—a huge billiard-table without the cloth, and with pockets as deep as the bottomless pit; but mainly a billiard-table, after all.

[From a lecture at the Town Hall, Bradford, in 1864] You know that we are speaking always of the real, active, continual, national worship; that by which men act, while they live; not that which they talk of, when they die. Now, we have, indeed, a nominal religion, to which we pay tithes of property and sevenths of time; but we have also a practical and earnest religion, to which we devote nine-tenths of our property, and six-sevenths of our time. And we dispute a great deal about the nominal religion: but we are all unanimous about this practical one; of which . . . the ruling goddess may be best generally described as the 'Goddess of Getting-on,' or 'Britannia of the Market.' The Athenians had an 'Athena Agoraia,' or Athena of the Market; but she was a subordinate type of their goddess, while our Britannia Agoraia is the principal type of ours. And all your great architectural works are, of course, built to her. It is long since you built a great cathedral; and how you would laugh at me if I proposed building a cathedral on the top of one of these hills of yours, to make it an Acropolis! But your railroad mounds, vaster than the walls of Babylon; your railroad stations, vaster than the temple of Ephesus, and innumerable; your chimneys, how much more mighty and costly than cathedral spires! your harbour-piers; your warehouses; your exchanges!—all these are built to your great Goddess of 'Getting-on'; and she has formed, and will continue to form, your architecture, as long as you worship her; and it is quite vain to ask me to tell you how to build to *her*; you know far better than I.

[From a lecture at the Royal Artillery Institution, Woolwich, in 1869] And this is the race, then, that we know not any more how to govern! and this the history which we are to behold broken off by sedition! and this is the country, of all others, where life is to become difficult to the honest, and ridiculous to the wise! And the catastrophe, forsooth, is to come just when we have been making swiftest progress beyond the wisdom and wealth of the past. Our cities are a wilderness of spinning wheels instead of palaces; yet the people have not clothes. We have blackened every leaf of English greenwood with ashes, and the people die of cold; our harbours are a forest of merchant ships, and the people die of hunger.

Whose fault is it? Yours, gentlemen; yours only. You alone can feed them, and clothe, and bring into their right minds, for you only can govern—that is to say, you only can educate them.

33   The idea of the State, 1869

Extracts from Matthew Arnold, *Culture and Anarchy* (1869),
introduction and chs 1, 2 and 6.

See document 26. Culture and Anarchy was a collection of periodical
articles written in 1867–8 when Matthew Arnold had been alarmed
by the popular disturbances over the Second Reform Bill. Now
'a Liberal tempered by experience', he had become less tolerant of
city society which he summed up as consisting of middle-class
Philistines and of a Populace for whose poverty and political
disorder the panaceas of provincial Liberalism provided no remedy.
The anarchy which Arnold saw in the cities was both a propensity
to disorder and a lack of cultural standards; his ideal of 'sweetness
and light' or 'Hellenizing' was intended to provide both a higher
culture to civilize the cities and an idea of the State which alone
could control the cities and elevate the condition of the slum-
dwellers.

[Mr Bright] keeps repeating, with all the powers of his noble oratory,
the old story, how to the thoughtfulness and intelligence of the people
of great towns we owe all our improvements in the last thirty years,
and how these improvements have hitherto consisted in Parliamentary
reform, and free trade, and abolition of Church rates, and so on; and
how they are now about to consist in getting rid of minority-members,
and in introducing a free breakfast-table, and in abolishing the Irish
Church by the power of the Nonconformists' antipathy to establishments, and much more of the same kind. And though our pauperism
and ignorance, and all the questions which are called social, seem now
to be forcing themselves upon his mind, yet he still goes on with his
glorifying of the great towns, and the Liberals, and their operations
for the last thirty years. It never seems to occur to him that the present
troubled state of our social life has anything to do with the thirty
years' blind worship of their nostrums by himself and our Liberal
friends, or that it throws any doubts upon the sufficiency of this

worship. But he thinks what is still amiss is due to the stupidity of the Tories, and will be cured by the thoughtfulness and intelligence of the great towns, and by the Liberals going on gloriously with their political operations as before; or that it will cure itself. . . .

It is delusion on this point which is fatal, and against delusion on this point culture works. It is not fatal to our Liberal friends to labour for free-trade, extension of the suffrage, and abolition of church-rates, instead of graver social ends; but it is fatal to them to be told by their flatterers, and to believe, with our pauperism increasing more rapidly than our population, that they have performed a great, an heroic work, by occupying themselves exclusively, for the last thirty years, with these Liberal nostrums, and that the right and good course for them now is to go on occupying themselves with the like for the future. . . . It is not fatal to the Nonconformists to remain with their separated churches; but it is fatal to them to be told by their flatterers, and to believe, that theirs is the one pure and Christ-ordained way of worshipping God, that provincialism and loss of totality have not come to them from following it, or that provincialism and loss of totality are not evils. . . .

. . . We are all of us included in some religious organisation or other; we all call ourselves . . . *children of God*. Children of God;—it is an immense pretension!—and how are we to justify it? By the works which we do, and the words which we speak. And the work which we collective children of God do, our grand centre of life, our *city* which we have builded for us to dwell in, is London! London, with its unutterable external hideousness, and with its internal canker of *publice egestas, privatim opulentia*,—to use the words which Sallust puts into Cato's mouth about Rome,—unequalled in the world!. . . .

. . . Oxford, the Oxford of the past, has many faults; and she has heavily paid for them in defeat, in isolation, in want of hold upon the modern world. Yet we in Oxford, brought up amidst the beauty and sweetness of that beautiful place, have not failed to seize one truth:— the truth that beauty and sweetness are essential characters of a complete human perfection. When I insist on this, I am all in the faith and tradition of Oxford. I say boldly that this our sentiment for beauty and sweetness, our sentiment against hideousness and rawness, has been at the bottom of our attachment to so many beaten causes, of our opposition to so many triumphant movements. And the sentiment is true, and has never been wholly defeated, and has shown its power even in its defeat. . . .

. . . Well, then, what if we tried to rise above the idea of class to the idea of the whole community, *the State*, and to find our centre of light

and authority there? Every one of us has the idea of country, as a
sentiment; hardly any one of us has the idea of *the State*, as a working
power. And why? Because we habitually live in our ordinary selves,
which do not carry us beyond the ideas and wishes of the class to
which we happen to belong. And we are all afraid of giving to the
State too much power, because we only conceive of the State as
something equivalent to the class in occupation of the executive
government, and are afraid of that class abusing power to its own
purposes. . . .

. . . We are on our way to what the late Duke of Wellington, with
his strong sagacity, foresaw and admirably described as 'a revolution
by due course of law.' . . . Great changes there must be, for a revolution
cannot accomplish itself without great changes; yet order there must
be, for without order a revolution cannot accomplish itself by due
course of law. So whatever brings risk of tumult and disorder, multitudinous processions in the streets of our crowded towns, multitudinous
meetings in their public places and parks,—demonstrations perfectly
unnecessary in the present course of our affairs,—our best self, or right
reason, plainly enjoins us to set our faces against. It enjoins us to
encourage and uphold the occupants of the executive power, whoever
they may be, in firmly prohibiting them. But it does this clearly and
resolutely, and is thus a real principle of authority, because it does it
with a free conscience; because in thus provisionally strengthening the
executive power, it knows that it is not doing this merely to enable
[one class to assert itself against another] . . . It knows that it is stablishing
the State, or organ of our collective best self, of our national right
reason; and it has the testimony of conscience that it is stablishing the
State on behalf of whatever great changes are needed, just as much as
on behalf of order; . . .

. . . We have already seen how these things,—trade, business, and
population,—are mechanically pursued by us as ends precious in
themselves, and are worshipped as what we call fetishes; and Mr.
Bright, I have already said, when he wishes to give the working class
a true sense of what makes glory and greatness, tells it to look at the
cities it has built, the railroads it has made, the manufactures it has
produced. So to this idea of glory and greatness the free-trade which
our Liberal friends extol so solemnly and devoutly has served,—to
the increase of trade, business, and population; and for this it is prized.
. . . we cannot precisely say that we have fewer poor men than we had
before free-trade, but we can say with truth that we have many more
centres of industry, as they are called, and much more business,

population, and manufactures. And if we are sometimes a little troubled by our multitude of poor men, yet we know the increase of manufactures and population to be such a salutary thing in itself, and our free-trade policy begets such an admirable movement, creating fresh centres of industry and fresh poor men here, while we were thinking about our poor men there, that we are quite dazzled and borne away, and more industrial movement is called for, and our social progress seems to become one triumphant and enjoyable course of what is sometimes called, vulgarly, outrunning the constable.

If, however, taking some other criterion of man's well-being than the cities he has built and the manufactures he has produced, we persist in thinking that our social progress would be happier if there were not so many of us so very poor, and in busying ourselves with notions of in some way or other adjusting the poor man and business one to the other, and not multiplying the one and the other mechanically and blindly, then our Liberal friends, the appointed doctors of free-trade, take us up very sharply. . . .

But, if we still at all doubt whether the indefinite multiplication of manufactories and small houses can be such an absolute good in itself as to counterbalance the indefinite multiplication of poor people, we shall learn that this multiplication of poor people, too, is an absolute good in itself, and the result of divine and beautiful laws. This is indeed a favourite thesis with our Philistine friends. . . .

. . . And a line of poetry, which Mr. Robert Buchanan throws in . . . —'Tis the old story of the fig-leaf time—this fine line, too naturally connects itself, when one is in the East of London, with the idea of God's desire to *swarm* the earth with beings; because the swarming of the earth with beings does indeed, in the East of London, so seem to revive *the old story of the fig-leaf time,* such a number of the people one meets there having hardly a rag to cover them; and the more this swarming goes on, the more it promises to revive this old story. And when the story is perfectly revived, the swarming quite completed, and every cranny choke full, then, too, no doubt, the faces in the East of London will be gleaming faces, which Mr. Robert Buchanan says it is God's desire they should be, and which every one must perceive they are not at present, but, on the contrary, very miserable. . . . '

. . . I remember, only the other day, . . . a multitude of children who were gathered before us in one of the most miserable regions of London,—children eaten up with disease, half-sized, half-fed, half-clothed, neglected by their parents, without health, without home, without hope . . . so long as these children are there in these festering masses,

... and so long as their multitude is perpetually swelling, charged with misery they must still be for themselves, charged with misery they must still be for us, ... and the knowledge how to prevent their accumulating is necessary, even to give their moral life and growth a fair chance!

34 Appealing to voluntary action, 1871

Extracts from the Earl of Derby's speech at Liverpool in June 1871, printed in *Speeches and Addresses*, ed. Sanderson and Roscoe, i, pp. 129–35.

By 1871 the former Lord Stanley, now 15th Earl of Derby, was one of the leaders of the Conservative party. Still believing that the working of economic forces needed to be tempered by paternalism and civic pride (see document 30), Derby, like other philanthropists, had become concerned with the problems of 'overcrowding' and working-class housing. He insisted that voluntary action should provide the remedy and remained fearful of the implications of governmental interference in the question.

We are all, unfortunately, too well acquainted with the sanitary and social condition of a large part of this town. Taking Liverpool as a whole, and adopting no very high standard of comparison, our deaths are at least 10 per 1,000 yearly more numerous than they ought to be or need be. In a population of nearly half a million you can calculate for yourselves what is the waste of life represented by these figures. It would be bad enough if it was equally distributed over the town, but it is not equally distributed. It is concentrated in a few districts, inhabited mostly by the poorest part of the population, and in those districts the amount of preventable mortality is larger than would be endurable to reflect upon, but for the consideration that the state of things which it indicates need not and will not continue.

... first, What are the causes of this excessive disease and mortality? And, next, How are we to find a remedy? The causes, I think, are few and simple—overcrowding, drunkenness, and immorality; and among a certain class a want of a sufficiency of wholesome food. I say nothing of the temporary mischief produced by epidemics, except so far as they are aggravated by unfavourable physical conditions; nor do I touch upon the subject of drunkenness, because . . . if a man or a woman has to live in a hole where cleanliness and decency are impossible, you must not wonder if they try to drown—I will not call it their misery, but their discomfort, in drink.

There is a kind of action and reaction in this matter. Crowded lodgings and poisoned air produce the craving for stimulants, and drunken homes keep the family from ever moving into a more respectable home. I hear many people say, 'Oh, education will set all that right.'. . . I am not quite so sanguine. If a man is placed in a position where moderately pure air is unattainable, and self-respect almost impossible, it is not being able to read and write that will keep him out of the gin-shop. . . . if it were possible that every man, woman, and child in Liverpool should have a clean, wholesome, and decent lodging, you would have struck a heavier blow at intemperance than could be struck by all the School Boards and all the teetotal gatherings in England put together. . . .

. . . the fact that overcrowding does prevail to an enormous extent, and has done so since the days of the Irish famine, will not be disputed. . . . about 25,000 houses are occupied by families in single rooms. That is, in plain words, that their inmates are living under conditions necessarily unhealthy, and hardly consistent with decency. If you take only the average of six persons to a house . . . you have 150,000 persons, or a third of the whole population, in this unsatisfactory position. It is quite clear that that is not an arrangement which can be allowed to continue longer than we can help. But how are we to deal with it? There are only two things to do—to build fresh houses, and to get hold of and improve the best of the old. . . . They have been combined, and successfully combined, by many societies. The doubt has always been, can you do this work so as to make it pay a fair or even a moderate return as an investment? . . .

I am a member of five or six different societies of this kind. The largest—the Improved Industrial Dwellings Company—pays a steady dividend of 5 per cent, putting by, at the same time, an ample fund for repairs and casualties. The London Labourers' Dwellings Company also pays 5 per cent. . . . On the whole, it may be taken as proved that, with ordinary good and economical management, a return of 5 per cent. in average years can be got from investments of this kind without either giving less in the way of accommodation than health and decency require, or . . . asking more than the working class are willing to pay, and actually do pay, for the wretched hovels they live in now. . . .

Now, I do not contend that the return I spoke of would tempt a speculator, or that better investments may not be found; but if a man can get 5 per cent., or even 4½ or 4 per cent., with scarcely any risk of losing the principal, and, at the same time, have the satisfaction of knowing that he is helping on a good work, it seems to me that he might do worse with his savings, both for his pocket and his conscience. . . .

Only one more word. Objection has been taken to this movement on the ground that the means employed are inadequate to the object. My answer is, that depends on the spirit in which it is taken up. If we cannot do all that we could wish, we can at least set an example and make a beginning, and it is to my mind vitally essential that the work we have in hand should be done by private enterprise. Either it will pay or it will not. If it will, there is no need to call on any public authority to help us. If it will not—but that is an hypothesis I do not accept for an instant—it is no light matter to require the local governing body of the town to provide homes for the poor at less than their cost price. You would by that course be sanctioning a principle of which it would not be easy to see how or where you could limit the application. For if a poor man, not being a pauper, has a right to be supplied with lodging at less than it costs, why not the food also?— the one is as necessary as the other—and then you come to what would be nothing less than a system of universal outdoor relief. I only indicate the difficulties of that alternative. By voluntary action we avoid them altogether. It is to voluntary action, to individual and collective effort, that we appeal; and, for the honour of Liverpool and the welfare of its inhabitants, I hope and I believe that we shall not fail.

35   The dignity of the municipality, 1874–6

Extracts from two speeches of Joseph Chamberlain printed in *Mr. Chamberlain's Speeches* (1914), ed. C. W. Boyd, i, pp. 41–2 and 71–3.

Joseph Chamberlain (1836–1914) was the son of a London master-cordwainer. After making a fortune as a screw-manufacturer in Birmingham, he turned first to local, then to national, politics as a radical Liberal. As mayor of Birmingham in the middle-1870s, he presided over a programme of reform which included the municipal ownership of utilities, the erection of civic buildings and the redevelopment of parts of the city centre. Though little of it was wholly novel, Chamberlain elaborated and propagated a gospel of civic activism which combined pride in the city and its 'local self-government' with a concept of the corporation as the embodiment of the community's dignity and political will. After his election as M.P. for Birmingham in 1876, Chamberlain carried this approach into parliamentary politics, where he tried to make the Liberal party the voice of the political culture of the provincial cities.

[Speech as mayor of Birmingham at the laying of the foundation stone of the municipal buildings, June 1874] For my part, I have an abiding faith in municipal institutions, an abiding sense of the value and importance of local self-government, and I desire therefore to surround them by everything which can mark their importance, which can show the place they occupy in public estimation and respect, and which can point to their great value to the community. Our corporations represent the authority of the people. Through them you obtain the full and direct expression of the popular will, and consequently any disrespect to us . . . necessarily degrades the principles which we represent. Therefore, just as in past times we have provided for our monarchs and our princes palaces in which to live . . . so now it behoves us to find a fitting habitation for our local Parliament, to show the value we put upon our privileges and our free institutions.

Let me remind you that those old communities from whom we derive the model of our municipal institutions were never behind-hand in the discharge of this duty. We find in the old cities of the Continent— of Belgium, and Germany, and Italy—the free and independent burghers of the Middle Ages have left behind them magnificent palaces and civic buildings—testimonies to their power and public spirit and munificence, memorials of the time when those communities maintained the liberties and protected the lives of the people against the oppression, and the tyranny, and the rapacity of their rulers. We have fallen upon less stirring times, but if our duties are humble they are not less important, for it is not too much to say that upon the proper conduct of our local legislation depend the lives, the health, and the happiness of communities at all events vaster than ever were gathered together in those mediaeval cities. Therefore I claim that in the erection of buildings worthy of the population and importance of Birmingham, we are not seeking to gratify any personal vanity or petty sense of self-importance, but are endeavouring to do honour to great principles, and to show our respect for institutions upon which the welfare and happiness of the community very largely depend.

[Speech to the Birmingham town council upon his election as M.P., November 1876] You have spoken of certain great undertakings which have been carried to a successful issue, during the period of my Mayoralty. . . . you referred to the new duties and extended work which that has imposed upon the Town Council. . . . this in itself is one of those objects which we have always had in view . . . because these increased responsibilities bring with them a higher sense of the dignity and importance of municipal work, without which there can be no efficient and satisfactory performance of it. They have brought with them, on the part both of our fellow-citizens and their representa- tives, higher appreciations of our obligations, a broader view of our duties, and they have promoted a pride and interest in our local work, which will always be the best incentives for the good government of the town. . . . In our local parliament we want men of the highest ability and culture to keep alive . . . a love of knowledge and the appreciation of the highest intellectual requirements. On the other hand, it is absolutely necessary that we should remain in close sympathy and relationship with the mass of the people, whose daily needs and common wants should find fitting and frequent expression in our midst. . . . we are actuated by an earnest and hearty desire to promote the welfare of the town of Birmingham. During the last three years we have had to make amends for lost time. We have gladly availed ourselves of the powers that have been placed in our hands. We have accepted onerous duties in the conduct of business in which all have a common interest, and which . . . therefore ought to be managed for all, and by the representatives of all. We have opened a new park and a new reading-room. We have built new baths, we have improved the health of the town, and we have tried to improve its appearance. We have done something to the roadways, we have done more for the footpaths, and we have promoted that great scheme of improvement which will change the face of a large part of the town, and which we are confident will conduce to higher morality, greater happiness, and better health in very many of the poorest and most unfortunate of our population. And for the completion of all this work, and for all the other work which lies before us, we need and we ask the assistance and support of all who sympathise with those objects. If a man has leisure, and wants occupation, his taste must be difficult indeed if he cannot find some congenial employment in connection with the multifarious duties of the Town Council of Birmingham. If he is ambitious, what nobler position can he hope to fill than that of the first citizen of this great community? If he is a philanthropist, where else can he expect to be influential in saving the lives of thousands of persons and in bringing health to tens of thousands of homes? For myself, I shall always look back with pride on the lengthened term of my office as chief of this great municipality.

36   Utopia–another word for time, 1876

Extracts from B. W. Richardson, *Hygeia. A City of Health* (1876), pp. 10–47.

Benjamin Ward Richardson (1828–96), physician and sanitary reformer, delivered his address as president of the Health section of the Social Science Association in 1875. Published with a dedication to Edwin Chadwick, it outlined a model city of health with 100,000 inhabitants which would achieve the lowest possible mortality by elaborately careful design, extensive municipal provision of amenities, and strict sanitary and social regulation. His vision illustrated not only the public health movement's concentration on health and mortality as indices and determinants of social welfare but also the contemporary faith in social progress and the high expectations of civic government.

. . . It is my object to put forward a theoretical outline of a community so circumstanced and so maintained by the exercise of its own freewill, guided by scientific knowledge, that in it the perfection of sanitary results will be approached, if not actually realised, in the co-existence of the lowest possible general mortality with the highest possible individual longevity. I shall try to show a working community in which death . . . is kept as nearly as possible in its proper or natural place in the scheme of life. . . .

. . . From the study of the past we are warranted, then, in assuming that civilisation, unaided by special scientific knowledge, reduces disease and lessens mortality, and that the hope of doing so still more by systematic scientific art is fully justified.

. . . it may be urged, that as mere civilising influences can of themselves effect so much, they might safely be left to themselves to complete, through the necessity of their demands, the whole sanitary code. If this were so, a formula for a city of health were practically useless. The city would come without the special call for it.

I think it probable the city would come in the manner described, but how long it would be in coming is hard to say, for whatever great results have followed civilisation, the most that has occurred has been an . . . uncertain arrest of the spread of the grand physical scourges of mankind. The phenomena have been suppressed, but the root of not one of them has been touched. Still in our midst are thousands of enfeebled human organisms which only are comparable with the savage. Still are left amongst us the bases of all the diseases that, up to the present hour, have afflicted humanity. . . .

. . . Mr. Chadwick has many times told us that he could build a city that would give any stated mortality, from fifty, or any number more, to five, or perhaps some number less, in the thousand annually. I believe Mr. Chadwick to be correct . . . and for that reason I have projected a city that shall show the lowest mortality. I need not say that no such city exists . . . Depicting nothing whatever but what is at this present moment easily possible, I shall strive to bring into ready and agreeable view a community not abundantly favoured by natural resources, which, under the direction of the scientific knowledge acquired in the past two generations, has attained a vitality not perfectly natural, but approaching to that standard. In an artistic sense it would have been better to have chosen a small town or large village than a city for my description; but as the great mortality of States is resident in cities, it is practically better to take the larger and less favoured community. If cities could be transformed, the rest would follow.

Our city, which may be named *Hygeia*, has the advantage of being a new foundation, but it is so built that existing cities might be largely modelled upon it. . . .

. . . There is in the city one principal sanitary officer, a duly qualified medical man elected by the Municipal Council, whose sole duty it is to watch over the sanitary welfare of the place. Under him, as sanitary officers, are all the medical men who form the poor law medical staff. To him these make their reports on vaccination and every matter of health pertaining to their respective districts; to him every registrar of births and deaths forwards copies of his registration returns; and to his office are sent, by the medical men generally, registered returns of the cases of sickness prevailing in the district. His inspectors likewise make careful returns of all the known prevailing diseases of the lower animals and of plants. To his office are forwarded, for examination and analysis, specimens of foods and drinks suspected to be adulterated, impure, or otherwise unfitted for use. For the conduct of these researches the sanitary superintendent is allowed a competent chemical staff. Thus, under this central supervision, every

M

death, every disease of the living world in the district, and every assumable cause of disease, comes to light and is subjected, if need be, to inquiry.

. . . in our model city certain forms of disease would find no possible home, or, at the worst, a home so transient as not to affect the mortality in any serious degree. . . .

. . . calculating the mortality which would be saved, and comparing the result with the mortality which now prevails in the most favoured of our large English towns, I conclude that an average mortality of eight per thousand would be the maximum in the first generation living under this salutary *régime*. That in a succeeding generation Mr. Chadwick's estimate of a possible mortality of five per thousand would be realised, I have no reasonable doubt, since the almost unrecognised, though potent, influence of heredity in disease would immediately lessen in intensity, and the healthier parents would bring forth the healthier offspring.

As my voice ceases to dwell on this theme of a yet unknown city of health, do not, I pray you, wake as from a mere dream. The details of the city exist. They have been worked out by those pioneers of sanitary science . . . I am, therefore, but as a draughtsman, who . . . have drawn a plan, which you in your wisdom can modify, improve, perfect. . . though the ideal we all of us hold be never reached during our lives, we shall continue to work successfully for its realisation. Utopia itself is but another word for time; and some day the masses, who now heed us not, or smile incredulously at our proceedings, will awake to our conceptions. . . .

37   The backbone of the nation, 1877–81

Extracts from two speeches of Joseph Cowen printed in *The Life and Speeches of Joseph Cowen, M.P.* (1885), E. R. Jones, pp. 403–6 and 428–31.

Joseph Cowen (1831–1900) was the son of a wealthy Tyneside manufacturer whom he succeeded as Liberal M.P. for Newcastle in 1873. A sympathizer with working-class aspirations at home and with nationalist movements abroad, Cowen remained an independent radical in Parliament, unashamedly provincial, with a strong personal following on Tyneside where he ran the *Newcastle Chronicle*. He shared the mid-Victorian pride in the industrial cities, especially in their economic achievement, their local institutions and their self-liberation from old hierarchy and obscurantism.

[Speech on 'The Spirit of our Time' to the Newcastle College of Physical Science in October 1877] Another feature of our age has been the growth of great cities. The gathering of men into crowds has some drawbacks. It has, in the past, not contributed to the public health, and there are those who maintain that it has dwarfed and enervated our race. But the application of science to the wants of common life has minimized the evils complained of. London, the largest city in Europe, is now one of the healthiest. The concentration of citizens, like the concentration of soldiers, is a source of strength. The ancient boroughs were the arks and shrines of freedom. They put a bridle upon the warsteed of the haughty baron, who . . . could not destroy the principle of municipal combination which secured their liberty. . . . Behind the dull roar of our machinery, the bellowing ot our blast-furnaces, the panting of the locomotive, and the gentle ticking of the electric telegraph . . . we can hear the songs of children who are fed and clad, and the acclaim of a world made free by these agencies. When people talk of trade institutions, when they declaim . . . against the noise and the dirt of the busy centres of population, they should remember the liberty we enjoy as a consequence of the mental activity and enterprise which have been generated by the contact of mind with mind brought together in great towns. Science has passed from speculation; it has now become a matter of life. It is no longer the toy of the dreamer, the schoolman, and the ascetic. . . . It is thrown upon the whole world, and is as much the birthright of the plebian as the patrician, of the artisan as of his employer. The master-minds of science do not bury their achievements in their studies. The leaders in literature do not now seek . . . an aristocratic patron to whom to dedicate their books. The labours of the philosopher are designed for, and now find their way into, the humblest dwellings of the poor as well as the denizens of castles and halls. This tendency to expansion, this inroad upon the spirit of exclusiveness and monopoly in things of knowledge, is one of the most gratifying signs of the times.

[Speech on 'The Rise and Strength of Great Towns' at the Middlesbrough Jubilee in October, 1881] Those who can only detect beauty in pastoral and primitive pursuits, those who can only find sentiment in struggling streams and dreamy sunsets, will be unable to discover either in the incessant roar of the machinery, that 'dirls' in the ears of the men of Middlesbrough, or in the murky clouds that float above them. Yet, those who dip below the surface will be able to trace the broad outlines of a mighty poem of moving human interest in those bellowing blast-furnaces and grimy workshops. They are carving out of raw materials the means of social elevation, amelioration and enjoyment. They are breaking down old asperities, indefinitely adding to the usefulness of existence, linking town to town, uniting in the bonds of amity long-estranged and oft-embattled lands, and binding all classes in the rough but genial poetry of real life. . . .

Middlesbrough is an epitome of modern times—of that irresistible and victorious civilization which has for its foundation, industry and freedom—freedom of thought, of labour, of sale and exchange, which is the guiding principle of commercial success, and which furnishes as complete a model of public and private prosperity, and as stable a fabric of social happiness and national grandeur as the world has ever seen. Many bemoan the Arcadian association and romantic solitude that has retreated before the era of hammers and anvils, of looms and furnaces. . . . I have a sneaking sympathy with the plaintive wail that Mr. Ruskin and others so often . . . raise over a vanished and irrecoverable past. But the Fates are against them. The minister of civilization preached from the railway-car and the telegraph. In the great battle between movement and stagnation, the cry is ever onward . . . The towns of which Middlesbrough is a type are the indices of our advance: they record the rise of a nation. As the barons of Runnymede put a check on the arbitrary power of the king, so the burghers, in after years, curbed the pretensions of the barons. The boroughs built by these doughty traders were the citadels of freedom ... The noise of the workshops rose, like the music of another epoch, ... and proclaimed the dawn of the day when trade asserted its independence, and industry claimed its rights.

Our towns are the backbone of the nation. They give it strength, cohesion, vitality. Scattered populations are usually ignorant, and oppression is always most easily established over them. The power conferred by concentration may be abused, has been abused, but when regulated by vigilantly supervised representative institutions there is no fear either for the liberty of the individual or the community.

Four   From the 1880s: The doubts return

In the early 1880s the prevailing mood changed to gloom and
alarm with surprising suddenness. The city now seemed not just to
contain problems but to be itself a complex of them, above all the
problem of mass poverty, with its components of unemployment,
physical degeneracy, overcrowding, inadequate housing and economic
exploitation, and with concomitants like immorality, vice, crime,
irreligion and political disaffection. London, particularly its East
End, dominated the argument, and the sensationalist pamphlet
The Bitter Cry (38) made a remarkable impact upon opinion. It
also showed Liberal nonconformity, previously in the van of the
city's admirers, becoming disenchanted with the cities and querying
the virtues of mid-Victorian liberal individualism. Mearns and his
collaborators relied partly on 'the State' for solutions. Gissing's
novels (40) drew an equally grim picture of London's overwhelming
intolerability and of the crushing of human potentialities by
destitution and deprivation. Gissing only despaired; Morris (41),
who saw the cities in the same terms of misery, degradation and
exploitation, saw hope in the prospect of a revolt of the oppressed.
A disciple of Ruskin, he found in Marxist revolution the means
to a dream-civilization of arts and crafts, co-operation and community,
material sufficiency and free-expression, in which there would be
no room for cities as his own century knew them. The Fabian
Wells (45) feared the intensification of capitalist exploitation of
labour until, in a society of pleasure cities for the rich and cities
of toil for the workers, monopoly capitalism would bring revolt
upon its own head.

Some now sought the transformation of society by means beyond
those which earlier decades had thought necessary or tolerable.
The Liberal economist Hobson (43) rejected the 'anarchic'
tendencies of unrestrained capitalist enterprise in the cities and
argued for public control of transport systems and of urban land-
utilization, even for a regulation of terms of employment, in order
to facilitate the decentralization of the city population and create
a civic culture of 'spiritual cohesiveness' and social progress. Even
Booth (42), an admirer of the cities and of free enterprise, saw

the need for government to intervene and care for the most depressed classes, and Rowntree (48) pursued Booth's methods of social investigation to gloomier conclusions on the nature and extent of poverty which he showed to be a nationwide problem of the large towns, not something identifiable with London alone. Emphasizing the physical depression of the poor, in contrast to Booth's picture of vitality and energy, he held the prevailing economic system partly responsible and proposed a larger social role for government, extending even to the redistribution of wealth. Another Liberal nonconformist, Howard (44), proposed the creation of 'garden cities' combining municipal collectivism with private enterprise. His hostility to the 'vested interests' of urban landlords and his insistence upon the elimination of private rent showed the influence of the American social theorist Henry George. The whole scheme, like Morris's vision of the future, had something of the rural nostalgia, the back-to-the-land impulse, of the period; the garden city, indeed, was meant to restore vitality and viability to rural society as well as to create a new urban civilization in face of which London and the other cities would be forced to transform themselves. Wells's version of the marriage of town and country appeared in *Anticipations* (49) where he argued that transport and communications improvements would lead inevitably to a decentralization of the cities, spreading London's population over most of England and creating a variegated suburban civilization.

The unease of the political left was not confined to the poverty question. The young radical intellectuals writing in *The Heart of the Empire* desponded at the vastness of the transition from an England of villages to an England of cities, at the current enthusiasm of the city electorate for Tory imperialism, and at the inadequacy of the ethic of individualism as well as at the condition of 'the ghetto'. Trevelyan (47) regretted the loss of the natural beauty and the stimulation to thought and character of rural life and attacked *laissez-faire* Conservatism for impeding collective action to harness for the general welfare the forces of industry and science which, potentially beneficial, had often been socially harmful. Masterman (46), the volume's editor, argued the need for govern- ment and individual action for the benefit of the slum population but was even more troubled by what he regarded as the absence of spirituality in city life. With religious practice declining and the wealthy evading their social responsibilities, society seemed to have been fragmented by a social individualism bereft of higher purpose and to have lost its traditional values, indeed any shared values beyond the material and the trivial. Masterman believed Christianity alone to be capable of the redemption of urban civilization by giving impetus to social reform and a spiritual ideal to the masses. By 1909 (53) he was more optimistic about the progress of social reform but less hopeful of religious revival. Convinced that the break with traditional values through urbanization was too complete, he now saw the necessity for novel collectivist ideals to animate and elevate urban society, even if they weakened institutions like the family. Collectivism was now to provide not merely the means of social improvement but also a spiritual ideal and purpose, a 'spirit of the hive' of the sort towards which the nature of 'the Crowd' seemed to point. Failing that, he could imagine the self-destruction of the cities as the consummation of their existing tendencies.

There were still optimists and admirers of the cities. Booth (42) investigated London poverty to test the pessimistic generalizations current in the 1880s and concluded that the worst poverty was less extensive and more easily remediable within the existing economic system than the alarmists suggested. He delighted in the diversity and vitality of cities, especially in the sense of competition between individuals, and he feared the socialism which some now held to be the requisite of city life. The spirit of 'getting-on' which Ruskin loathed was what Booth admired most, and he thought it operative among the great majority of the working classes. He advocated State institutionalization of the debased and helpless poor in order to leave the independent poor better able to compete in the free economy of the cities. By 1902 he had also taken up the idea of a decentralization of the city population by transport improvements, much like Wells (49) whose technological determinism had now enlisted him in the ranks of the optimists. Booth (50) looked forward to London spreading itself over the Home Counties with a consequent reduction of central overcrowding and a release of the expansionary energies of which the metropolis was the aggregate. He proposed a metropolitan transport authority to control and facilitate the process, though collectivism was to stop short of housing provision. The Scottish evolutionist Geddes (52) was less concerned with London. Combining scientific empiricism and evolutionary optimism with a patent affection for cities, he insisted on the uniqueness of each city and its experience. Like many people at that time he emphasized the importance of community and the need for creative civic government. 'Civics', a comprehensive urban planning comparable to eugenics, the science of selective breeding, was to guide the future evolution of cities towards Eu-topia, the best possible development from the actual, an approach distinct from the more familiar utopianism.

The American expatriate and novelist James (39) was equally fascinated by cities, those at least of the European civilizations. His excitement at the diversity, the stir, the 'momentary concussion of a million of atoms' in London was only increased during the 1880s by the sense of revolutionary undercurrents and of the great divide between wealth and poverty. The city offered psychological experience and literary inspiration, and James relished the roles of observer and participant in 'the largest chapter of human accidents'. The native novelist Gissing came to reflect the more relaxed attitudes towards the cities in the Edwardian period. His ruminations in *Ryecroft* (51) were mellow, almost good-natured, by his earlier standards. Though regretful at the decline of rural life and exultant at his own escape from London, which he regarded as the antithesis of true English social ideals, Gissing was prepared to admire the grit of the industrial North and to see in the 'triumph of artificial circumstance' in London life, even low life, something in which youth at least might revel.

38   An exceeding bitter cry, 1883

Extracts from A. Mearns *et al.*, *The Bitter Cry of Outcast London. An Inquiry into the Condition of the Abject Poor* (1883), pp. 3–20.

The Bitter Cry was the product of collaboration among a group of nonconformist ministers of whom Andrew Mearns (1837–1925), then secretary of the Congregational Union, was the organizing spirit. The pamphlet, which attracted considerable attention, marked a new phase of criticism of the cities, especially of London, and in particular the turning of Liberal nonconformity from defence and praise of the city to a questioning of the condition of the poorest classes and of government's relationship to urban society.

There is no more hopeful sign in the Christian Church of to-day than the increased attention which is being given by it to the poor and outcast classes of society . . . but by all only the merest edge of the great dark region of poverty, misery, squalor and immorality has been touched. . . . the churches are making the discovery that seething in the very centre of our great cities, concealed by the thinnest crust of civilization and decency, is a vast mass of moral corruption, of heart-breaking misery and absolute godlessness, and that scarcely anything has been done to take into this awful slough the only influences that can purify or remove it.

Whilst we have been building our churches and solacing ourselves with our religion and dreaming that the millennium was coming, the poor have been growing poorer, the wretched more miserable, and the immoral more corrupt; the gulf has been daily widening which separates the lowest classes of the community from our churches and chapels, and from all decency and civilization. . . . We must face the facts; and these compel the conviction that THIS TERRIBLE FLOOD OF SIN AND MISERY IS GAINING UPON US. . . .

It is perhaps scarcely necessary to say of the hundreds of thousands who compose the class referred to, that very few attend any place of worship. . . . Indeed, with the exception of a very small proportion, the idea of going has never dawned upon these people. And who can wonder? Think of

THE CONDITION IN WHICH THEY LIVE

We do not say the condition of their homes, for how can those places be called homes, compared with which the lair of a wild beast would be a comfortable and healthy spot? Few who will read these pages have any conception of what these pestilential human rookeries are, where tens of thousands are crowded together amidst horrors which call to mind what we have heard of the middle passage of the slave ship. To get into them you have to penetrate courts reeking with poisonous and malodorous gases arising from accumulations of sewage and refuse scattered in all directions and often flowing beneath your feet; courts, many of them which the sun never penetrates, which are never visited by a breath of fresh air, and which rarely know the virtues of a drop of cleansing water. . . .

That people condemned to exist under such conditions take to drink and fall into sin is surely a matter for little surprise. . . . One of the saddest results of this over-crowding is the inevitable association of honest people with criminals. . . . Who can wonder that every evil flourishes in such hotbeds of vice and disease? . . . Who can wonder that young girls wander off into a life of immorality, which promises release from such conditions? Who can wonder that the public-house is 'the Elysian field of the tired toiler?'

. . . Incest is common; and no form of vice and sensuality causes surprise or attracts attention. . . . The vilest practices are looked upon with the most matter-of-fact indifference. The low parts of London are the sink into which the filthy and abominable from all parts of the country seem to flow. Entire courts are filled with thieves, prostitutes and liberated convicts. . . .

Another difficulty with which we have to contend, and one in large measure the cause of what we have described, is the

POVERTY

of these miserable outcasts. The poverty, we mean, of those who try to live honestly; for notwithstanding the sickening revelations of immorality which have been disclosed to us, those who endeavour to earn their bread by honest work far outnumber the dishonest. . . . And then it should not be forgotten how hardly upon poverty like this must press the exorbitant demand for rent. Even the rack-renting of Ireland, which so stirred our indignation a little while ago, was merciful by comparison. If by any chance a reluctant landlord can be induced to execute or pay for some long-needed repairs, they become the occasion for new exactions. . . . This is what the helpless have to submit to; they are charged for these pestilential dens a rent which consumes half the earnings of a family, and leaves them no more than from 4*d.* to 6*d.* a day for food, clothing and fire; a grinding of the faces of the poor which could scarcely be paralleled in lands of slavery and of notorious oppression.

That something needs to be done for this pitiable outcast population must be evident . . . Despair of success in any such undertaking may paralyse many. We shall be pointed to the fact that without State interference nothing effectual can be accomplished upon any large scale. And *it is* a fact. These wretched people must live somewhere. They must live near the centres where their work lies. They cannot afford to go out by train or tram into the suburbs; and how, with their poor emaciated, starved bodies, can they be expected—in addition to working twelve hours or more, for a shilling, or less—to walk three or four miles each way to take and fetch? . . . Large spaces have been cleared of fever-breeding rookeries, to make way for the building of decent habitations, but the rents of these are far beyond the means of the abject poor. They are driven to crowd more closely together in the few stifling places still left to them; and so Dives makes a richer harvest out of their misery, buying up property condemned as unfit for habitation, and turning it into a gold-mine because the poor must have shelter somewhere, even though it be the shelter of a living tomb.

The State must make short work of this iniquitous traffic, and secure for the poorest the rights of citizenship; the right to live in something better than fever dens; the right to live as something better than the uncleanest of brute beasts. This must be done before the Christian missionary can have much chance with them. . . .

It is little creditable to us that all our wealth and effort should be devoted to providing for the spiritual needs of those who are comfortably conditioned, and none of it expended upon the abject poor. . . . An 'exceeding bitter cry' is this which goes up to heaven from the misery of London against the apathy of the Church. . . .

39   The largest chapter of human accidents, 1886–8

Extracts from (a) the retrospective preface to Henry James, *The Princess Casamassima* (1886); (b) the essay 'London' (1888) reprinted in Henry James, *Essays in London and elsewhere* (1893).

Henry James (1843–1916), the American-born novelist, settled in London in 1876. Fascinated by the older civilization of western Europe, he found in London not only educated and cultured society but also imaginative stimulation in the sheer multiplicity and diversity of metropolitan life. The novel *The Princess Casamassima*, which appeared in serial form in 1885–6, explored the theme, unusual for James, of political discontent amidst London's extremes of wealth and poverty. His preface, written for the collected edition of his works published in 1907–9, recalls the mood of the 1880s and the author's reaction as a literary artist to 'the thick tribute of the London streets.' The essay on London, which first appeared in the *Century Magazine* in 1888, celebrated the capital as a way of life and a state of mind.

---

a.

. . . this fiction proceeded, quite directly, during the first year of a long residence in London, from the habit and the interest of walking the streets. . . . as to do this was to receive many impressions, so the impressions worked and sought an issue, so the book after a time was born. . . . the attentive exploration of London, the assault directly made by the great city upon an imagination quick to react, fully explains a large part of it. . . . One walked of course with one's eyes greatly open, and . . . such a practice, carried on for a long time and over a considerable space, positively provokes, all round, a mystic solicitation, the urgent appeal, on the part of everything, to be interpreted and . . . reproduced. 'Subjects' and situations, character and history, the tragedy and comedy of life, are things of which the common air, in such conditions, seems pungently to taste; and to a mind curious, before the human scene, of meanings and revelations the great grey Babylon easily becomes, on its face, a garden bristling with an immense illustrative flora. Possible stories, presentable figures, rise from the thick jungle as the observer moves, fluttering up like startled game, and before he knows it indeed he has fairly to guard himself against the brush of importunate wings. . . .

. . . [The experiences of the streets] offered me no image more vivid than that of some individual sensitive nature or fine mind, some small obscure intelligent creature whose education should have been almost wholly derived from them, capable of profiting by all the civilisation, all the accumulations to which they testify, yet condemned to see these things only from outside—in mere quickened consideration, mere wistfulness and envy and despair. . . . I had only to imagine such a spirit intent enough and troubled enough, and to place it in presence of . . . the more fortunate than himself—all on the scale on which London could show them . . . I had only to conceive his watching the same public show, the same innumerable appearances, I had watched myself, and of his watching very much as I had watched; save indeed for one little difference. This difference would be that so far as all the swarming facts should speak of freedom and ease, knowledge and power, money, opportunity, and satiety, he should be able to revolve around them but at the most respectful of distances and with every door of approach shut in his face. . . .

. . . Truly, of course, there are London mysteries (dense categories of dark arcana) for every spectator, and it's in a degree an exclusion and a state of weakness to be without experience of the meaner conditions, the lower manners and types, the general sordid struggle, the weight of the burden of labour, the ignorance, the misery and the vice. With such matters as those my tormented young man would have had contact—they would have formed . . . his natural and immediate London. But the reward of a romantic curiosity would be the question of what the total assault, that of the world of his work-a-day life and the world of his divination and his envy together, would have made of him, and what in especial he would have made of them. As tormented, I say, I thought of him . . . .

. . . My scheme called for the suggested nearness (to all our apparently ordered life) of some sinister anarchic underworld, heaving in its pain, its power and its hate; a presentation not of sharp particulars, but of loose appearances, vague motions and sounds and symptoms, just perceptible presences and general looming possibilities. . . .

. . . To haunt the great city and by this habit to penetrate it, imaginatively, in as many places as possible—*that* was to be informed, *that* was to open doors, *that* positively was to groan at times under the weight of one's accumulations.

. . . the value I wished most to render and the effect I wished most to produce were precisely those of our not knowing, of society's not knowing, but only guessing and suspecting and trying to ignore, what 'goes on' irreconcilably, subversively, beneath the vast smug surface . . . I might perhaps . . . catch some gust of the hot breath that I had at many an hour seemed to see escape and hover. . . . if you haven't, for fiction, the root of the matter in you, haven't the sense of life and the penetrating imagination, you are a fool in the very presence of the revealed and assured; but . . . if you *are* so armed you are not really helpless, not without your resource, even before mysteries abysmal.

b.

. . . for the real London-lover the mere immensity of the place is a large part of its merit. A small London would be an abomination, as it fortunately is an impossibility, for the idea and the name are beyond everything an expression of extent and number. Practically, of course, one lives in a quarter, in a plot; but in imagination and by a constant mental act of reference the sympathising resident inhabits the whole . . . He fancies himself, as they say, for being a particle in so unequalled an aggregation; and its immeasurable circumference, even though unvisited and lost in smoke, gives him the sense of a social, an intellectual margin. . . . if small questions play a part, they play it without illusions about its importance. There are too many questions, small or great . . . Therefore perhaps the most general characteristic is the absence of insistence. Habits and inclinations flourish and fall, but intensity is never one of them. . . .

The compensation is that material does arise; that there is great variety, if not morbid subtlety; and that the whole of the procession of events and topics passes across your stage. . . . I am speaking of the inspiration there may be in the sense of far frontiers; the London-lover loses himself in this swelling consciousness, delights in the idea that the town which incloses him is after all only a paved country, a state by itself. . . . London is indeed an epitome of the round world, and . . . there is nothing one can't study at first hand.

. . . the British capital is the particular spot in the world which communicates the greatest sense of life.

London is so clumsy and so brutal, and has gathered together so many of the darkest sides of life, that it is almost ridiculous to talk

of her as a lover talks of his mistress, and almost frivolous to appear
to ignore her disfigurement and cruelties. She is like a mighty ogress
who devours human flesh; but to me it is a mitigating circumstance
. . . that the ogress herself is human. It is not in wantonness that she fills
her maw, but to keep herself alive and do her tremendous work. She
has no time for fine discriminations, but after all she is as good-natured
as she is huge . . . It is mainly when you fall on your face before her that
she gobbles you up. . . . It is not to be denied that the heart tends to
grow hard in her company, but she is a capital antidote to the morbid
. . . She teaches her victims not to 'mind,' and the great danger for them
is perhaps that they shall learn the lesson too well.

One has not the alternative of speaking of London as a whole,
for the simple reason that there is no such thing as the whole of it.
It is immeasurable—embracing arms never meet. Rather it is a collection
of many wholes . . . Inevitably there must be a choice . . . The ugliness,
the 'rookeries,' the brutalities, the night-aspects of many of the streets,
the gin-shops and the hour when they are cleared out before closing—
there are many elements of this kind which have to be counted out
before a genial summary can be made.

And yet I should not go so far as to say that it is a condition of such
genialities to close one's eyes upon the immense misery; on the
contrary, I think it is partly because we are irremediably conscious of
that dark gulf that the most general appeal of the great city remains
exactly what it is, the largest chapter of human accidents. . . . the
impression of suffering is a part of the general vibration; it is one of the
things that mingle with all the others to make the sound that is
supremely dear to the consistent London-lover—the rumble of the
tremendous human mill. This is the note which, in all its modulations,
haunts and fascinates and inspires him. . . . We are far from liking
London well enough till we like its defects . . . .

It is not what London fails to do that strikes the observer, but the
general fact that she does everything in excess. Excess is her highest
reproach, and it is her highest misfortune that there is really too much
of her. She overwhelms you by quantity and number—she ends by
making human life, by making civilisation appear cheap to you. . . .
And as the monster grows and grows forever, she departs more and
more . . . from the ideal of a convenient society, a society in which
intimacy is possible, in which the associated meet often and sound and
select and measure and inspire each other, and relations and combinations have time to form themselves. The substitute for this, in London,
is the momentary concussion of a million of atoms. . . .

40   A city of the damned, 1889

Extracts from George Gissing, *The Nether World* (1889), chapters 2, 19, 28 and 30.

George Gissing (1857–1903), the novelist, was the son of a Wakefield chemist and attended Owens College, Manchester. As a struggling writer, he lived amidst and experienced poverty in London. Though interested by socialism in the 1880s, Gissing was unable to identify with the London poor whom he saw as brutalized beyond redemption by the conditions of their existence. This novel about the nether world of poverty and disappointed aspiration conveys his sense of London as oppressive and over-whelming.

It was the hour of the unyoking of men. In the highways and byways of Clerkenwell there was a thronging of released toilers, of young and old, of male and female. Forth they streamed from factories and workrooms, anxious to make the most of the few hours during which they might live for themselves. Great numbers were still bent over their labour, and would be for hours to come, but the majority had leave to wend stablewards. Along the main thoroughfares the wheel-track was clangorous; every omnibus that clattered by was heavily laden with passengers . . . This way and that the lights were blurred into a misty radiance; overhead was mere blackness, whence descended the lashing rain. There was a ceaseless scattering of mud; there were blocks in the traffic, attended with rough jest or angry curse; there was jostling on the crowded pavement. Public-houses began to brighten up, to bestir themselves for the evening's business. Streets that had been hives of activity since early morning were being abandoned to silence and darkness and the sweeping wind.

At noon today there was sunlight on the Surrey hills; the fields and lanes were fragrant with the first breath of spring, and from the shelter of budding copses many a primrose looked tremblingly up to the vision of blue sky. But of these things Clerkenwell takes no count;

N

here it had been a day like any other, consisting of so many hours, each representing a fraction of the weekly wage. Go where you may in Clerkenwell, on every hand are multiform evidences of toil, intolerable as a nightmare. It is not as in those parts of London where the main thoroughfares consist of shops and warehouses and work-rooms, whilst the streets that are hidden away on either hand are devoted in the main to dwellings. Here every alley is thronged with small industries; all but every door and window exhibits the advertise-ment of a craft that is carried on within. Here you may see how men have multiplied toil for toil's sake, have wrought to devise work superfluous, have worn their lives away in imagining new forms of weariness. The energy, the ingenuity daily put forth in these grimy burrows task the brain's power of wondering. But that those who sit here through the livelong day, through every season, through all the years of the life that is granted them, who strain their eyesight, who overtax their muscles, who nurse disease in their frames, who put resolutely from them the thought of what existence *might* be—that these do it all without prospect or hope of reward save the permission to eat and sleep and bring into the world other creatures to strive with them for bread, surely that thought is yet more marvellous.

Workers in metal, workers in glass and enamel, workers in wood, workers in every substance on earth, or from the waters under the earth, that can be made commercially valuable. In Clerkenwell the demand is not so much for rude strength as for the cunning fingers and the contriving brain. . . . Wealth inestimable is ever flowing through these workshops, and the hands that have been stained with gold-dust may, as likely as not, some day extend themselves in petition for a crust. In this house . . . business is carried on by a trader in diamonds, and next door is a den full of children who wait for their day's one meal until their mother has come home with her chance earnings. A strange enough region wherein to wander and muse. Inextinguishable laughter were perchance the fittest result of such musing; yet somehow the heart grows heavy, somehow the blood is troubled in its course, and the pulses begin to throb hotly. . . .

. . . [The Snowdons and Sidney Kirkwood take a train from Liverpool Street to rural Essex] Over the pest-stricken regions of East London, sweltering in sunshine which served only to reveal the intimacies of abomination; across miles of a city of the damned, such as thought never conceived before this age of ours; above streets swarming with a nameless populace, cruelly exposed by the unwonted light of heaven; stopping at stations which it crushes the heart to think should be the destination of any mortal; the train made its way at length beyond the outmost limits of dread, and entered upon a land of level meadows, of hedges and trees, of crops and cattle. . . .

With the first breath of winter there passes a voice half-menacing, half-mournful, through all the barren ways and phantom-haunted refuges of the nether world. Too quickly has vanished the brief season when the sky is clement, when a little food suffices, and the chances of earning that little are more numerous than at other times; this wind that gives utterance to its familiar warning is the vaunt-courier of cold and hunger and solicitude that knows not sleep. Will the winter be a hard one? It is the question that concerns this world before all others, that occupies alike the patient work-folk who have yet their home unbroken, the strugglers foredoomed to loss of such scant needments as the summer gifted them withal, the hopeless and the self-abandoned and the lurking creatures of prey. To all of them the first chill breath from a lowering sky has its voice of admonition; they set their faces; they sigh, or whisper a prayer, or fling out a curse, each according to his nature.

And as though the strife here were not already hard enough, behold from many corners of the land come needy emigrants, prospectless among their own people, fearing the dark season which has so often meant for them the end of wages and of food, tempted hither by thought that in the shadow of palaces work and charity are both more plentiful. Vagabonds, too, no longer able to lie about the country roads, creep back to their remembered lairs and join the combat for crusts flung forth by casual hands. Day after day the stress becomes more grim. One would think that hosts of the weaker combatants might surely find it seasonable to let themselves be trodden out of existence, and so make room for those of more useful sinew; somehow they cling to life; so few in comparison yield utterly. The thoughtful in the world above look about them with contentment when carriage-ways are deep with new-fallen snow. 'Good; here is work for the unemployed.' Ah, if the winter did but last a few months longer, if the wonted bounds of endurance were but, by some freak of nature, sensibly overpassed, the carriage-ways would find another kind of sweeping! . . .

. . . [The Hewett family live in a block of tenements] The economy prevailing in to-day's architecture takes good care that no depressing circumstance shall be absent from the dwellings in which the poor find shelter. What terrible barracks, those Farringdon Road Buildings! Vast, sheer walls, unbroken by even an attempt at ornament; row above row of windows in the mud-coloured surface, upwards, upwards, lifeless eyes, murky openings that tell of bareness, disorder, comfortlessness within. . . . An inner courtyard, asphalted, swept clean—looking up to the sky as from a prison. Acres of these edifices, the tinge of grime declaring the relative dates of their erection; millions of tons of brute brick and mortar, crushing the spirit as you gaze. Barracks, in truth; housing for the army of industrialism, an army fighting with itself, rank against rank, man against man, that the survivors might have whereon to feed. Pass by in the night, and strain imagination to picture the weltering mass of human weariness, of bestiality, of unmerited dolour, of hopeless hope, of crushed surrender, tumbled together within those forbidding walls.

41   The Clearing of Misery, 1890

Extracts from William Morris, *News from Nowhere* (1890), chapters 10 and 18.

William Morris (1834–96), son of a London businessman and Oxford-educated, was a follower of Ruskin, sharing his mediaevalism, his distaste for modern city life, industrialism and commercial values, and his yearning for social and artistic regeneration. Eventually, impatient of ideals which lacked any means of realization, Morris accepted the necessity of class-conflict and a rising of the city masses. In 1883 he joined Hyndman's Social Democratic Federation and threw himself into socialist agitation. In *News from Nowhere* a socialist of Morris's own time dreams of post-revolutionary England and finds a Utopian society almost the reverse-image of Morris's analysis of the late-Victorian cities.

After a pause, I said: 'Your big towns, now; how about them? London . . . the modern Babylon of civilization, seems to have disappeared.'
   'Well, well,' said old Hammond, 'perhaps after all it is more like ancient Babylon now than the "modern Babylon" of the nineteenth century was. . . .'

'Tell me, then,' said I, 'how is it towards the east?'

Said he: 'Time was when if you mounted a good horse and rode . . . for an hour and a half, you would still be in the thick of London, and the greater part of that would be "slums", as they were called; that is to say, places of torture for innocent men and women; or worse, stews for rearing and breeding men and women in such degradation that that torture should seem to them mere ordinary and natural life.'

'I know, I know,' I said . . . 'That was what was. . . . Is any of that left?'

'Not an inch,' said he; 'but some memory of it abides with us . . . Once a year, on May-day, we hold a solemn feast in those easterly communes of London to commemorate The Clearing of Misery, as it is called. On that day we have music and dancing, and merry games and happy feasting on the site of some of the worst of the old slums, the traditional memory of which we have kept. On that occasion the custom is for the prettiest girls to sing some of the old revolutionary songs, and those which were the groans of the discontent, once so hopeless, on the very spots where those terrible crimes of class-murder were committed day by day for so many years. . . .'

'Tell me in detail,' said I, 'what lies east of Bloomsbury now?'

Said he: 'There are but few houses between this and the outer part of the old city; but in the city we have a thickly dwelling population. Our forefathers, in the first clearing of the slums were not in a hurry to pull down the houses in what was called at the end of the nineteenth century the business quarter of the town, and what later got to be known as the Swindling Kens. . . . it remains the most populous part of London, or perhaps of all these islands. . . . However, this crowding, if it may be called so, does not go further than a street called Aldgate, a name which perhaps you may have heard of. Beyond that the houses are scattered wide about the meadows there, which are very beautiful, especially when you get on to the lovely river Lea . . . about the places called Stratford and Old Ford. . . .'

. . . How strange! that I who had seen the very last remnant of the pleasantness of the meadows by the Lea destroyed, should have heard them spoken of with pleasantness come back to them in full measure.

Hammond went on: 'When you get down to the Thames side you come on the Docks, which are works of the nineteenth century, and are still in use, although not so thronged as they once were, since we discourage centralization all we can, and we have long ago dropped the pretension to be the market of the world. About these Docks are a good few houses, which, however, are not inhabited by many people permanently; I mean, those who use them come and go a good deal, the place being too low and marshy for pleasant dwelling. Past the Docks eastward and landward it is all flat pasture, once marsh, except for a few gardens, and there are very few permanent dwellings there. . . . There is a place called Canning's Town, and further out, Silvertown, where the pleasant meadows are at their pleasantest: doubtless they were once slums, and wretched enough.'

. . . 'So much for what was once London,' said I. 'Now tell me about the other towns of the country.'

He said: 'As to the big murky places which were once . . . the centres of manufacture, they have, like the bricks and mortar desert of London, disappeared; only, since they were centres of nothing but "manufacture", and served no purpose but that of the gambling market, they have left less signs of their existence than London. Of course, the great change in the use of mechanical force made this an easy matter, and some approach to their break-up as centres would probably have taken place, even if we had not changed our habits so much; but they being such as they were, no sacrifice would have seemed too great a price to pay for getting rid of the "manufacturing districts", as they used to be called. . . .One is tempted to believe from what one has read of the condition of those districts in the nineteenth century, that those who had them under their power worried, befouled, and degraded men out of malice prepense: . . .'

. . . Said I: 'How about the smaller towns? I suppose you have swept those away entirely?'

'No, no,' said he, '. . . On the contrary, there has been but little clearance, though much rebuilding, in the smaller towns. Their suburbs, indeed, when they had any, have melted away into the general country, and space and elbow-room has been got in their centres: but there are the towns still with their streets and squares and market-places; so that it is by means of these smaller towns that we of today can get some kind of idea of what the towns of the older world were like—I mean to say at their best.'

. . . I said: 'We have heard about London and the manufacturing districts and the ordinary towns: how about the villages?'

Said Hammond: 'You must know that toward the end of the nineteenth century the villages were almost destroyed, unless where they became mere adjuncts to the manufacturing districts, or formed a sort of minor manufacturing district themselves. Houses were allowed to fall into decay and actual ruin; trees were cut down for the sake of the few shillings which the poor sticks would fetch . . . Labour was scarce; but wages fell nevertheless. All the small country arts of life which once added to the little pleasures of country people were lost. . . . Incredible shabbiness and niggardly pinching reigned over the fields and acres. . . .

'The change,' said Hammond, 'which in these matters took place very early in our epoch, was most strangely rapid. People flocked into the country villages, and, so to say, flung themselves upon the freed land like a wild beast upon his prey; and in a very little time the villages of England were more populous than they had been since the fourteenth century, and were still growing fast. Of course, this invasion of the country was awkward to deal with, and would have created much misery, if the folk had still been under the bondage of class monopoly. But as it was, things soon righted themselves. People found out what they were fit for, and gave up attempting to push themselves into occupations in which they must needs fail. The town invaded the country; but the invaders . . . yielded to the influence of their surroundings, and became country people; and in their turn, as they became more numerous than the townsmen, influenced them also; so that the difference between town and country grew less and less; and it was indeed this world of the country vivified by the thought and briskness of town-bred folk which has produced that happy and leisurely but eager life of which you have had a first taste. . . .'

'This is how we stand. England was once a country of clearings amongst the woods and wastes, with a few towns interspersed, which were fortresses for the feudal army, markets for the folk, gathering places for the craftsmen. It then became a country of huge and foul workshops and fouler gambling-dens, surrounded by an ill-kept, poverty-stricken farm, pillaged by the masters of the workshops. It is now a garden, where nothing is wasted and nothing is spoilt, with the necessary dwellings, sheds and workshops scattered up and down the country, all trim and neat and pretty. For, indeed, we should be too much ashamed of ourselves if we allowed the making of goods, even on a large scale, to carry with it the appearance, even, of desolation and misery. . . .'

. . . [Hammond tells the narrator how the rising of the London masses brought about the revolution] 'When the conflict was once really begun, it was seen how little of any value there was in the old world of slavery and inequality. . . . In the times . . . of which you seem to know so much, there was no hope; nothing but the dull jog of the mill-horse under compulsion of collar and whip; but in that fighting-time that followed, all was hope: "the rebels" at least felt themselves strong enough to build up the world again from its dry bones—and they did it, too! . . . In short, the two combatants, the workman and the gentleman, between them—'

'Between them,' said I, quickly, 'they destroyed commercialism!'

'Yes, yes, YES,' said he; 'that is it. Nor could it have been destroyed otherwise; except, perhaps, by the whole of society gradually falling into lower depths, till it should at last reach a condition as rude as barbarism, but lacking both the hope and the pleasures of barbarism. Surely the sharper, shorter remedy was the happiest?'

42 The absorbing interest of a battle-field, 1892

Extracts from Charles Booth, *Life and Labour of the People in London*
(1892 edn), i, part 1: East London.

Charles Booth (1840–1916), the social investigator, was a Liverpool
ship-owner with a Liberal nonconformist background. In the 1880s
he took up the much-publicized question of poverty in the cities and
set out to discover its nature and extent in London. The results of
the great investigation which he organized and financed appeared in
seventeen volumes from 1889 to 1902. An admirer of the free-
enterprise economy and of social individualism, Booth attacked
emotional exaggeration of the poverty problem and the tendency
to look to vague but threatening 'socialism' for a remedy. Carefully
distinguishing the different categories of the poor, he argued that
the most helpless and debased should be institutionalized by the
state to leave the respectable and independent working-classes better
able to compete in the free economy, a strictly limited form of
collectivism which he called 'Socialism in the arms of Individualism'.
Rejecting a gloomy picture of the city, he stressed the colour and
diversity of London life and the vitality and happiness of the poor.

E. Regular Standard Earnings: These are the bulk of Section 5, together
with a large proportion of the artisans and most other regular wage
earners. I also include here, as having equal means, the best class of
street sellers and general dealers, a large proportion of the small shop-
keepers, the best off amongst the home manufacturers, and some of
the small employers. This is by far the largest class of the population
under review, adding up to 377,000, or over 42 per cent.

Section No. 5 contains all, not artisans or otherwise, who earn
from 22*s* to 30*s* per week for regular work. There are some of them
who, when wages are near the lower figure, or the families are large,
are not lifted above the line of poverty; but few of them are *very poor*,

and the bulk of this large section can, and do, lead independent lives, and possess fairly comfortable homes.

The wage earners of Class E take readily any gratuities which fall in their way . . . but against anything which could be called charity their pride rises stiffly. This class is the recognized field of all forms of co-operation and combination, and I believe, and am glad to believe, that it holds its future in its own hands. No body of men deserves more consideration; it does not constitute a majority of the population in the East of London, nor, probably, in the whole of London, but it perhaps may do so taking England as a whole. It should be said that only in a very general way of speaking do these people form one class, and beneath this generality lie wide divergences of character, interests, and ways of life. This class owns a good deal of property in the aggregate. . . .

. . . Each district has its character—its peculiar flavour. One seems to be conscious of it in the streets. It may be in the faces of the people, or in what they carry—perhaps a reflection is thrown in this way from the prevailing trades—or it may lie in the sounds one hears, or in the character of the buildings.

Of all the districts of that 'inner ring' which surrounds the City, St George's-in-the-East is the most desolate. The other districts have each some charm or other—a brightness not extinguished by, and even appertaining to, poverty and toil, to vice, and even to crime—a clash of contest, man against man, and men against fate—the absorbing interest of a battle-field—a rush of human life as fascinating to watch as the current of a river to which it is so often likened. But there is nothing of this in St George's, which appears to stagnate with a squalor peculiar to itself.

The feeling that I have just described—this excitement of life which can accept murder as a dramatic incident, and drunkenness as the buffoonery of the stage—is especially characteristic of Whitechapel. And looked at this way, what a drama it is! Whitechapel is a veritable Tom Tiddler's ground, the Eldorado of the East, a gathering together of poor fortune seekers; its streets are full of buying and selling, the poor living on the poor. . . .

The neighbourhood of old Petticoat Lane on Sunday is one of the wonders of London, a medley of strange sights, strange sounds, and strange smells. Streets crowded so as to be thoroughfares no longer, and lined with a double or treble row of hand-barrows . . . the salesmen with stentorian voices cry their wares, vying with each other in introducing to the surrounding crowd their cheap garments, smart braces, sham jewellery, or patent medicines. . . . Other stalls supply daily wants—fish is sold in large quantities—vegetables and fruit—queer cakes and outlandish bread. In nearly all cases the Jew is the seller, and the Gentile the buyer; Petticoat Lane is the exchange of the Jew, but the lounge of the Christian. . . .

. . . we have in Classes B, C, and D the problem of poverty. In the population under review the 100,000 of 'very poor' (Class B) are at all times more or less 'in want.' They are ill-nourished and poorly clad. But of them only a percentage—and not, I think, a large percentage—would be said by themselves, or by anyone else, to be 'in distress.' From day to day and from hand to mouth they get along; sometimes suffering, sometimes helped, but not always unfortunate, and very ready to enjoy any good luck that may come in their way. They are, very likely, improvident, spending what they make as they make it; but the 'improvidence of the poor has its bright side.' . . . Some may be semi-paupers, going into the 'house' at certain seasons, and some few receive out-door relief, but on the whole they manage to avoid the workhouse. On the other hand, the 200,000 of 'poor' (Classes C and D), though they would be much the better for more of everything, are not 'in want.' They are neither ill-nourished nor ill-clad, according to any standard that can reasonably be used. Their lives are an unending struggle, and lack comfort, but I do not know that they lack happiness. . . .

. . . To the rich the very poor are a sentimental interest; to the poor they are a crushing load. The poverty of the poor is mainly the result of the competition of the very poor. The entire removal of this very poor class out of the daily struggle for existence I believe to be the only solution of the problem. . . .

If it is true, as we are taught and as I believe, that the standard of life is rising, and that the proportion of the population in very poor circumstances never has been less, and is steadily decreasing, it follows, as I think, that some day the individualist community, on which we build our faith, will find itself obliged for its own sake to take charge of the lives of those who, from whatever cause, are incapable of independent existence up to the required standard, and will be fully able to do so. Has this time come yet? . . .

Beyond the malefic influence which the imperative needs and ill-regulated lives of the class we are considering exercise over the fortunes of those who might otherwise do well enough, and beyond the fact that they do not support themselves, but absorb the charities of both rich and poor, they are also a constant burthen to the State. . . . Their presence in our cities creates a costly and often unavailing struggle to raise the standard of life and health.

The question of those who actually suffer from poverty should be considered separately from that of the true working classes, whose desire for a larger share of wealth is of a different character. It is the plan of agitators and the way of sensational writers to confound the two in one, to talk of 'starving millions,' and to tack on the thousands of the working classes to the tens or hundreds of distress. Against this method I protest. To confound these essentially distinct problems is to make the solution of both impossible; it is not by welding distress and aspirations that any good can be done. . . .

. . . The children in class E, and still more in class D, have when young less chance of surviving than those of the rich, but I certainly think their lives are happier . . . They are more likely to suffer from spoiling than from harshness, for they are made much of, being commonly the pride of their mother, who will sacrifice much to see them prettily dressed, and the delight of their father's heart. This makes the home, and the happiness of their parents; but it is . . . the constant occupation, which makes the children's lives so happy. They have their regular school hours, and when at home, as soon as they are old enough, there is 'mother' to help, and they have numbers of little friends. In class E they have for playground the back yard, in class D the even greater delights of the streets. With really bad parents the story would be different, but men and women may be very bad, and yet love their children and make them happy. . . .

. . . I see nothing improbable in the general view that the simple natural lives of working-class people tend to their own and their children's happiness more than the artificial complicated existence of the rich. Let it not be supposed, however, that on this I propose to base any argument against the desire of this class to better its position. Very far from it. Their class ambition as well as their efforts to raise themselves as individuals deserve the greatest sympathy. They might possess and spend a good deal more than they do without seriously endangering the simplicity of their lives or their chances of happiness, and it would be well if their lot included the expenditure of a larger proportion of our surplus wealth than is now the case. . . .

. . . East London lay hidden from view behind a curtain on which were painted terrible pictures:—Starving children, suffering women, over-worked men; horrors of drunkenness and vice; monsters and demons of inhumanity; giants of disease and despair. Did these pictures truly represent what lay behind, or did they bear to the facts a relation similar to that which the pictures outside a booth at some country fair bear to the performance or show within? This curtain we have tried to lift.

. . . those who have had a lengthened experience of East London, agree that its state was much worse when they first knew the district than it is now. Beyond this, such glimpses as we can obtain of a remoter past seem to tell a similar story of improvement, and however we test the question the same answer is given; so that I am inclined to think that if an inquiry, such as the present, had been made at any previous time in the history of London, it would have shown a greater proportion of depravity and misery than now exists, and a lower general standard of life. . . .

Whatever the miseries of Class A, they are not the result of a too exalted ideal, nor due to any consciousness of degradation. . . . On the other hand, the impression of horror that the condition of this class makes upon the public mind today is out of all proportion to that made when its actual condition was far worse, and consequently the need to deal with the evils involved becomes more pressing. This, moreover, is no mere question of sentiment, but (if we admit a general all-round improvement) an imperative need of the rising standard of life. What might be an admissible state of things in days past is admissible no longer. It drags us back, and how to put an end to it has become a question of the first importance. . . .

43   The breath of social life, 1894

Extracts from J. A. Hobson, *The Evolution of Modern Capitalism. A Study of Machine Production* (1894), chapter 13.

John A. Hobson (1858–1940), the economist, was the son of a provincial newspaper proprietor and editor. In 1894 he was a university extension lecturer and becoming recognized as one of the most radical critics among Liberal progressives of the social consequences of unrestrained industrial capitalism. Though Hobson, who admired Ruskin, had some sympathy with back-to-the-land ideas, he looked in *The Evolution of Modern Capitalism*, perhaps his major work of economic theory, to a transformation of the existing cities through a decentralization of population and an extension of collectivism to control the working of economic forces.

The biggest, and in some respects the most characteristic of machine-products is the modern industrial town. . . .

This rapid appreciation of the economies of centralised production, heedless of all considerations, sanitary, aesthetic, moral, found a hasty business expression in these huge hideous conglomerations of factory buildings, warehouses, and cheap workmen's shelters, which make the modern industrial town. The requirements of a decent, healthy, harmonious individual or civic life played no appreciable part . . . Considerations of cheap profitable work were paramount; considerations of life were almost utterly ignored. So swift, heedless, anarchic has this process been, that no adequate provisions were made for securing the prime conditions of healthy, physical existence required to maintain the workers in the most profitable state of working efficiency. Only of recent years in a few of the larger manufacturing towns has some slow revival of the idea of civic life, as distinct from the organised manipulation of municipal affairs for selfish business purposes, begun to manifest itself. The typical modern town is still a place of workshops, not of homes. . . .

. . . If the town were a social organism formed by men desirous of living together for mutual support, comfort, and enjoyment in their lives, . . . a wholesome public feeling would be so strongly operative as to outweigh the increased opportunities of crime. But . . . the modern town is a result of the desire to produce and distribute most economically the largest aggregate of material goods. . . . Now, the economy of factory co-operation is only social to a very limited extent; anti-social feelings are touched and stimulated at every point by the competition of workers with one another, the antagonism between employers and employed, between sellers and buyers, factory and factory, shop and shop.

Perhaps the most potent influence in breaking the strength of the *morale* of the town worker is the precarious and disorderly character of town work. . . . Town work . . . is more irregular than country work, and this irregularity has a most pernicious effect upon the character of the worker. . . .

. . . The average townsman is more developed morally as well as intellectually [than the countryman] for good and for evil. That the good does not more signally predominate is in no small measure due to the feeble social environment . . . where the density of population is determined by industrial competition, rather than by human-social causes, . . . the force of public opinion is in inverse proportion to the density of population, being weakest in the most crowded cities. In spite of the machinery of political, religious, social, trade organisations in large towns, it is probable that the true spiritual cohesiveness between individual members is feebler than in any other form of society. If it is true that as the larger village grows into the town, and the town into the ever larger city, there is a progressive weakening of the bonds of moral cohesion between individuals, that the larger the town the feebler the spiritual unity, we are face to face with the heaviest indictment that can be brought against modern industrial progress, and the forces driving an increased proportion of our population into towns are bringing about a decadence of *morale* which is the necessary counterpart of the deterioration of national physique.

. . . The free play of economic forces under the guidance of the selfish instincts of commercial individuals, or groups of individuals, is driving an increased proportion of the population of civilised countries into a town life which is injurious to physical and moral health, and provides no security for the attainment of an intellectual life which is worth living. . . .

. . . it is to improved transport services that we may look to facilitate a kind of decentralisation, the net gain of which is less dubious than that arising from the substitution of a large number of industrial villages for a small number of industrial towns. Is it not possible for more town-workers to combine centralised work with decentralised life—to work in the town but to live in the country? May not this advantage, at present confined to the wealthier classes, be brought within the reach of the poorer classes? . . . Three chief difficulties stand in the way of success: the length of the working day, which makes the time required for travelling to and from a distant home a matter of serious consideration; the defective supply of convenient, cheap, and frequent trains or other quick means of conveyance; the irregularity and un-certainty of tenure in most classes of labour, which prevents the establishment of a settled house chosen with regard to convenient access to a single point of industry. . . . considerable extension of direct public control over the means of transport will be required . . . A firm public control in the common interest over the steam and electric railways of the future seems essential to the attainment of adequate decentralisation for dwelling purposes. Private enterprise in transport, working hand in hand with private ownership of land, will only substitute for a single mass of over-crowded dwellings a number of smaller suburban areas of over-crowded dwellings. . . .

The removal of the other two barriers belongs to that joint action of labour organisation and legislation which aims at building up a condition of stable industrial economy. One of the most serviceable results of that shortening of the working-day . . . would be . . . to enable workmen and workwomen to live at a longer distance from their work. So long, however, as a large proportion of city workers have no security of tenure in their work . . . these schemes of decentrali-sation can be but partial in their application. . . .

It is, however, unlikely, that any wide or lasting solution of the problem of congested town life will be found in a sharp local severance of the life of an industrial society which shall abandon the town to the purpose of a huge workshop, reserving the country for habitation. . . . It is only in the case of the largest and densest industrial cities, swollen to an unwieldly and dangerous size, that such methods of decentralisa-tion can in some measure be applied. . . . In smaller towns . . . a spread-ing of the close-packed population over an expanded town-area will be more feasible, and will form the first step in that series of reforms which shall humanise the industrial town. The congestion of the poorer population . . . is the most formidable barrier to the work of transforming the town from a big workshop into a human dwelling-place, with an individual life, a character, a soul of its own. The true reform policy is not to destroy the industrial town but to breathe into it the breath of social life, to temper and subordinate its industrial machine-goods-producing character to the higher and more complex purposes of social life. An ample, far-sighted, enlightened, social control over the whole area of city ground, whether used for dwellings or for industrial purposes, is the first condition of the true municipal life. The industrial town, left for its growth to individual industrial control, compresses into unhealthily close proximity large numbers . . . with different and often antagonistic aims, with little knowledge of one another, with no important common end to form a bond of social sympathy. The town presents the single raw material of local proximity out of which municipal life is to be built. The first business of the municipal reformer then is to transform this excessive proximity into wholesome neighbourhood, in order that true neighbourly feelings may have room to grow and thrive, and eventually to ripen into the flower of a fair civic life . . . To evoke the personal human qualities of this medley of city workers so as to reach within the individual the citizen, to educate the civic feeling until it take shape in civic activities and institutions, which not only safeguard the public welfare against the encroachments of private industrial greed, but shall find an ever ampler and nobler expression in the aesthetic beauty and spiritual dignity of a complex, common life—all this work of transformation lies in front of the democracy, grouped in its ever-increasing number of town-units.

44   Marrying town and country, 1898

Extracts from Ebenezer Howard, *To-morrow: a Peaceful Path to Real Reform* (1898). (The edition used is the slightly-revised one of 1902 entitled *Garden Cities of To-morrow*, introduction and chapters 4, 6, 11, 12 and 13.)

Ebenezer Howard (1850–1928) was the son of a City shopkeeper and worked as a shorthand writer in London. A Liberal and a nonconformist, Howard rejected the existing cities and proposed the creation of a new civilization based on a marriage of town and country in the 'garden city', which he later defined as 'a Town designed for healthy living and industry; of a size that makes possible a full measure of social life, but not larger; surrounded by a rural belt; the whole of the land being in public ownership or held in trust for the community.' He founded the Garden City Association in 1903 and was soon building a prototype garden city at Letchworth.

There is . . . a question in regard to which one can scarcely find any difference of opinion. It is wellnigh universally agreed by men of all parties, not only in England, but all over Europe and America and our colonies, that it is deeply to be deplored that the people should continue to stream into the already over-crowded cities, and should thus further deplete the country districts.

. . . Yes, the key to the problem how to restore the people to the land—that beautiful land of ours . . . the very embodiment of Divine love for man—is indeed a *Master Key*, for it is the key to a portal through which . . . will be seen to pour a flood of light on the problems of intemperance, of excessive toil, of restless anxiety, of grinding poverty—the true limits of Governmental interference, ay, and even the relations of man to the Supreme Power.

. . . Whatever may have been the causes which have operated in the past, and are operating now, to draw the people into the cities, those causes may be summed up as 'attractions'; and . . . no remedy can

possibly be found effective which will not present to the people . . .
greater 'attractions' than our cities now possess . . . Each city may be
regarded as a magnet, each person as a needle; and . . . nothing short
of the discovery of a method for constructing magnets of yet greater
power than our cities possess can be effective for redistributing the
population in a spontaneous and healthy manner.

 . . . The subject is treated continually in the public press, and in all
forms of discussion, as though men, or at least working men, had not
now, and never could have, any choice or alternative, but either . . .
to stifle their love for human society—at least in wider relations than
can be found in a straggling village—or . . . to forgo almost entirely
all the keen and pure delights of the country. The question is universally
considered as though it were now, and for ever must remain, quite
impossible for working people to live in the country and yet be engaged
in pursuits other than agricultural; as though crowded, unhealthy
cities were the last word of economic science; and as if our present
form of industry, in which sharp lines divide agricultural from
industrial pursuits, were necessarily an enduring one. . . . There are in
reality not only . . . two alternatives—town life and country life—but
a third alternative, in which all the advantages of the most energetic
and active town life, with all the beauty and delight of the country,
may be secured in perfect combination; . . . this life will be the magnet
which will produce the effect for which we are all striving—the
spontaneous movement of the people from our crowded cities to the
bosom of our kindly mother earth, at once the source of life, of
happiness, of wealth, and of power. The town and the country may,
therefore, be regarded as two magnets, each striving to draw the
people to itself—a rivalry which a new form of life, partaking of the
nature of both, comes to take part in. . . .

The Town magnet . . . offers, as compared with the Country magnet,
the advantage of high wages, opportunities for employment, tempting
prospects of advancement, but these are largely counter-balanced by
high rents and prices. Its social opportunities and its places of amusement are very alluring, but excessive hours of toil, distance from work,
and the 'isolation of crowds' tend greatly to reduce the value of these
good things. The well-lit streets are a great attraction, especially in
winter, but the sunlight is being more and more shut out, while the air
is so vitiated that the fine public buildings . . . rapidly become covered
with soot . . . Palatial edifices and fearful slums are the strange, complementary features of modern cities.

The Country magnet declares herself to be the source of all beauty and wealth; but the Town magnet mockingly reminds her that she is very dull for lack of society, and very sparing of her gifts for lack of capital. . . . Rents, if estimated by the acre, are certainly low, but such low rents are the natural fruit of low wages rather than a cause of substantial comfort; while long hours and lack of amusements forbid the bright sunshine and the pure air to gladden the hearts of the people. The one industry, agriculture, suffers frequently from excessive rainfalls . . . Even the natural healthfulness of the country is largely lost for lack of proper drainage and other sanitary conditions, while, in parts almost deserted by the people, the few who remain are yet frequently huddled together as if in rivalry with the slums of our cities.

But neither the Town magnet nor the Country magnet represents the full plan and purpose of nature. Human society and the beauty of nature are meant to be enjoyed together. The two magnets must be made one. . . . The town is the symbol of society—of mutual help and friendly co-operation, of . . . wide relations between man and man—of broad, expanding sympathies—of science, art, culture, religion. And the country! The country is the symbol of God's love and care for man. All that we are and all that we have comes from it. . . . It is the source of all health, all wealth, all knowledge. But its fullness of joy and wisdom has not revealed itself to man. Nor can it ever, so long as this unholy, unnatural separation of society and nature endures. Town and country *must be married*, and out of this joyous union will spring a new hope, a new life, a new civilization. . . .

. . . the town is definitely planned, so that the whole question of municipal administration may be dealt with by one far-reaching scheme. . . . It will no doubt be the work of many minds—the minds of engineers, of architects and surveyors, of landscape gardeners and electricians. But it is essential . . . that there should be unity of design and purpose—that the town should be planned as a whole, and not left to grow up in a chaotic manner as has been the case with all English towns, and more or less so with the towns of all countries. A town, like a flower, or a tree, or an animal, should, at each stage of its growth, possess unity, symmetry, completeness, and the effect of growth should never be to destroy that unity, but to give it greater purpose, nor to mar that symmetry, but to make it more symmetrical . . .

Garden City is not only planned, but it is planned with a view to the very latest of modern requirements, and it is obviously always easier, and usually far more economical and completely satisfactory, to make out of fresh material a new instrument than to patch up and alter an old one. . . .

. . . A most important question now arises regarding the extent to which municipal enterprise is to be carried, and how far it is to supersede private enterprise. We have already . . . stated that the experiment advocated does not involve, as has been the case in so many social experiments—the complete municipalization of industry and the elimination of private enterprise. . . . But probably the true answer is to be found at neither extreme, is only to be gained by experiment, and will differ in different communities and at different periods. With a growing intelligence and honesty in municipal enterprise, with greater freedom from the control of the Central Government, it may be found—especially on municipally owned land—that the field of municipal activity may grow so as to embrace a very large area, and yet the municipality claim no rigid monopoly and the fullest rights of combination exist. . . .

. . . there is a path along which both the Individualist and the Socialist must inevitably travel; for . . . on a small scale society may readily become more individualistic than now—if by Individualism is meant a society in which there is fuller and freer opportunity for its members to do and to produce what they will, and to form free associations, of the most varied kinds; while it may also become more socialistic—if by Socialism is meant a condition of life in which the well-being of the community is safeguarded, and in which the collective spirit is manifested by a wide extension of the area of municipal effort. . . .

. . . Some of my friends have suggested that such a scheme of town clusters is well enough adapted to a new country, but that in an old-settled country, with its towns built, and its railway 'system' for the most part constructed, it is quite a different matter. But surely to raise such a point is to contend . . . that the existing wealth forms of the country are permanent, and are forever to serve as hindrances to the introduction of better forms: that crowded, ill-ventilated, unplanned, unwieldly, unhealthy cities—ulcers on the very face of our beautiful island—are to stand as barriers to the introduction of towns in which modern scientific methods and the aims of social reformers may have the fullest scope in which to express themselves. . . . What Is may hinder What Might Be for a while, but cannot stay the tide of progress. These crowded cities have done their work; they were the best which a society largely based on selfishness and rapacity could construct, but they are in the nature of things entirely unadapted for a society in which the social side of our nature is demanding a larger share of recognition. . . . The large cities of today are scarcely better adapted for the expression of the fraternal spirit than would a work on astronomy which taught that the earth was the centre of the universe be capable of adaptation for use in our schools. Each generation should build to suit its own needs; and it is no more in the nature of things that men should continue to live in old areas because their ancestors lived in them, than it is that they should cherish the old beliefs which a wider faith and a more enlarged understanding have outgrown. . . . The simple issue to be faced, and faced resolutely, is: Can better results be obtained by starting on a bold plan on comparatively virgin soil than by attempting to adapt our old cities to our newer and higher needs? Thus fairly faced, the question can only be answered in one way; and when that simple fact is well grasped, the social revolution will speedily commence. . . .

. . . The effects produced on our over-crowded cities, whose forms are at once, by the light of a new contrast, seen to be old-fashioned and effete, will be so far-reaching in their character that, in order to study them effectively, it will be well to confine our attention to London, which, as the largest and most unwieldly of our cities, is likely to exhibit those effects in the most marked degree.

. . . assume . . . that the remedy advocated in this work is effective; that new garden cities are springing up all over the country on sites owned by the municipalities . . . What, then, must in the nature of things be the more noticeable effects upon London and the population of London? . . .

For observe what must inevitably happen. A vast field of employment being opened outside London, unless a corresponding field of employment is opened within it, London must die . . . Elsewhere new cities are being built: London then must be transformed. Elsewhere the town is invading the country: here the country must invade the town. Elsewhere cities are being built on the terms of paying low prices for land, and of then vesting such land in the new municipalities: in London corresponding arrangements must be made or no one will consent to build. Elsewhere, owing to the fact that there are but few interests to buy out, improvements of all kinds can go forward rapidly and scientifically: in London similar improvements can only be carried out if vested interests recognize the inevitable and accept terms. . . .

. . . a new city [will] rise on the ashes of the old. The task will indeed be difficult. Easy, comparatively, is it to lay out on virgin soil the plan of a magnificent city . . . Of far greater difficulty is the problem—

even if all vested interests freely efface themselves—of rebuilding a new city on an old site, and that site occupied by a huge population. But this, at least, is certain, that the present area of the London County Council ought not . . . to contain more than, say, one-fifth of its present population; and that new systems of railways, sewerage, drainage, lighting, parks, etc., must be constructed if London is to be saved, while the whole system of production and of distribution must undergo changes. . . .

The time for the complete reconstruction of London . . . has, however, not yet come. A simpler problem must first be solved. One small Garden City must be built as a working model, and then a group of cities such as that dealt with in the last chapter. These tasks done, and done well, the reconstruction of London must inevitably follow, and the power of vested interests to block the way will have been almost, if not entirely, removed.

45   The new tyranny of cities, 1899

Extracts from H. G. Wells, *The Sleeper Awakes* (1899), chapters 7, 14, 18 and 23.

Herbert George Wells (1866–1946) was the son of a gardener and small shopkeeper in Bromley. Climbing the examination ladder and obtaining a scientific education, Wells reacted against the confinement society seemed to impose on talents like his. A member of the socialist Fabian Society in the 1890s, he achieved popular success as the writer of 'fantasies of possibility', stories speculating on the shape of the future in the light of scientific and social progress. *The Sleeper Awakes* expressed, as Wells wrote later, the current 'idea of the growth of the towns and the depopulation of the countryside and the degradation of labour through the higher organization of industrial production.' In the story Graham, a man of Wells's own time, falls into a trance and awakes in London two centuries on to find 'a nightmare of Capitalism triumphant' unredeemed by the quirk of monopoly capitalism which has made him owner of the world.

... It seemed to him beyond measure incredible that in his thirty years of life he had never tried to shape a picture of these coming times. 'We were making the future,' he said, 'and hardly any of us troubled to think what future we were making. And here it is!'
   ... The vastness of street and house he was prepared for, the multitudes of people. But conflicts in the city ways! And the systematised sensuality of a class of rich men!
   He thought of Bellamy, the hero of whose Socialistic Utopia had so oddly anticipated this actual experience.[1] But here was no Utopia, no Socialistic state. He had already seen enough to realise that the ancient antithesis of luxury, waste and sensuality on the one hand and abject poverty on the other, still prevailed. . . . And not only were the buildings of the city gigantic and the crowds in the street gigantic,

but the voices he had heard in the ways, the uneasiness of Howard, the very atmosphere spoke of gigantic discontent. What country was he in? Still England it seemed, and yet strangely 'un-English. . . .'
. . . A thing Graham had already learnt . . . was that nearly all the towns in the country and almost all the villages had disappeared. . . . Yet the officer had speedily convinced him how inevitable such a change had been. The old order had dotted the country with farmhouses, and every two or three miles was the ruling landlord's estate, and the place of the inn and cobbler, the grocer's shop and church—the village. Every eight miles or so was the country town . . . But directly the railways came into play, and after them the light railways, and all the swift new motor cars that had replaced wagons and horses . . . the necessity of having such frequent market towns disappeared. And the big towns grew. They drew the worker with the gravitational force of seemingly endless work, the employer with their suggestion of an infinite ocean of labour.

And as the standard of comfort rose, as the complexity of the mechanism of living increased, life in the country had become more and more costly, or narrow and impossible. . . . to live outside the range of the electric cables was to live an isolated savage. In the country were neither means of being clothed nor fed . . . no efficient doctors for an emergency, no company and no pursuits.

Moreover, mechanical appliances in agriculture made one engineer the equivalent of thirty labourers. So . . . the labourers now came to the city and its life and delights at night to leave it again in the morning. The city had swallowed up humanity; man had entered upon a new stage in his development. First had come the nomad, the hunter, then had followed the agriculturist of the agricultural state, whose towns and cities and ports were but the headquarters and markets of the countryside. And now, logical consequence of an epoch of invention, was this huge new aggregation of men.

Such things as these . . . strained Graham's imagination to picture. And when he glanced 'over beyond there' at the strange things that existed on the Continent, it failed him altogether.

He had a vision of city beyond city; cities on great plains, cities beside great rivers, vast cities along the sea margins, cities girdled by snowy mountains. . . .

And everywhere now through the city-set earth, save in the administered 'black belt' territories of the tropics, the same cosmopolitan social organization prevailed, and everywhere from Pole to Equator his property and his responsibilities extended. The whole world was civilised; the whole world dwelt in cities; the whole world was his property. . . .

Out of the dim south-west, glittering and strange, voluptuous, and in some way terrible, shone those Pleasure Cities . . . Strange places reminiscent of the legendary Sybaris, cities of art and beauty, mercenary art and mercenary beauty, sterile wonderful cities of motion and music, whither repaired all who profited by the fierce, inglorious, economic struggle that went on in the glaring labyrinth below.

Fierce he knew it was. How fierce he could judge from the fact that these latter-day people referred back to the England of the nineteenth century as the figure of an idyllic easy-going life. He turned his eyes to the scene immediately before him again, trying to conceive the big factories of that intricate maze. . . .

. . . She turned a flushed face upon him, moving suddenly. 'Your days were the days of freedom. . . . Men are no longer free—no greater, no better than the men of your time. That is not all. This city—is a prison. Every city now is a prison. Mammon grips the key in his hand. Myriads, countless myriads, toil from the cradle to the grave. Is that right? Is that to be—for ever? Yes, far worse than in your time. All about us, beneath us, sorrow and pain. All the shallow delight of such life as you find about you, is separated by just a little from a life of wretchedness beyond any telling. Yes, the poor know it—they know they suffer. . . .'

'You come,' she said, 'from the days when this new tyranny of the cities was scarcely beginning. It is a tyranny—a tyranny. In your days the feudal war lords had gone, and the new lordship of wealth had still to come. Half the men in the world still lived out upon the free country-side. The cities had still to devour them. . . .'

'It was not—But never mind. How is it now—?'

'Gain and the Pleasure Cities! Or slavery—unthanked, unhonoured slavery. . . .'

. . . [Graham speaks to the people of the world] 'I come out of the past to you,' he said, 'with the memory of an age that hoped. My age was an age of dreams—of beginnings, an age of noble hopes; throughout the world, we had made an end of slavery; throughout the world, we had spread the desire and anticipation that wars might cease, that all men and women might live nobly, in freedom and peace . . . So we hoped in the days that are past. And what of those hopes? How is it with man after two hundred years?'

'Great cities, vast powers, a collective greatness beyond our dreams. For that we did not work, and that has come. But how is it with the little lives that make up this greater life? How is it with the common lives? As it has ever been—sorrow and labour, lives cramped and unfulfilled, lives tempted by power, tempted by wealth, and gone to waste and folly. The old faiths have faded and changed, the new faith—Is there a new faith?'

Note

1 The American Edward Bellamy's *Looking Backward* (1888) used the Rip van Winkle formula to depict an idealized socialistic society of the future.

46   The problem of the coming race, 1901

Extracts from C. F. G. Masterman, 'Realities at Home', in *The Heart of the Empire: Discussions of problems of modern city life in England* (1901), pp. 1–52.

C. F. G. Masterman (1874–1927) was a fellow of Christ's College, Cambridge, when he edited *The Heart of the Empire*, a collection of essays by Liberal intellectuals on the social questions of the English city. At a time when an imperialistic mood dominated politics, the contributors argued for more determined action by government, the churches and individuals to remedy the condition of 'the ghetto', and Masterman's introductory chapter considered the failures of Christianity and Liberal individualism among the city populations created by the nineteenth century, matters which, as a Liberal Churchman involved in social work in the London slums, he felt keenly.

... great changes, and in many respects great improvements, have taken place in large areas since men first awakened in the mid-century to the vital importance of the 'Condition of the People' problem. ...

But while men have slept other forces have arisen and changes taken place even as yet unappreciated by the majority of the people. Throughout the century the population of England has exhibited a continuous drift into the great cities; and now, at the opening of a new era, it is

necessary to recognise that we are face to face with a phenomenon
unique in the world's history. Turbulent rioting over military successes,
Hooliganism, and a certain temper of fickle excitability has revealed
to observers during the past few months that a new race, hitherto
unreckoned and of incalculable action, is entering the sphere of practical
importance—the 'City type' of the coming years; the 'street-bred'
people of the twentieth century; the 'new generation knocking at our
doors.'

The England of the past has been an England of reserved, silent men,
dispersed in small towns, villages, and country homes. The England
of the future is an England packed tightly in such gigantic aggregations of population as the world has never before seen. The change
has been largely concealed by the perpetual swarm of immigrants
from the surrounding districts, which has permeated the whole of
such a town as London with a healthy, energetic population reared
amidst the fresh air and quieting influences of the life of the fields.
But in the past twenty-five years a force has been operating in the
raw material of which the city is composed. The texture itself has been
transformed as by some subtle alchemy. The second generation of the
immigrants has been reared in the courts and crowded ways of the
great metropolis, with cramped physical accessories, hot, fretful life,
and long hours of sedentary or unhealthy toil. The problem of the
coming years is just the problem of this New Town type. . .

. . . it is physically, mentally, and spiritually different from the type
characteristic of Englishmen during the past two hundred years. The
physical change is the result of the city up-bringing in twice-breathed
air in the crowded quarters of the labouring classes. This as a substitute
for the spacious places of the old, silent life of England; close to the
ground, vibrating to the lengthy, unhurried processes of Nature. The
result is the production of a characteristic *physical* type of town
dweller: stunted, narrow-chested, easily wearied; yet voluble, excit-
able, with little ballast, stamina, or endurance—seeking stimulus in
drink, in betting, in any unaccustomed conflicts at home or abroad.
Upon these city generations there has operated the now widely spread
influence of thirty years of elementary school teaching. The result is a
mental change; each individual has been endowed with the power of
reading, and a certain dim and cloudy capacity for comprehending
what he reads. Hence the vogue of the new sensational press, with its
enormous circulation and baneful influence; the perpetual demand of
the reader for fiercer excitement. . . .

A change more vital and more ominous for the future is widely attested by those familiar with this new City type: the almost universal decay, amongst these massed and unheeded populations, of any form of spiritual religion. Morally, indeed, they for the most part accept a standard which is the astonishment of their friends.... But the spiritual world, whether in Nature, in Art, or in definite Religion, has vanished, and the curtain of the horizon has descended round the material things and the pitiful duration of human life. In former time in England, for better or worse, the things of the earth were shot with spiritual significance; heaven and hell stretched out as permanent realities ... To-day amongst the masses of our great towns God is faintly apprehended as an amiable but absentee ruler; heaven and hell are passing to the memories of a far-off childhood ... The full effect of this change has yet to be demonstrated; but certain results are already discernible. And increasing craving for material satisfaction ... and a fiercer refusal to endure hardship and privation ... and a concentration on the purely earthly outlook of a commercial Imperialism, heedless of abstract spiritual ideas, will be some of the least results of this change in human character.

... The problem, in effect the same in all these gigantic aggregations, has reached its fullest development in London; and we shall do well to concentrate our attention upon this enormous mass of population, where we shall be able to trace most clearly the lines of progress and the change from the old conditions to the new.

... in London we shall find manifest both the diminishing virulence of the older social diseases and the steadily deepening gravity of the problem of the coming race....

... What are the characteristic features of these unknown regions? ...
Once to apprehend the noise of chaffering, the shrill, unmusical voices, the sounds of a drifting population wedged together under the quiet stars, the mere physical discomforts of evil odour, unkempt humanity, and the packed mob of struggling human life, is to be filled with mournful inquiry as to the meaning or utility of such cramped and shabby existence, as to the possibilities of a development in which the individual appears equally negligible in the sight of man and of God.

The first impression obtained is the utter ugliness of it all. Here is a life from which the apprehension of beauty has visibly departed. Whatever may be the pleasures, existence here is set in grey—grey streets, grey people, a drab monotony, which after a time gets on one's nerves with a sense of personal injury. Gazing ... upon the multitudinous desolation of a great city in its interminable acreage of

crowded humanity, one realises as never before the Burden of London
—London as it has been called, 'the visible type of a Universe hastening
confusedly to unknown ends and careless of individual pain.' Here are
lives not even kindled by the resourcefulness, subtlety, and individual
enterprise of the avowed criminal; but in incredible multitude, shabby,
ineffective, battered into futility by the ceaseless struggle of life. . . .

. . . The second of the special scourges is the Overcrowding. While men
slept the evil has swollen into colossal dimensions; until now suddenly
awakened we find ourselves jammed in hopeless numbers within a
limited area and fiercely elbowing ourselves for room to live. *Laissez
faire* has here presented an object-lesson which he that runs may read:
the squalid inequality of unchecked private enterprise, operating
through the greater part of the nineteenth century, has bound an
almost insupportable burden upon the shoulders of the succeeding
generations. . . . No one observant of even the superficial characteristics
of the ghetto population could fail to note the result of . . . overcrowding: the listlessness and lassitude so manifest in the people of our
crowded streets; the anaemia of town life so strikingly prevalent in
our city children . . . Before the virility and health of the country life
that has been entering the city during the past half-century, the street-
reared population crumples up almost without a struggle. . . . Partially
concealed by this impetuous influx, the results of the congestion are
but now commencing to show themselves. As the proportion of the
town bred to the country bred increases these will become more
widely manifest. . . .

. . . Even a few years spent actually living in the ghetto will exhibit how
far the fancy picture of happiness, effort, and multifarious energies
unfolded to the occasional visitor is distant from the true facts. Despite
all the apparent stir, life for the great majority of the denizens of the
dull streets is incredibly monotonous and mean. 'Merrie England' is
emphatically a place of villages and small towns, with open spaces and
the perpetual presence of the natural world. Englishmen packed for
their lives in the labyrinths of drab streets that make up the greater
part of London acquire a life of 'mechanic pacing to and fro,' varied
only by occasional outbursts of brutalising and unlovely pleasure.
The mind thus 'cabined, cribbed, confined' turns instinctively to any
course of stimulating excitement. Betting, the unlimited abuse of
stimulants, and the noisy boisterousness of the modern English crowd
reveal the ravages of the disease of modern life. . . . The existence of
this unparalleled aggregation, the dying out of the industrial energy,
initiative, and determination to 'get on' so characteristic of the North,

the inevitable isolation and loneliness of the competing units in a monstrous and chaotic aggregation such as London, and the absence of a background setting present action, however obscure, into some large framework of meaning, and enforcing on the individual the sense of immediate personal responsibility—these are the general conditions which are filling observers of the ghetto life with dreary forebodings for the future. . . .

. . . A background to life—some common bond uniting, despite the discordance of the competitive struggle—some worthy subject of enthusiasm or devotion . . .—some spiritual force or ideal elevated over the shabby scene of temporary failure—this is the deep, imperative need of the masses in our great cities to-day. With this the mere discomforts incidental to changing conditions of life and the specific remediable social evils can be contemplated with equanimity; without it the drifting through time of the interminable multitude of the unimportant becomes a mere nightmare vision of a striving signifying nothing. . . .

But the progress of the century has seen the breaking down, at least in the great cities, of this consciousness of individual responsi-bility and consecration of individual energies; until now in the broken populations of the congested districts all religious agencies find them-selves baffled amidst masses heedless of their message. Spiritual presences, naturally congruous to the perpetual miracle of nature, do not haunt the streets of the great city; they are lost in the continual echo of moving feet, the absence of privacy and silence, the limitation of human energies along narrow grooves of wage-earning toil. That the population have now abandoned church-going is a commonplace. . . . with the older faiths largely inoperative, and no new enthusiasm to occupy their places, life becomes more and more approximated either to a dull persistence in routine, with no attempt to look before and after and to estimate the worth of action, or else to a fierce and uncontrolled individualism, concentrated only on the pleasures and advancement of the family, tearing the social fabric into its component threads, and destined on the arrival of troublous times to ensure its speedy destruction. . . .

. . . Virtually . . . the only forces operating among the new city race, the only attempts at spiritual or collective effort with which any dweller in it is ever likely to come into contact, are the forces of the older creeds of Christianity. Developing as they are today from their limited other-worldly outlook into systems endeavouring by every possible means, through direct spiritual energy, through instruction, through recreation, through political and social effort, to penetrate into the lives of the people, with widespread organisation and the possibility of unlimited store of energy upon which to draw, the Churches to-day present to the observer the most hopeful machinery to the warfare against the degenerating influences of modern town life. . . . they offer the only adequate machinery for the humanising, civilising, and Christianising of masses upon whom the advancement of science has bestowed little benefit, and into whose life the growth of democratic government has brought no illuminating ideal. . . .

. . . 'a menace to the future progress of humanity' is now silently, without observation, developing in the great cities of England. The old astonishing creed that if each man assiduously minds his own business and pursues his own individual advancement and the welfare of his family, somehow by some divinely ordered interconnections and adjustments the success and progress of the whole body politic will be assured, may at least perhaps be relegated to the limbo of forgotten illusions. . . . from an aggregation of individual selfishness no healthy, consistent, harmonious social fabric can be woven . . . No commercial success, climatic advantage, or universal domination can ever resist the dry rot of isolated effort after material satisfaction, tearing individuals and classes apart, and breaking up the organism into an aggregation of isolated atoms.

Back to the land, from gigantic massed populations to healthier conditions of scattered industry; housing reform; temperance reform; a perfected system of national education; the elimination of the submerged; the redemption of women's labour—all these are immediate necessaries. But all these are but palliatives of the one fundamental malady—attempts in some degree to check the ravages of selfishness, indifference, and isolation. Accompanying all these must be wholehearted endeavour to deal with the disease at its very centre. We would plead for the service of all who love for all who suffer . . . as the only possibility of peaceful escape from the gathering difficulties of the future, we need a real and living religion—some outpouring of spiritual effort which will revitalise dogmas and injunctions now entombed in neglected and unrealised creeds. . . . Before such a spirit the technical questions would find moving power adequate to their speedy solution; the polarisation of society into those who get and those who lack, produced by forces seemingly so impersonal, gigantic, beyond the interference of human agency, would collapse before the determination that all may be one; . . . and the ghetto, in its vastness, its gloomy endurance, its multitudinous desolation, would vanish before the eager and passionate sympathy of those for whom in reality the wilderness and the solitary place would be glad, and the desert rejoice and blossom as the rose. . . .

47 Deflecting the Titan forces, 1901

Extracts from G. M. Trevelyan, 'Past and Future', in *The Heart of the Empire* (1901), pp. 398–415.

Among the Liberal intellectuals contributing to Masterman's symposium was George Macaulay Trevelyan (1876–1962), son of the Liberal politician, Sir G. O. Trevelyan, grand-nephew of Macaulay, and a future Regius Professor of Modern History at Cambridge. His analysis of the vulgarizing tendencies of modern city life and his bitter attack on *laissez-faire* Conservatism took Arnold's 'The Future' (see document 26) as its text.

. . . we must ask what is the difference between the banks of Time which the English used to see and those which they see to-day. The difference is this: in the past life was naturally—that is, by the process of existing social and economic conditions—beautiful and instructive; while to-day life moves in conditions which tend to make it ugly and trivial. It can still be made more beautiful and instructive than ever, but if so it will be by artificial means and by conscious effort of our own. The world on the banks, having become naturally ugly, must be made artificially beautiful.

. . . whatever may be the mutual relations of the fellow travellers on the deck of the ship, the banks of the stream have changed for the worse. The second of the great moulding forces—the surroundings of life that strike the senses—no longer beautify but degrade by their touch. It is not the decadence of the race but the chance of economic law that has caused this change. Economy, which then fixed men under the habitual sway of the country, to-day compels him to live where he can never see the earth for the pavement, or the breadth of heaven for the chimney-tops. Of our forefathers, nine out of ten lived in the rural parts; and the remainder, the busiest and best tithe of

P

English humanity, in towns whose darkest lane was never a mile from the orchards round the town, so that the recreation of the city dweller was by the hedgerows and river-banks . . . The spring and the winter came unsought into every man's life, not as they come to-day, wayfarers bewandered among the house-tops, feebly whispering of unknown things in far salubrious lands, but fresh with bursting boughs, or strong in glowing frost. . . . Whether they knew it or not, the Cavaliers drew their charm from the fields, and the Puritans their strength from the earth. . . .

. . . The examples we have given demonstrate that what is ugly in modern life is natural, that unloveliness comes of following the law of need as it is written to-day. *Laissez-faire* and mere competition are fast building 'a hell in heaven's despite.' But here steps in the guardian angel of the modern world—Artifice or Conscious Effort. . . .

The way back to Nature herself lies now through dexterous use of Artifice and modern inventions towards that end. Although for most men the country can never again be brought to their doors every evening, it can be brought into their lives every holiday by the train, the tram, and the bicycle. And if the dwellers in the smithy of Lancashire are ever again to see the stars in heaven or to feel the joys of cleanliness on earth, it will not be by reviving the old life of manor-house and village green, but by using the pure electric current in place of the forces that are fed on smoke, and rearing through the cleansed air into the recovered sky warehouse and workshop, no longer sordid as poverty, but worthy of the world's new wealth and strength.

Such is the law of our modern era. Economy and natural process, unguided, work for evil. But to check them we have in our hands the new powers of science and industry; Titan forces, themselves neutral in the warfare between gods and demons; but infinitely strong for good, whenever we take the pains to use them for ideal ends. We have shown this law applying to those influences which attack the mind through bodily sense. . . . it applies no less to instruction by direct intellectual process. . . .

. . . Among the old English who lived in the country, whether in town or village, the natural course of economy and society supplied the instruction of the mind. . . . But . . . in the future, activity of mind must be developed by a scheme of artificial education growing ever more and more *elaborate*, consciously constructed at great pains and expense; for we have lost by the introduction of machinery the old natural school of craftsmanship and art, that quickened and instructed the mind of him who laboured with his hands. . . .

But in England of the past, not only the intelligence but the character received instruction by the ordinary working of society. Each shire, each town, each village, had its own local piety, its customs, its anniversaries, its songs, its ethics, the indefinable but peculiar tone that marked it off from its neighbour. . . . undisturbed and unspoiled by imperfect knowledge of other codes and customs, the life of the village realised a limited ideal. The agricultural labourer, though he did not share with the craftsman the benefit of an intelligent training and profession, shared with him in these traditions of a simple life.

The agricultural labourer is now fast disappearing. He has suffered city change into something poor and strange. Rumours coming thick and fast from the great cities have destroyed for him the traditional piety and the honest customs of the countryside. He apes what he does not understand,—what indeed no one can understand, for it has no meaning,—the variegated, flaunting vulgarity of the modern town. . . .

Such is the fate of the agricultural labourer. His brother of the town, whose influence is now spreading so strongly and so far, is equally without loadstar of local piety or healthy reverence. Omnivorous inquisitiveness into the trivial and the important alike, destroying all sense of proportion and all chance of real knowledge, is taught him by the respectable papers, and magazines. The lower class of prints teach what is worse, a low cunning in the latest conventions of folly, which is termed 'knowing' or 'up to date.' The music-halls proclaim those ideals so loud on the housetops that even the well educated of late years have to listen . . . Our ancestors were coarse but they were not vulgar. Vulgarity—that indefinable essence and spirit of the very mean and foolish—is a creature of the nineteenth-century conditions. It came in gradually as the old natural education, limited in area and knowledge, gave way to the present chaotic turmoil of everything under heaven. Such has been the most rapid achievement, so far, of the new powers of rapid locomotion and reproduction; instead of being chained to the chariot of virtue and intelligence they have been let loose on the world—the blind foolish Titans. And yet it is by these same foolish Titans . . . that the better future must be built up.

There is no cause for despair, though much for alarm. The old life was so narrow and sluggish that we may improve upon it yet. The modern city man is better than his conditions, and better than his teachers—or rather caterers—who supply him with what they think he wants. The inanities of the Jingo and Little England press have forced the nation to become silly on an occasion when it might otherwise have kept its head. . . . At any rate there is no cause for despair, if only men will use the forces of machinery and industry to combat those grave evils which these very forces are now creating by process of economic law.

. . . The old view of life seen through piety and tradition was narrow, and in many ways both false and bad; the new views of life seen through printed matter will be infinitely broad and various; they may, therefore, be either infinitely better or infinitely worse. . . . The capability of the city-bred man, with his undoubtedly keen intellect and brain, . . . to understand good literature and complex ideas when presented to him, is a fact insufficiently recognised by those who abuse the modern man instead of his modern surroundings. The hope of the future is very great, if only pains are taken to present good intellectual food for habitual consumption, to meet this terrible free trade in garbage. . . .

. . . We have now sufficiently illustrated . . . the rule that will be found to govern modern life in almost every branch. The natural process of modern economy is on the whole towards evil rather than good, but the way of salvation does not lie backwards in vain regret; it consists in deflecting the Titan forces with which the modern world is armed from purely economic to partly ideal ends. . . . In the future nothing will take care of itself, and no nation will ever again 'muddle through' . . . either in material things or in things of higher import. This is the theoretical basis for that cry for more strenuous common action, for more interference by the State with the organs of society, for the increased efforts of individuals in the common cause . . . Individual action is quickened not deadened by this creed of interference. For Individualism, like Socialism, is perennial and never dies. . . .

But while individualism is of eternity, *laissez-faire* was of the day, and that day is gone. The spirit of *laissez-faire*, once the salvation, is now the bane of England. . . .

. . . For the good new world MUST BE MADE, IT CANNOT GROW. It must be artificial, not natural. And it can only be made on two conditions now conspicuously absent. First, a POLITICAL PARTY that believes not in *laissez-faire* but in action—a party led by men who are reformers themselves . . . Secondly, by the enthusiastic EFFORT OF INDIVIDUALS in the spheres of economy, social work, religion, science, education, literature, journalism, and art, all parts of the variegated whole out of which the glorious world of the future will be built up, if man will be true to himself. If he will not, life will become a dingy chaos of distraction and meaningless vulgarity, where rich and poor will be equally far from blessedness or perception of any real value in life.

... the grim alternative of the world growing ever blacker, uglier, noisier, more meaningless, must be faced if it is to be prevented.

48   Great searchings of heart, 1901

Extracts from B. Seebohm Rowntree, *Poverty. A Study of Town Life* (1901), pp. 144–5, 215–16 and 300–5.

Seebohm Rowntree (1871–1954), a major figure in twentieth-century social investigation and reform, was a member of the Quaker family which built up the cocoa and confectionery business in York and had a tradition of enlightened paternalism in its welfare provision and labour-management. Educated as a chemist at Owens College, Manchester, and in charge of labour relations in the family firm, Rowntree was inspired by Booth's work in London to organize a similar enquiry in York. He took his investigation further than Booth, especially into family budgets and nutritional standards, and drew a gloomier picture of the extent and nature of poverty, emphasizing its connection with economic factors, such as low wages, which Booth had ignored or underplayed. The solutions to which Rowntree pointed were more drastic than Booth's in their questioning of the merits of the free economy and in the role they indicated for central government.

Though we speak of the above causes as those mainly accounting for most of the 'secondary' poverty, it must not be forgotten that they are themselves often the outcome of the adverse conditions under which too many of the working classes live. Housed for the most part in sordid streets, frequently under overcrowded and unhealthy conditions, compelled very often to earn their bread by monotonous and laborious work, and unable, partly through limited education and partly through overtime and other causes of physical exhaustion, to enjoy intellectual recreation, what wonder that many of these people fall a ready prey to the publican and the bookmaker? ...

The writer is not forgetful of the larger questions bearing upon the welfare of human society which lie at the back of the considerations just advanced. . . . Probably it will be admitted that they include questions dealing with land tenure, with the relative duties and powers of the State and of the individual, and with legislation affecting the aggregation or the distribution of wealth. While the immediate causes of 'secondary' poverty call for well-considered and resolute action, its ultimate elimination will only be possible when these causes are dealt with as part of, and in relation to, the wider social problem. . . .

. . . And all three tests point clearly to the low standard of health amongst those living in poverty. Some of the unhealthy conditions here noted are removable by the application of existing Public Health Acts, and it is of the utmost importance that the community should insist upon the vigorous enforcement of their provisions. Yet even if this were done there would still remain the fact that *nearly 30 per cent of the population are living in poverty and are ill-housed, ill-clothed, and under-fed.* So long as this state of things continues a low average standard of physical efficiency among the wage-earning classes is inevitable. . . .

. . . We have been accustomed to look upon the poverty in London as exceptional, but when the result of careful investigation shows that the proportion of poverty in London is practically equalled in what may be regarded as a typical provincial town, we are faced by the startling probability that from 25 to 30 per cent of the town populations of the United Kingdoms are living in poverty. If this be the fact, its grave significance may be realised when it is remembered that, in 1901, 77 per cent of the population . . . is returned as 'urban' and only 23 per cent as 'rural'. . . .

. . . That in this land of abounding wealth, during a time of perhaps unexampled prosperity, probably more than one-fourth of the population are living in poverty, is a fact which may well cause great searchings of heart. There is surely need for a greater concentration of thought by the nation upon the well-being of its own people, for no civilisation can be sound or stable which has at its base this mass of stunted human life. The suffering may be all but voiceless, and we may long remain ignorant of its extent and severity, but when once we realise it we see that social questions of profound importance await solution. What, for instance, are the primary causes of this poverty? How far is it the result of false social and economic conditions? . . .

The dark shadow of the Malthusian philosophy has passed away, and no view of the ultimate scheme of things would now be accepted under which multitudes of men and women are doomed by inevitable law to a struggle for existence so severe as necessarily to cripple or destroy the higher parts of their nature.

49   Centrifugal possibilities, 1901

Extracts from H. G. Wells, *Anticipations of the Reaction of Mechanical
and Scientific Progress upon Human Life and Thought* (1901), chapter 2.

By 1901 Wells's technological determinism had revised his earlier
pessimism about the evolution of the city (see document 45). His
belief that transport and communications systems dictated the size
and population-density of cities now led him to forecast the diffusion
of the cities over 'urban regions' through the influence of motor
vehicles, improved railways and the telephone. Overcrowding in
the city would end, and a new type of suburban society would
develop, combining the merits of both city and countryside.

Now, is this growth of large towns really . . . a result of the development of railways in the world, or is it simply a change in human
circumstances that happens to have arisen at the same time? . . . the
former is probably the true answer.

   It will be convenient to make the issue part of a more general
proposition, namely, that *the general distribution of population in a
country must always be directly dependent on transport facilities.* . . .

   . . . We have heard so much of the 'problem of our great cities' . . .
the belief in the inevitableness of yet denser and more multitudinous
agglomerations in the future is so widely diffused, that at first sight it
will be thought that no other motive than a wish to startle can dictate
the proposition that not only will many of these railway-begotten
'giant cities' reach their maximum in the commencing century, but
that in all probability they . . . are destined to such a process of dis-
section and diffusion as to amount almost to obliteration, so far, at
least, as the blot on the map goes, within a measurable further space
of years.

   . . . the present writer is disagreeably aware that in this matter he
has expressed views entirely opposed to those he now propounds . . .
At the outset he took for granted . . . that the future of London, for
example, is largely to be got as the answer to a sort of rule-of-three

sum. If in one hundred years the population of London has been multiplied by seven, then in two hundred years—! And one proceeds to pack the answer in gigantic tenement houses, looming upon colossal roofed streets . . . and develop its manners and morals in accordance with the laws that will always prevail amidst over-crowded humanity so long as humanity endures. . . . if, instead of that obvious rule-of-three sum, one resorts to an analysis of operating causes, its plausibility crumbles away, and it gives place to an altogether different forecast . . . that is in almost violent contrast to the first anticipation. It is much more probable that these coming cities will not be, in the old sense, cities at all; they will present a new and entirely different phase of human distribution. . . .

. . . As a consequence [of the railway and the steamship] the social history of the middle and later thirds of the nineteenth century, not simply in England but all over the civilized world, is the history of a gigantic rush of population into the magic radius of—for most people—four miles, to suffer there physical and moral disaster less acute but, finally, far more appalling to the imagination than any famine or pestilence that ever swept the world. Well has Mr. George Gissing named nineteenth-century London in one of his great novels the 'Whirlpool,' the very figure for the nineteenth-century Great City, attractive, tumultuous, and spinning down to death.

But, indeed, these great cities are no permanent maelstroms. These new forces, at present still so potently centripetal in their influence, bring with them, nevertheless, the distinct promise of a centrifugal application that may be finally equal to the complete reduction of all our present congestions. The limit of the pre-railway city was the limit of man and horse. But already that limit has been exceeded, and each day brings us nearer to the time when it will be thrust outward in every direction with an effect of enormous relief.

We are—as the Census Returns for 1901 quite clearly show—in the early phase of a great development of centrifugal possibilities. . . . the available area of a city which can offer a cheap suburban journey of thirty miles an hour is a circle with a radius of thirty miles. And is it too much . . . to expect that the available area for even the common daily toilers of the great city of the year 2000, or earlier, will have a radius very much larger even than that?. . . . Indeed, it is not too much to say that the London citizen of the year 2000 A.D. may have a choice of nearly all England and Wales south of Nottingham and east of Exeter as his suburb. . . .

. . . And so, though the [city] centre will probably still remain the centre and 'Town,' it will be essentially a bazaar, a great gallery of shops and places of concourse and rendezvous, a pedestrian place, . . . and altogether a very spacious, brilliant, and entertaining agglomeration.

Enough now has been said to determine the general nature of the expansion of the great cities in the future, so far as the more prosperous classes are concerned. It will not be a regular diffusion . . . but a process of throwing out the 'homes' and of segregating various types of people. The omens seem to point . . . to a wide and quite unprecedented diversity in the various suburban townships and suburban districts. . . .

. . . But the diffusion of the prosperous, independent, and managing classes involves in itself a very considerable diffusion of the purely 'working' classes also. Their centres of occupation will be distributed, and their freedom to live at some little distance from their work will be increased. . . . ugliness and squalor upon the main road will appeal to the more prosperous for remedy with far more vigour than when they are stowed compactly in a slum.

Enough has been said to demonstrate that old 'town' and 'city' will be, in truth, terms as obsolete as 'mail coach.' . . . We may for our present purposes call these coming town provinces 'urban regions.' Practically, by a process of confluence, the whole of Great Britain south of the Highlands seems destined to become such an urban region, laced all together not only by railway and telegraph, but by novel roads such as we forecast . . . and by a dense network of telephones, parcels delivery tubes, and the like nervous and arterial connections.

It will certainly be a curious and varied region, far less monotonous than our present English world . . . perhaps rather more abundantly wooded, breaking continually into park and garden, and with everywhere a scattering of houses. . . . Each district, I am inclined to think, will develop its own differences of type and style. . . .

And as for the world beyond our urban regions? The same line of reasoning that leads us to the expectation that the city will diffuse itself until it has taken up considerable areas and many of the characteristics, the greenness, the fresh air, of what is now country, leads us to suppose also that the country will take to itself many of the qualities of the city. The old antithesis will indeed cease, the boundary lines will altogether disappear; it will become, indeed, merely a question of more or less populous. There will be horticulture and agriculture going on within the 'urban regions,' and 'urbanity' without them.

50   The aggregate of vitality and expansion, 1902

Extracts from Charles Booth, *Life and Labour of the People in London*, final volume (1902), pp. 179–206.

In the volume concluding and reflecting upon his investigations, Booth, resolutely optimistic, looked beyond his earlier proposal of State care for the lowest of the poor (document 42) to envisage a great dispersal of the metropolitan population aided by transport improvements and the creation of a London transport authority, though collectivist intervention was not to extend to the provision of working-class housing. This process would release and itself be promoted by the expansive energies of the city, the natural energies of free enterprise and social individualism.

. . . if our national prosperity is maintained, London will share in it, and her growth continue. Whether this be within or without the present county boundary is immaterial . . . it will not be long before a 'Greater London' will have to be reckoned with for administrative purposes. . . .

In all other departments of life the methods of transit have, during the nineteenth century, been quickened nearly tenfold and increased a hundred-fold. But in cities . . . the past hangs around us, and has made progress very slow. Let anyone now design a place of residence for four or five million inhabitants, and how greatly it would differ in plan and structure from London! The improved methods for the application of mechanical force now available are, as compared with steam traction, of very recent date, and even now are only year by year becoming perfected. At every point we have yet much to learn, and we are still timid; but great possibilities clearly lie before us in the reorganization of urban life within itself, as well as in its relations with the surrounding country and with the (still) wide world beyond. It is to these possibilities that I desire to draw attention in connection with the comfort and welfare of the people of London, and especially in regard to their house accommodation.

. . . the increase of population in urban centres (however objectionable in some of its aspects), and the concurrent need of space for industrial purposes or civic development, are the results of, and factors in, general prosperity; not the congestion of decadence or of economic disaster; while pressure [on residential space] arising from the attempt to introduce and enforce a higher standard of life among the poor is mainly due to the effect on our minds of the contrast between national prosperity and the miserable and unhealthy conditions in which many of our people live. . . . as the causes of pressure are resultants of prosperity, there can be no permanent or absolute economic difficulty in dealing with the inter-connected evils of overcrowding. On the contrary . . . freer expansion, while mitigating these evils, would redound to the general prosperity. . . .

. . . We have not to create, or even arouse, the forces which tend to expansion; we have only to give them play, and then to make use of them; guiding them towards the desired end, and averting, so far as may be, concurrent evils. . . .

There are some who would limit the collective interference of the community to the enforcement of a certain standard of life as to crowding and sanitation, leaving locomotion as well as building to private enterprise . . . I do not myself think that the evils of a congested city population . . . could ever be cured on these lines . . . the proposals I make as regards means of locomotion, interfere with private enterprise only in a direction in which even now no step can be taken without powers granted by Parliament, and in which some kind of monopoly is inevitable. As a rule, however, the necessity for intervention is not questioned; on this subject the doctrine of *laissez faire* has few supporters. . . .

The futility of municipal action for the direct supply of dwellings on the scale hitherto adopted, is patent, and the dangers of this course, if pursued far, are very serious. By confining the corporate efforts of the community to the task of making the means of communication comprehensive and adequate and efficient, private enterprise would be encouraged to provide all the houses needed, and to private enterprise the local authorities would do well to relinquish that portion of the tremendous task of re-organization and reconstruction on which the welfare of the people of London depends. . . .

. . . It may perhaps be objected that the effect of providing better and more rapid communication would be to foster centralization, and so increase the evil we are trying to amend. But in many ways it would have the opposite result. Wherever a man may go to find his work it is near home that he will seek his pleasure, and his wife will find her shopping, and thus a local centre is formed. Such centres are to be found now all around London, with brilliant shops, streets full of people, churches, and chapels certainly, perhaps a Town Hall, and probably a theatre. The growth of such local life . . . during the past decade is very noticeable, and would undoubtedly play an increasing part in the greater and happier London I desire to see.

. . . in conclusion I would emphasize once more . . . the crying necessity for forethought and plan in the arrangement of our metropolis, with its great past and, I hope, still greater future. . . .

. . . We see life cursed by drink, brutality and vice, and loaded down with ignorance and poverty . . . Such is the dark side of the picture, which, perhaps, looks the more black to our eyes owing to the heightened demands of a rising standard of life, and the expectancy of better things; as it is said that the greatest darkness precedes the dawn.

Improvement certainly there has been at every point. As to drink . . . though there may be more drinking, there is, undoubtedly, less drunken rowdiness. . . . there is much less street violence; and such scenes of open depravity as occurred in years gone by do not happen now. There is greater intelligence . . . and wider interests prevail, even if they be too much absorbed in pleasure seeking. Side by side with these improvements the whole level of poverty has been pressed upwards by increasing demands on life—demands which were unthought of forty, thirty, or even twenty years ago. But the gulf is still wide which separates the poor from such a degree of confident comfort as civilization calls for . . . .

While the whole of life may well be lifted on to a higher plane, we cannot dare to wish that the struggle should be avoided. And light breaks through the darkness. Destitution degrades, but poverty is certainly no bar to happiness. If we permit our minds to dwell upon the masses in London who exist under its disabilities, we may think also of thousands of poor but wholesome homes; of husbands and wives happy in working for each other and rejoicing in their children...

And if we turn to industry, the Atlas on whose broad shoulders our whole world rests . . . we are conscious of a power and vigour in the impulses of trade, which can wipe out mistakes.

Closely connected with the vitality and expansion of industry, we trace the advancement of the individual which in the aggregate is represented by the vitality and expansion of London. This it is that draws from the provinces their best blood, and amongst Londoners selects the most fit. Amongst such it is common for the children to aim at a higher position than their parents held; and for the young people when they marry to move to a new house in a better district. A new middle class is thus forming, which will, perhaps, hold the future in its grasp. Its advent seems to me the great social fact of today. Those who constitute this class are the especial product of the push of industry; within their circle religion and education find the greatest response; amongst them all popular movements take their rise, and from them draw their leaders. To them, in proportion as they have ideas, political power will pass. . . .

. . . I have spoken of structural expansion as the first need of London, with administrative expansion following naturally in its train. The further need, which includes everything else, is the mental expansion which will make full use of opportunities. We want to see London spreading itself over the Home counties, not as an escape from evil left behind, but as a development of energy which will react for good over the whole area as it now exists, even in its blackest and most squalid centres.

51   The triumph of artificial circumstance, 1903

Extracts from George Gissing, *The Private Papers of Henry Ryecroft* (1903), sections 'Spring', 2 and 16, and 'Winter', 5, 11 and 14.

Since *The Nether World* (see document 40), Gissing had moved to Devon on the proceeds of modest literary success. The semi-autobiographical reflections of *Ryecroft*, published in the year of Gissing's death, celebrated rural peace after the stresses of London and revealed a mellower, more fatalistic attitude to the continuing process of urbanization.

I think with compassion of the unhappy mortals for whom no such sun will ever rise. I should like to add to the Litany a new petition: 'For all inhabitants of great towns, and especially for all such as dwell in lodgings, boarding-houses, flats, or any other sordid substitute for Home which need or foolishness may have contrived.' ...

... I am no friend of the people. As a force, by which the tenor of the time is conditioned, they inspire me with distrust, with fear; as a visible multitude, they make me shrink aloof, and often move me to abhorrence. For the greater part of my life, the people signified to me the London crowd, and no phrase of temperate meaning would utter my thoughts of them under that aspect. ... Every instinct of my being is anti-democratic, and I dread to think of what our England may become when Demos rules irresistibly.

Right or wrong, this is my temper. But he who would argue from it that I am intolerant of all persons belonging to a lower social rank than my own would go far astray. Nothing is more rooted in my mind than the vast distinction between the individual and the class. Take a man by himself, and there is generally some reason to be found in him, some disposition for good; mass him with his fellow creatures in the social organism, and ten to one he becomes a blatant creature, without a thought of his own, ready for any evil to which contagion prompts him. ...

Walking along the road after nightfall, I thought all at once of London streets, and, by a freak of mind, wished I were there. I saw the shining of shop-fronts, the yellow glistening of a wet pavement, the hurrying people, the cabs, the omnibuses—and I wished I were amid it all.

What did it mean, but that I wished I were young again? Not seldom I have a sudden vision of a London street, perhaps the dreariest and ugliest, which for a moment gives me a feeling of home-sickness. Often it is the High Street of Islington . . . no thoroughfare in all London less attractive to the imagination, one would say; but I see myself walking there—walking with the quick, light step of youth, and there, of course, is the charm. I see myself, after a long day of work and loneliness, setting forth from my lodgings. For the weather I care nothing; rain, wind, fog—what does it matter! The fresh air fills my lungs; my blood circles rapidly; I feel my muscles, and have a pleasure in the hardness of the stone I tread upon. Perhaps I have money in my pocket; I am going to the theatre, and afterwards, I shall treat myself to supper—sausage and mashed potatoes, with a pint of foaming ale. The gusto with which I look forward to each and every enjoyment! At the pit-door, I shall roll and hustle amid the throng, and find it amusing. Nothing tires me. Late at night, I shall walk all the way back to Islington, most likely singing as I go. Not because I am happy—nay, I am anything but that; but my age is something and twenty; I am strong and well.

Put me in a London street this chill, damp night, and I should be lost in barren discomfort. But in those old days, if I am not mistaken, I rather preferred the seasons of bad weather; I had, in fact, the true instinct of townfolk, which finds pleasure in the triumph of artificial circumstance over natural conditions, delighting in a glare and tumult of busy life under hostile heavens which, elsewhere, would mean shivering ill-content. The theatre, at such a time, is doubly warm and bright; every shop is a happy harbour of refuge . . . the supper-bars make tempting display under their many gas-jets; the public-houses are full of people who all have money to spend. Then clangs out the piano-organ—and what could be cheerier!

I have much ado to believe that I really felt so. But then, if life had not somehow made itself tolerable to me, how should I have lived through those many years? Human creatures have a marvellous power of adapting themselves to necessity. Were I, even now, thrown back into squalid London, with no choice but to abide and work there— should I not abide and work? . . . I suppose I should.

... Of course, the vilest cooking in the kingdom is found in London; is it not with the exorbitant growth of London that many an ill has spread over the land? London is the antithesis of the domestic ideal; a social reformer would not even glance in that direction, but would turn all his zeal upon small towns and country districts, where blight may perhaps be arrested, and whence, some day, a reconstituted national life may act upon the great centre of corruption. ...

If the ingenious foreigner found himself in . . . manufacturing Lancashire . . . something of the power of England might be revealed to him, but of England's worth, little enough. Hard ugliness would everywhere assail his eyes; the visages and voices of the people would seem to him thoroughly akin to their surroundings. ...

Yet Lancashire is English, and there among the mill chimneys, in the hideous little street, folk are living whose domestic thoughts claim undeniable kindred with those of the villages of the kinder south. ... After all, this grimy row of houses, ugliest that man ever conceived, is more representative of England today than the lovely village among the trees and meadows. More than a hundred years ago power passed from the south of England to the north. The vigorous race on the other side of the Trent only found its opportunity when the age of machinery began; . . . In Sussex or in Somerset, however dull and clownish the typical inhabitant, he plainly belongs to an ancient order of things, represents an immemorial subordination. The rude man of the north is—by comparison—but just emerged from barbarism . . . By great misfortune, he has fallen under the harshest lordship the modern world has known—that of scientific industrialism—and all his vigorous qualities are subdued to a scheme of life based upon the harsh, the ugly, the sordid. . . . the frank brutality of the man in all externals has been encouraged, rather than mitigated, by the course his civilization has taken, and hence it is that, unless one knows him well enough to respect him, he seems even yet stamped with the half-savagery of his folk as they were a century and a half ago. ... And now one can only watch the encroachment of his rule upon that old, that true England whose strength and virtue were so differently manifested. This fair, broad land of the lovely villages signifies little save to the antiquary, the poet, the painter. Vainly, indeed, should I show its beauty and its peace to the observant foreigner; he would but smile, and, with a glance at the traction-engine just coming along the road, indicate the direction of his thoughts.

52   Evolving Eu-topia, 1905

Extracts from P. Geddes, 'Civics: as Applied Sociology', in F. Galton *et al.*, *Sociological Papers* (1905), pp. 103–18.

The Scot Patrick Geddes (1854–1932) studied biology under T. H. Huxley and became Professor of Botany at Dundee. He turned to 'civics', the study of social function in civic development, stressing the idea of community and the need for civic planning. His paper read before the Sociological Society in 1904 outlined his idea of studying the historical development and contemporary condition of individual cities in order to understand and control their future evolution. This approach, strongly influenced by evolutionary and eugenic theory, rejected utopianism, the reliance on state socialism and the sufficiency of merely empirical improvement of the cities.

This department of sociological studies should evidently be, as far as possible, concrete in treatment. If it is to appeal to practical men and civic workers, it is important that the methods advocated for the systematic study of cities, and as underlying fruitful action, be not merely the product of the study, but rather be those which may be acquired in course of local observation and practical effort... observation of city after city, now panoramic and impressionistic, again detailed, should gradually develop towards an orderly Regional Survey. This point of view has next to be correlated with the corresponding practical experience, that which may be acquired through some varied experiences of citizenship, and thence rise toward a larger and more orderly conception of civic action—as Regional Service. .... Applied Sociology in general, or Civics, as one of its main departments, may be defined as the application of Social Survey to Social Service.

.... there is emerging more and more clearly for sociological studies in general, and for their concrete fields of application in city after city, the conception of a scientific centre of observation and record on the one hand, and of a corresponding centre of experimental endeavour on the other—in short of Sociological Observatory and Sociological

Laboratory, and of these as increasingly co-ordinated . . . the intimate connection between a scientific demography and a practical eugenics has been clearly set forth. But this study of the community in the aggregate finds its natural parallel and complement in the study of the community as an integrate, with material and immaterial structures and functions, which we call the City. Correspondingly, the improvement of the individuals of the community, which is the aim of eugenics, involves a corresponding civic progress . . . we see that the sociologist in concerned not only with 'demography' but with 'politography,' and that 'eugenics' is inseparable from 'politogenics.' For the struggle for existence, though observed mainly from the side of its individuals by the demographer, is not only an intra-civic but an inter-civic process; and if so, ameliorative selection, now clearly sought for the individuals in detail as eugenics, is inseparable from a corresponding art—a literal 'Eu-politogenics.' . . .

. . . But a city is more than a place in space, it is a drama in time. Though the claim of geography be fundamental, our interest in the history of the city is supremely greater . . .

. . . in all this I am but recalling what every tourist in some measure knows; yet his impressions and recollections can become an orderly politography, only as he sees each city in terms of its characteristic social formations, and as he utilises the best examples from each phase towards building up a complete picture of the greatest products of civic evolution, temporal and spiritual, of all places and times up to the present.

. . . Viewed as Science, Civics is that branch of Sociology which deals with Cities—their origin and distribution; their development and structure; their functioning, internal and external, material and psychological; their evolution, individual and associated. Viewed again from the practical side, that of applied science, Civics must develop through experimental endeavour into the more and more effective Art of enhancing the life of the city and of advancing its evolution. . . .

As primarily a student of living nature in evolution, I have naturally approached the city from the side of its geographic and historic survey, its environment and functional change; yet it is but a step from these to the abstract interpretations of the economist or the politician, even of philosopher and moralist. . . .

But what of the opening Future? May its coming developments not be discerned by the careful observer in germs and buds already formed or forming, and deduced by the thinker from sociological principles? I believe in large measure both. . . . Enough for the present, if it be admitted that the practical man in his thought and action in the present is mainly the as yet too unconscious child of the past, and that in the city he is still working within the grasp of natural conditions.

To realise the geographic and historic factors of our city's life is thus the first step to comprehension of the present, one indispensable to any attempt at the scientific forecast of the future, which must avoid as far as it can the dangers of mere utopianism. . . .

. . . After this general and preliminary survey of geographic environment and historic development, there nowadays begins to appear the material of a complementary and contemporary volume, the Social Survey proper. . . . Mr. Booth's monumental Survey of London, followed by others, such as Mr. Rowntree's of York, have already been so widely stimulating and suggestive that it may safely be predicted that before many years the Social Survey of any given city will be as easily and naturally obtainable as is at present its guide-book. . . .

But these two volumes—'The City: Past and Present,'—are not enough. Is not a third volume imaginable and possible, that of the opening Civic Future? Having taken full note of places as they were and are, of things as they have come about, and of people as they are— of their occupations, families, and institutions, their ideas and ideals— may we not to some extent discern, then patiently plan out, at length boldly suggest, something of their actual or potential development? And may not, must not, such discernment, such planning, while primarily, of course, for the immediate future, also take account of the remoter and higher issues which a city's indefinitely long life and correspondingly needed foresight and statesmanship involve? Such a volume would thus differ widely from the traditional and contem-porary 'literature of Utopias' in being regional instead of non-regional, indeed ir-regional; and so realisable, instead of being unrealisable and unattainable altogether. The theme of such a volume would thus be to indicate the practicable alternatives, and to select and to define from these the lines of development of the legitimate *Eu-topia* possible in the given city, and characteristic of it; obviously, therefore, a very different thing from a vague *Ou-topia*, concretely realisable nowhere. Such abstract counsels of perfection as the descriptions of the ideal city, from Augustine through More or Campanella and Bacon to Morris, have been consolatory to many, to others inspiring. Still, a Utopia is one thing, a plan for our city improvement is another.

Some concrete, if still fragmentary, materials towards such a volume are, of course, to be found in all municipal offices, though scattered between the offices of the city engineer and health officer, the architect and park superintendent. . . . But though our cities are still as a whole planless, their growth as yet little better than a mere casual accretion and agglomeration, if not a spreading blight, American and German cities are now increasingly affording examples of comprehensive design of extension and of internal improvement.

. . . what we have reached is really the conception of an *Encyclopaedia Civica*, to which each city should contribute the Trilogy of its Past, its Present, and its Future. Better far, as life transcends books, we may see, and, yet more, foresee, the growth of civic consciousness and conscience, the awakening of citizenship towards civic renascence. . . .

53   The tyranny of the present, 1909

Extracts from C. F. G. Masterman, *The Condition of England* (1909), pp. 90–5, 118–25, 140–1 and 282–9.

In 1909 Masterman, now a Liberal M.P., was a junior minister in the Liberal government. Now less preoccupied with 'the ghetto', Masterman developed further in *The Condition of England* his analysis of a society which had lost its spiritual health in the cities (see document 46). Convinced that society needed a collective, indeed collectivist, ideal for its regeneration, he now had little faith in the capacity of religious institutions and ideas to produce the transformation. Fearful of the psychology of 'the Crowd', depressed by the inanities and vulgarities of 'the suburbans', puzzled by 'a society beyond measure complex, baffling and uncertain in its energies and aims', Masterman even toyed with visions of an apocalyptic ending for the cities.

This loss of religion would not, indeed, be so serious a matter if it were being replaced by any other altruistic and impersonal ideal. Such have been found in a conception of patriotism, in efforts towards social redemption, even in a vision of duty. . . . It is to be feared that these are not universal amongst the suburban peoples. Their lives are laborious and often disappointing. . . . And as with the body so with

the soul. Considerable hours spent in not too exacting but conspicuously cheerless occupations, the natural harassments of Middle Class
poverty . . . leave little surplusage of mental energy to be devoted to
larger issues. Those who are intimate with the modern phases of
suburban life think that they can detect a slackening of energy and
fibre in a generation which is much preoccupied with its pleasures. . . .
The young men of the suburban society, especially, are being accused
of a mere childish absorption in vicarious sport and trivial amusements. . . .

. . . Divorced from the ancient sanities of manual or skilful labour,
of exercise in the open air, absorbed for the bulk of his day in crowded
offices . . . each a unit in a crowd which has drifted away from the
realities of life in a complex, artificial city civilisation, he comes to
see no other universe than this—the rejoicing over hired sportsmen
who play before him, the ingenuities of sedentary guessing com-
petitions, the huge frivolity and ignorance of the world of the music
hall and the Yellow newspaper. . . .

. . . the Crowd: the special product of modern industrial civilisation.
Those who would attempt a diagnosis of the present must find themselves more and more turning their attention from the individual to
the aggregation: upon the individuals which act in an aggregation in
a manner different from their action as isolated units of humanity.
We have to deal, in fact, not only with the Crowd casually collected
in sudden movement by persons accustomed to live alone, but with
whole peoples which in London and the larger cities are reared in a
Crowd, labour in a Crowd, in a Crowd take their enjoyments, die in
a Crowd, and in a Crowd are buried at the end. . . .

There is a note of menace in it, in the mixed clamour which rises
from its humours and angers, like the voice of the sea in gathering
storm. There is the evidence of possibilities of violence in its way-
wardness, its caprice, its always incalculable mettle and temper, forming
in the aggregate a personality differing altogether from the personali-
ties of its component atoms. . . . one feels that the smile might turn
suddenly into fierce snarl or savagery, and that panic and wild fury
are concealed in its recesses, no less than happiness and foolish praise.
But more than the menace, the overwhelming impression is one of
ineptitude; a kind of life grotesque and meaningless. It is in the City
crowd, where the traits of individual distinction have become merged
in the aggregate . . . that the scorn of the philosopher for the mob,
the cynic for humanity, becomes for the first time intelligible. . . .

Why is it that this writing down of values takes place when mankind is thus collected into aggregations . . . ? In part, perhaps, because the trivial and vacant elements are uppermost amongst a city race whose aspirations and purposes are independent of organised collective energies and aims . . . the Crowd remains, to-day as yesterday, an instrument which the strong man has always used and always despised in the using. The new features of it come from the change that has gathered men from the countryside and the tiny town and hurried them into the streets of an immense city; henceforth always to move in a company, each tied as with a chain to his fellows, never to stand alone. In such a transformation there would seem some danger of the normal life of man becoming the life of the Crowd, with features intensified and distorted when collected in tumult or demonstration. We seem to see in the experience of a generation an increasing tendency thus to merge the individual in the mass, more frequent and unfailing response to the demand for agitation. . . . In our own 'mafficking,' . . . in unemployed demonstrations, even in a spectacle so diverting and yet so foreboding as the 'sieges of St. Stephen's' by the 'Suffragettes,' there are traces of similar if less exaggerated emotion: as man, communicating the infection of the Crowd consciousness to his fellowmen, suddenly abandons his individual volitions and restraints, and loses himself in the volition of the Crowd. A note of hysteria may seem to be an inevitable accompaniment of a city life so divorced from the earth's ancient tranquillity as never to appear entirely sane. And the future of the city populations, ever 'speeded up' by more insistent bustles and noises and nervous explosions, takes upon itself, in its normal activities, something hitherto abnormal to humanity. We shall probably encounter more appeals to the multiplied power of assembly, more determination to find a short cut in lawlessness towards attainment, more passive and active resistance in attempts at government by violence rather than government by reason. . . .

. . . the Crowd consciousness and the city upbringing must of necessity act as a disintegrating force, tearing the family into pieces. If the Crowd condition, which, in part, is to supplement it, may be made a dignified and noble thing, there need be less regret over a change which, desirable or otherwise, would appear to be inevitable. . . . And the spirit of a collective mind, 'the spirit of the hive,' residing in the various industrial cities, may find expression and a conscious revelation of itself, in something more beautiful and also more intelligible than the chaotic squalor of uniformly mean streets and buildings which make up the centres of industrial England.

Certainly, unless the life of the Crowd can be redeemed, all other redemption is vain. Here is the battle-ground for the future of a race and national character. . . .

. . . This tyranny of the present upon the imagination is perhaps the greatest of all obstacles to reform. It is not only that the inhabitants of London cannot picture what London was when the Abbey of Westminster stood up white from green gardens . . . It is that they are unable even to imagine a time when Cadogan Square was a huddle of slum tenements, and Islington an expanse of meadow land, and the places they now occupy, quiet fields. Lacking such imagination, they find it impossible to stand up and face the domination of the present with the naked vision of the future. . . . Here in part is the insistence of things against ideas, the dominance of the material . . . no first visitor to the newer industrial centres but is aware of a certain shrivelling up of man's importance before the aggregate of material construction. The sense of proportion is dwarfed by the mere divergence in size and stability, as the weak, unprotected human body is contrasted with vast levers and furnaces which at any moment could crack him like an eggshell, or shrivel him up like sawdust. Human life and mechanical life come to be pictured in permanence like those gaunt and sullen streets of East London, where tiny cottages crouch beneath tall encompassing walls so high that between them men scarce can see the sun. And behind the weight laid upon the imagination by mass and matter is the perhaps more oppressive weight of custom and convention. . . .

Yet against this tyranny of the present the reformer, after all, has some sources of protection. . . . as of Nineveh there remains but a heap, and of Tyrus a spit of sandy shore, and of Sagesta but one solemn temple looking down the valley to the sea, so a triumphant imagination can fling off the yoke of the present, to see in solid England dynamic instead of static forces, and all the cities in motion and flow towards some unknown ends. This may not provide any peculiar satisfaction for present endeavour. There is no guarantee, because change is inevitable, that change will come along desirable ways. Nor does consolation reside in the knowledge that one day, without a shadow of uncertainty, great London itself will become but a vast tomb for all its busy people, and of its splendour and pride not one stone be left upon another. But it does release from the tyranny of a present which sees no change possible. If change must come, then it may be deflected along desirable ways. . . .

And of all illusions of the opening twentieth century perhaps the most remarkable is that of security. Already gigantic and novel forces of mechanical invention, upheavals of people, social discontents, are exhibiting a society in the beginnings of change. . . .

A few years back men loved to anticipate an age of innocence and gold; with humanity at last tranquil and satisfied, in the socialistic millennium or the anarchic heaven of childhood. To-day the critic of a less sanguine outlook proclaims that modern civilisation carries within itself the seeds of its own destruction. . . . And if not in this way, yet in any similar and entirely unexpected fashion, arising out of that present danger: the instability which of necessity must prevail when vast implements of destruction are placed in the hands of a civilisation imperfectly self-controlled, and subject to panic fears and hatreds. . . .

Select Bibliography

Further reading might well begin with some of the works already quoted. Short selections cannot always do justice to lengthy works, particularly of course to novels. Apart from the novels and the poems of Cowper and Wordsworth, the works by Southey, Chadwick, Vaughan, Engels, Booth, Morris, Howard and Masterman quoted here would repay further attention.

Other works by our novelists relevant to the subject include Dickens's *Bleak House* (1852–3) and *Little Dorritt* (1855–7); Gissing's *Demos* (1886) and *The Whirlpool* (1897); and Wells's *The War in the Air* (1908) and *Tono-Bungay* (1909). Anthologies and collections which indicate the range and evolution of an author's opinions include *Wordsworth: Poetry and Prose*, ed. W. M. Merchant (1967); *Carlyle: Selected Works, Reminiscences and Letters*, ed. J. Symons (1955); *William Morris*, ed. G. D. H. Cole (1934 and 1948); and *William Morris: Selected Writings and Designs*, ed. A. Briggs (1962). Among individual works Ruskin's *Fors Clavigera* (1871–84) and Geddes's *Cities in Evolution* (1915) are particularly interesting.

Useful biographies and studies of figures featured in this volume include E. C. Batho, *The later Wordsworth* (1933); G. Carnall, *Robert Southey and his Age* (1960); S. E. Finer, *The Life and Times of Sir Edwin Chadwick* (1952) and M. W. Flinn's critical edition of Chadwick's report, *The Sanitary Condition of the Labouring Population of Great Britain* (1965); R. Blake, *Disraeli* (1966), especially chapter 9 on the novels; Edgar Wright, *Mrs. Gaskell: The Basis for Reassessment* (1965); John Lucas, *The Melancholy Man. A study of Dickens's novels* (1970), A. Welch, *The City of Dickens* (1971), Welch's article 'Satire and History. The City of Dickens' in *Victorian Studies* (**11**, no. 3), 1968, and P. Collins, 'Dickens and London', in *The Victorian City*, ed. Dyos and Wolff, of which further details are given below; G. Levine's chapter on 'The City in Carlyle, Ruskin and Morris', also in *The Victorian City;* J. A. Hobson, *John Ruskin, Social Reformer* (1898), which is revealing about Hobson as well as Ruskin; T. S. and M. B. Simey, *Charles Booth, Social Scientist* (1960); D. Macfadyen, *Sir Ebenezer Howard*

and the town planning movement (1933); A. Briggs, *A Study of the
Work of Seebohm Rowntree* (1961); and Lucy Masterman,
C. F. G. Masterman (1939 and 1968).

For readers who want to break new ground the following works
are of particular interest. Oliver Goldsmith's *The Deserted Village*
(1770) represents the Arcadian critique of the city. P. Gaskell's
The Manufacturing Population of Great Britain (1833) and Archibald
Alison's *The Principles of Population* (1840) were major contributions
to the 'condition of England' controversy. In *National Evils and
Practical Remedies* (1849) James Silk Buckingham, a critic of the
cities and of the new industrialism, projected a model town of
10,000 inhabitants, 'a proper union of agriculture and manufactures',
as the first step towards social regeneration. Thomas Guthrie's *The
City, its sins and its sorrows* (1859), sermons by a Scottish minister
and temperance enthusiast, balanced the city's political and material
achievements against its religious and moral deficiencies. Henry
Mayhew's *London Labour and the London Poor* (1851–62) has sections,
not all of them by Mayhew himself, of analysis and criticism of city
life. William Booth's *In Darkest England and the Way Out* (1890)
was the remedy for the slums proposed by the Salvation Army's
founder. W. R. Lethaby's 'Of Beautiful Cities' in *Art and Life, and
the building and decoration of Cities* (1897), lectures by members of the
Arts and Crafts Exhibition Society, showed a disciple of Ruskin
trying to incorporate the city into the vision of 'a dignified common
life' from which Morris had excluded it; while Robert Blatchford's
Merrie England (1894) was the ultimate in back-to-the-land
socialism, a rejection of the industrialism and exploitation of city
capitalism in favour of an agrarian life based on the public ownership
of land. George and Weedon Grossmith's *The Diary of a Nobody*
(1894), a humorous narrative of suburban petty gentility, and
Sidney J. Low's 'The Rise of the Suburbs' in *Contemporary Review*
(1891), an imperialist's celebration of the new suburban race, mark
the late-Victorian recognition of the suburbs as something distinct
from the city itself. In *The Town Child* (1907) R. A. Bray, a Fabian
L.C.C. member and a close friend of Masterman, considered the
city's problems of juvenile health, welfare and education; and
Florence, Lady Bell's *At the Works. A Study of a Manufacturing Town*
(1907) applied the approaches of Booth and Rowntree to
Middlesbrough. Apart from Masterman and Trevelyan the
contributors to *The Heart of the Empire* (1901) included Bray on
'The Children of the Town'. E. M. Forster's *Howards End* (1910)

hovered between the ambiguous and the ambivalent in its attitudes
towards city civilization, while F. M. Hueffer (better known as
Ford Madox Ford) enlisted with the optimists in *The Soul of London*
(1905) and in 'The Future of London' in W. W. Hutchings,
London Town Past and Present (1911), vol. 2.

Secondary works on and around the subject are led by Asa Briggs,
Victorian Cities (1963 and 1968); chapter 2 is particularly useful and
the bibliography is excellent. The editor's introductory chapter in
The Study of Urban History, ed. H. J. Dyos (1968), is also useful, and
a great deal can be gained, sometimes by reading between the lines,
from W. Ashworth, *The Genesis of Modern Town Planning* (1954);
two books by W. H. G. Armytage, *Heavens Below. Utopian
Experiments in England* (1961) and *Yesterday's Tomorrows: a Historical
Survey of Future Societies* (1968); and A. Chandler, *A Dream of Order.
The Medieval Ideal in Nineteenth-century English Literature* (1971). On
literary attitudes see also Ian Watt, *The Rise of the Novel* (1957 and
1963), K. Tillotson, *Novels of the Eighteen-Forties* (1954 and 1961),
and two articles by Raymond Williams on 'Literature and Rural
Society' and 'Literature and the City' in the *Listener*, numbers 2016
and 2017 (November 1967). A. S. Wohl's 'The Bitter Cry of
Outcast London' in *International Review of Social History*, **13** (1968),
is important for the 1880s. In 1968 the periodical *Victorian Studies*
devoted two numbers (vol. **11**, no. 3 and supplement) to the subject
of the Victorian city. The first included J. H. Raleigh, 'The Novel
and the City'; S. Meacham, 'The Church in the Victorian City';
and J. A. Banks, 'Population change and the Victorian city'; and the
second number G. R. Stange, 'The Victorian city and the frightened
poets', and A. Briggs, 'The Victorian City: Quantity and Quality'.
The publication is due in 1973 of *The Victorian City: Images and
Realities*, 2 volumes, ed. H. J. Dyos and M. Wolff, of which the
present author saw proofs when compiling this bibliography. In
addition to chapters listed above the following are recommended:
J. A. Banks, 'The Contagion of Numbers'; S. Marcus, 'Reading the
Illegible' (on Engels); U. C. Knoepflmacher, 'The Novel between
City and Country'; P. J. Keating, 'Fact and Fiction in the East End';
and G. Himmelfarb, 'The Culture of Poverty'.

Responses to the growth of cities in other countries are
discussed by various writers in *The Historian and the City*, ed.
O. Handlin and J. Burchard (Cambridge, Mass., 1963 and 1966); by
L. and M. White, *The Intellectual versus the City* (New York, 1964),
which deals with the U.S.A. and has a chapter on Henry James; and

by J. J. Sheehan, 'Liberalism and the city in nineteenth-century Germany', *Past & Present*, **51** (1971).

For discussions of urbanization in its historical perspective, see Handlin's introductory chapter in *The Historian and the City;* E. E. Lampard, 'Historical contours of contemporary urban society', *Journal of Contemporary History*, **4**, no. 3 (1969); and Lampard's chapter on 'The Urbanizing World' in *The Victorian City*. A. F. Weber, *The Growth of Cities in the Nineteenth Century* (New York, 1899 and 1963), provides comparative statistics of urbanization.

Index